# To Bella, Nelly & Jos:
letters from their grandmother about long ago & other places

To Veronica,
With best wishes from a near-neighbour of yours many years ago.
Sarah Bussey

*Though it is quite true, as one hears said, that we are
the sum of all that has happened to us,
the converse is quite true:
before anything whatever has happened to us
we are something,
and we continue to be that something
all the rest of our lives.*
William Maxwell

Written between March 2005 and September 2008

# To Bella, Nelly & Jos:
*letters from their grandmother*
*about long ago &*
*other places*

Sarah Bussy

Copyright © Sarah Bussy 2010
The moral right of the author has been asserted.

All rights reserved

Published and distributed by
HAREBELL BOOKS
Alresford, Hampshire SO24 0AG

British Library Cataloguing in Publication Data.
A catalogue record for this book is available from the British Library.

ISBN 978-0-9566241-0-9

Printed in Great Britain by the MPG Books Group, Bodmin and King's Lynn

When my mother bought me at the post office in Penge my knicker elastic even then must have been firmly in my armpits. The knickers in question were regulation brown bloomers required at the convent. If you pulled the legs down they'd reach your knees and show beneath your gymslip or candy-striped summer dress. So you yanked them up to the top of your thighs whence they flopped over and covered the sight of the elasticated bits. This made for a certain comfortable bulk but probably rather an odd silhouette.

But an odd silhouette was the least of your worries because you lived in ever-present terror of your knickers falling down. This was an all-too-feasible happening in those days back in the late forties and early fifties. It was in the nature of knickers. Either the elastic snapped or lost its elasticity to the point of uselessness. If it snapped then you had to grab your skirt around your knees in a desperate effort to keep the things hidden as you dashed to the lavatory. Considerable ingenuity was required once you'd reached this place of safety and it was vital for success to find a kirby grip somewhere on your head.

With this you tried to unpick the stitching at a point where you could catch hold of the elastic (even teeth might need to be employed). Then you threaded the elastic into the kirby grip and used it like a bodkin to reinsert it into the waist of the drawers. (This might not go right first time. If the elastic didn't stay threaded you'd have to start all over again.) Once you were holding both ends there were certain decisions to be made. Where were you going to make the knot and how much elastic could you afford to do without? If the elastic had not only broken but lost most of its stretchiness then it meant you'd performed this operation once or twice before on that particular garment. This would almost certainly mean that you'd have to make a knot while actually wearing the knickers. With little or no stretchiness left you were trapped inside until you could break out of them later at home.

This takes a lot of time and all too soon people start hammering on the door and asking what you're doing in there. 'I'm being excused' you'd reply. Thus there was apparently a verb 'to be excused' which meant doing whatever you had to do in the lavatory (except mending your knickers). It never occurred to me that it meant 'a plea for release from duty etc' as it says in the dictionary – a request in this case for permission to leave the classroom. I think it must have been the same for everyone at St Winefride's because even if someone enquired of a nun where a missing member of class was, the reply was invariably, 'Oh she's being excused'. Being excused seemed to be something only done by children and though passive in form was active in meaning.

However voluminous they were, knickers were virtually rude in themselves simply by virtue of what they covered. They covered that part of you which did the being excused business while you were in the lavatory and that part of you known as your bottom. Front bottom and back bottom were equal areas of shame and were never investigated except by a blind swipe with soap and flannel.

'We saw your knickers' whispered Mary Gibbs with a smirk. This had been as I was carried unconscious from chapel after executing a dramatic, head-cracking faint. Mary's face on its giraffe neck formed the apex of a crowded tableau of girls in the doorway of the staff room where I'd been laid out on the floor to recover. But I didn't mind about my knickers being seen while doing something that briefly made me the centre of concerned attention. They hadn't seen either of my bottoms and that was all that mattered.

You were allowed to leave the classroom to be excused but not if you were always asking to the way Jacqueline did when we were in the Lower Kindergarten. Most of the children had their hair in plaits or bunches but Jacqueline's was short, soft, blonde and apparently styled by her mother or aunt, both of whom always accompanied her to and from the convent. Instead of a satchel she came to school one day with an object of envy known as a vanity case – a squarish blue box with a locking lid that had a mirror on the inside of it. I don't know what she kept in the vanity case because I wasn't one of her special friends but you felt lipstick wouldn't have been much of a surprise even though she was only five. She was a perfect example of what people meant in those days when they referred to a child as spoilt. So although the nuns weren't unkind to her you could sense their disapproval of what she represented and their desire to keep her possible influence in check. The cluster round the vanity case was gently dispersed.

One day when Jacqueline asked, as she frequently did, to be excused she was told that she'd have to wait until break. She couldn't believe her ears – and neither could I. 'But I've got to be excused! I'm going to go! I'm going to go! I'm going to go all over the floor! I've got to be excused!' She spluttered on, tearful and red in the face, but the response was firm. 'I'm sorry Jacqueline but you'll have to wait. You should have been excused before you came into class.' Jacqueline roared on to no avail, eventually sat down sobbing, lapsed into silence and made it through until break without going all over the floor.

❋

'It's snowing!' These thrilling words cause an excited scramble to see out of the window. This means hauling ourselves onto our knees in the sand-tray underneath it. But when I look out it's still disappointingly green in the convent grounds and I haven't managed to spot a single happy flake before hopefulness turns into mortification and mystery.

'Sally Shervington – I'm surprised at *you*!' It's Mother Mary Agatha standing grimly in the now open doorway behind us. I'm back in my seat in an instant, face aflame and feeling slightly resentful towards the unknown individual, one of the few boys in the class, who has not only supplied the rest of us with faulty intelligence but has induced me to behave in a manner that's disappointing to grownups and apparently unworthy of me.

But why was I different from the others? Why wasn't she surprised and disappointed with *them*? What did she know about *me*? Was it something I didn't know about myself? I'd never spoken to her in my life. And I lived *miles* away from the school. If she was surprised that I behaved like other children then what kind of reputation had I got and where had it come from? Was it something to do with my father? Was it something to do with my name?

Well whatever it was that marked me out it seemed to have something to do with goodness and being pleasing to adults. It seemed that it was grownups who decided who you were and apparently they'd decided that I was an especially good child. And so it was I dimly reasoned that in order to be Sally Shervington I had to be good. If I wasn't good then I wouldn't be me. I'd cease to exist. Perhaps that's why the merest hint of being in trouble brought on the kind of terror that paralyses you in nightmares.

In addition to deciding who you were, adults (usually women in a bad temper) had a propensity to ask you who you thought you were. The funny thing is that when they asked you that, the last thing they wanted was an answer. 'Who do you think you are' wasn't a question at all but an exclamation. In those days girls often had this question that wasn't a question hurled at them. The emphasis might come on any of the six words (try it out for yourself) and be delivered within a tonal range from withering contempt to spit-laden rage. What had you or they done to deserve it? What did it imply? It implied that you were a nothing and yet were insolent enough to need reminding of the fact. It implied you had the presumption to think you might be something. Or rather that you dared to show signs of being a person; of having a mind capable of independent thought. Now that just wasn't allowed. It wasn't for you to question the workings of the world. Your part in the bewildering order of things was to be quiet and do as you were told. And of course to believe what you were told.

Not only that but they told you what you believed. What you believed was all set out in the catechism. This was a small, soft-covered book in red or blue containing questions and answers. You learnt the answers by heart so that you could shoot them back on demand. It began like this:

1  Who made you?
   God made me.
2  Why did God make you?
   God made me to know Him, love Him and serve Him in this world and to be happy with Him for ever in the next.

So it wasn't long after starting school that I was learning just how to know, love and serve God, someone invisible I'd never heard about before and who became linked in my mind with the highly visible and impressive person of my father. How to know, love and serve God meant knowing about sin. One day soon after moving up from the Lower Kindergarten into Miss Glover's class she tells us to take out our exercise books. (These exercise books which I still remember with affection had alternate unlined pages that were used for drawing and colouring.)

'Have you all got your RI exercise books out? Yes? Good. Now turn to the next unlined page and draw a nice big heart on the top part of it. When you've done that, do another heart the same size underneath it, like I've shown you on the board. Don't forget to leave a space between the two hearts and also below the second one. When you've all done that we'll be colouring them in.'

A buzz of pleasure runs round the room at the idea of colouring in and we settle down happily to work. After I've done my hearts which have gone quite well and aren't too wonky I select some bright crayons to fill them in with. But I have to put them back in the dingy green tin because Miss Glover's going to tell us what colours to use. We're to colour the top heart in yellow and the bottom heart in black.

'Go right up to the edges and make the black as black as you can.'

I'm keen to make a good job of this and so I press the black crayon too hard. It rips right through the paper and spoils the page underneath. I try not to let her notice even though I know she won't be cross. I just don't like being clumsy and making a mess of things. I'm always being clumsy and making a mess of things. Now she says,

'Have you all drawn your two hearts like these ones on the blackboard? Yes? Good. Now, in your best handwriting, I want you to copy this underneath the yellow heart.' It says – This is my soul full of grace.

'Have you all done that? Yes? Good. And now I want you to copy this under the bottom heart.' It says – This is my soul full of sin.

So your heart which was somewhere in the top part of your body and which thumped away keeping you alive was also where your soul was. And thus began the anxiety, pushed away into the background as much as possible, about my state of grace. You had to be in a state of grace at all times in case God called you suddenly in death. Because if you weren't in a state of grace when you died then you'd go to Hell for all eternity.

To be fair to the nuns they did at least indicate that as children we could hardly fail to be in a state of grace, however imperfect. We could only commit venial sins. The hint was though that when people became older there were terrible temptations that beset them and terrible sins they could commit which would put them in a state of mortal sin. Yet both mortal and venial sins could be wiped off your soul by confession,

contrition and a firm purpose of amendment (a resolve not to commit this sin again). If these conditions were met then the sinner's soul would change by the grace of God from a foul black to the colour of the sun. So there was at least some hope for you however awful you were.

This photograph was taken in Miss Glover's class. I'm sitting behind a little French boy called Patou who, not surprisingly, was my first love. Sitting next to me is Marianne, the sweetest-natured girl I've ever known. It doesn't look as if I was too worried about Hellfire – probably because at that time I didn't feel seriously sinful. I'm not prone to nostalgia but if I had to go back to any time in my life I'd choose to be six years old again in Miss Glover's class. You knew who you were then. And where you belonged. Well the two things go together don't they? You can't feel you know who you are unless you feel you know where you belong.

❋

Being good wasn't just a question of not committing sins such as being unkind and telling lies – the kind of things you'd later have to mumble miserably in the dismal darkness of the confessional box. It was much more complicated than that. There were all sorts of other things you weren't meant to do but you didn't find out you weren't meant to do them until you did them and got into trouble. And even when you did find out what you weren't meant to have done it didn't necessarily mean you had the slightest idea why you'd been wrong in doing it. The goodness expected of you embraced not only the way you spoke, the way you walked, the way you kept your elbows in while eating at the table but also the kind of company you kept. Let me give you an example.

One Monday morning at St Winefride's when I joined everyone else for assembly in the hall it was obvious from the atmosphere that something dreadful had happened. Or to be more precise – that someone (one of us) had *done* something dreadful. You knew this must be so because Reverend Mother Mary John was seated thin-lipped up on the stage whereas normally she was in her study at this time. Sure enough, once Mother Mary Ambrose had led us in prayer and in the singing of 'Daily, daily sing to Mary, sing my soul her praises due …' silence fell. Mother Mary Ambrose stepped aside and Reverend Mother replaced her at the front of the stage. She stood for some moments sweeping her eyes over the children sitting cross-legged below her. Faces of innocent and guilty alike burned with shame. Childish eyes were cast on the parquet floor to avoid meeting those behind the mannish horn-rimmed spectacles.

Eventually she spoke. Precisely what words she used over fifty years ago I can't remember now but I feel they must have included those of Lady Catherine de Bourgh to Elizabeth Bennett in *Pride and Prejudice* – namely that she had received a report of a most alarming nature. However, she probably just said something like this:

'It has been reported to me that there are some children in the hall this morning who do not seem to understand what is expected of pupils of the Ladies of Mary. I will not name any names on this occasion. The guilty children will know who they are when I tell you what it was that was reported to me. On Saturday morning last, three pupils from St Winefride's were seen queuing outside the cinema in Lower Sydenham. Three pupils from St Winefride's in such a place! This is not where the Ladies of Mary expect their pupils to be. Nor is it permitted. If any child in this school is ever seen again outside a cinema on a Saturday morning they will be expelled immediately. Is that clear children? Good. Now you may go to class.'

Interestingly, as I see it now, that meaning of the word class was the only one known to me as a child and young person. I'm sure I didn't hear people being referred to as working class, middle class or any other class. I don't think ordinary people used such expressions. Anyway, Reverend Mother's words were a source of relief (I wasn't there in Lower Sydenham last Saturday morning), disappointment (I'd expected something much worse and therefore more exciting) and puzzlement (why was it wrong to go to the pictures on a Saturday morning but all right on a Saturday afternoon as we sometimes did?)

Then I remembered (or was it later that I saw?) a noisy bunch of scruffy children cheerfully yelling and punching each other up outside the King's Hall in Penge one Saturday morning as they queued for the pictures. I was surprised the cinema was open and they seemed rather privileged to me; people who were on to something that hadn't come my way and which was closed to me because I wasn't like them. Their great privilege was to be what was called 'common'. They could get in to see a show for three pence (pronounced 'thruppence'), make a row, and shout and yell to their hearts' content. They were the kind of children I always eyed with envy in the side streets of Penge when I saw them racing along on their go-carts made out of pram wheels, planks and string. Their world was as foreign to me as mine was to them. And whereas they seemed to belong to the world around them, I was just meandering on my own through it trying to make sense of it all. They were too busy having a good time to notice me, which was probably just as well, although I think I usually imagined I was more or less invisible anyway.

I've just said that I was trying to make sense of it all, but I'm not sure that I was. Or if I was then it was being done unconsciously. I was merely receiving various impressions which added to the whole muddle of my existence. Looking back on us as a family it feels as if we were defined mostly by what we weren't. What we most emphatically weren't was *common*. Clearly it was only common children who went to the Saturday morning pictures and therefore it was a crime for us to do so too; so much so that it would lead to expulsion if we were ever caught doing it. There was a wonderful hypocrisy at work because adults made it quite clear to us that we must never be unkind to anyone or imagine that we were better than anyone else. This would be the kind of little homily delivered by my father. He wouldn't have used the word common but he was quite as alive as my mother and Reverend Mother herself to the dangers of contamination by the riff-raff.

There were certain indicators of non-commonness, the most important being the way in which you spoke. It was my mother who got especially worked up about this. One day I was in the garden, playing with Heather and a girl called Shiela from the flat above ours, when Fury in her shape swept down swift as a sparrow-hawk, dragged me indoors and raged at me for speaking like a common guttersnipe.

Not being common also meant not going to a council school. This was because you'd inevitably become common if you went to one. I was very bemused by the sightings I had of these places where children wore what they liked and had the most dismal-looking playgrounds in which to fight and push and shove and shriek like wild animals. Surely they weren't proper schools? How awful to have to go to one. The thought of it made me shudder. It was their ugliness that filled me with horror.

I made the assumption that common people not only spoke in an ugly way but were also poor. This assumption was quite natural if you kept your eyes and ears open in Penge where the majority of shoppers obviously were poor. Or perhaps it was just that poor people attracted my attention. (Penge started just round the corner from where we lived at the very edge of Sydenham's shabby respectability.) It was old people I used to notice. Like most children I suppose, I thought they'd always been old and I felt terribly sorry for them because they couldn't run and jump and skip and try to stand on their heads. There seemed to be so much sadness around. There was awful disfigurement and disablement. There were old men with trays suspended round their necks selling shoelaces and matches. There were one-legged old soldiers sawing away on violins, with the case open by their feet in the hope of receiving the odd penny or ha'penny. And there were at least two old women who had what looked like long bags of flesh hanging from one side of their face. Several inches long these fleshy bags seemed to have a rock in the bottom which made them waggle energetically in time to the brisk steps of the afflicted women as they went about their daily business.

We were told that it was rude to stare at people and so one's observations had to be made surreptitiously. It was rude to shout as well, but a lot of shouting went on in Maple Road market where cockney costermongers touted for customers. The memory of the din and bewildering crush of that market still seems more foreign to me than anywhere I've since been to abroad. The men who were shouting even spoke a language I didn't understand. What were they shouting about and how could they stand the cold? Why didn't they sell their stuff indoors? I couldn't make out why my mother and grandmother went to such a place. We didn't seem to belong there in the same way that we did in David Greig or Cullens. What I didn't understand then was that things were cheaper in the market and this mattered a lot because my mother had to manage her housekeeping down to the last penny.

Sometimes though she'd get some fruit and vegetables from an old woman called Mrs Price. Not very much because she had so little for sale – some King Edward potatoes, some onions and a few Bramley apples perhaps. Her shop was almost underneath the spooky railway bridge that made such a terrifying thunder of a din when the trains went over it and which you knew was going to fall down one day just as you were going underneath it. But Mrs Price didn't seem to mind it and was always cheerful. Her cheeks were the colour of old pink roses and had tiny red lines etched across them. She seemed to be all soft in spite of the fact she wore a rough old sack as an apron. There wasn't a scrap of lino or anything on the floor in there. It was just splintered boards. I have the impression it was always freezing too because I can't remember her without those gloves with the fingertips missing. When you went in she was usually out the back chopping firewood to put into bundles for sale and when she came out the front to serve you she always shut the door behind her.

But one day when my mother took me in, the door at the back of the shop had been left ajar. I sidled towards it while she and Mrs Price were exchanging pleasantries of some sort and I knew they wouldn't notice. My nosiness gave me a shock. What I saw when I peeped into the room behind was a pokey hole of a place with a shattered window pane, a split-open mattress on the bare floor and a broken down bit of a chair. That was all she had. That was how she lived. So then I understood why my mother sometimes bought things there that she could have got elsewhere. How Mrs Price made enough money to keep herself alive was a mystery.

A similar mystery was presented by the old Beano and Dandy woman. She made a pretence of being a newsagent about half way down the High Street from Mrs Price although there was a proper one a few doors away. Sometimes Heather would say, 'Come on! Let's go to Beano and Dandy's.' Hers was one of the few places where you could get warm in winter but the price you paid was bordering on the excessive. She always had a paraffin heater going and the stench it made, combined with the smell of heated newsprint mingled with cabbage and cat pee was overpowering. It inspired us with awe that life could be sustained in there. Five minutes was about all we could manage. In fact it seemed as if children in general had little stomach to explore the heap of Beanos and Dandys that cooked away in the window and which became progressively smothered by dead and dying flies.

A very different old woman used to push a battered pram up the path to our door every so often, usually on a Monday. She wore a stained white apron over whatever collection of clothes she had underneath. This was the rag-and-bone woman. 'Got anything for me today love?' she'd ask whoever opened the door to her. There was precious little waste in our place. In fact there was no waste at all – not even old newspapers because they were used to wrap up kitchen scraps before placing them in the dustbin. But my mother and grandmother would try to find things to put by ready for her next visit. There might be an old jumper with the elbows out of it and beyond darning, a pair of shoes that had been outgrown or perhaps an old school blouse if it hadn't already been ripped up to provide pieces of rag for cleaning purposes.

Whatever you gave her she thanked you with her toothless grin. (Well it wasn't quite toothless because if you looked hard enough you could see a tooth on either side at the top but they were so black they were almost invisible.) Then she'd fish around in a pocket in the front of her apron and produce a penny which you were told not to take. So then she'd give you a boiled sweet which you were allowed to accept but on no account put anywhere near your mouth. You didn't need to be told why. Her hands were unspeakably filthy and the sweets came unwrapped from a pocket in the stained apron – the same pocket that held the pennies.

Whereas the rag-and-bone woman pushed an old pram from door to door, the rag-and-bone man had a horse and cart and expected people to bring their unwanted stuff out to him. The slow clip-clop of the horse as it ambled up the hill was accompanied by the easy, unexpectant voice of its owner crying, 'Rag'n'bone! Rag'n'bone! Bring me your rag'n'bone! Any ole iron? Any ole iron? Rag'n'bone! Rag'n' bone! Bring me your rag'n'bone!' I never saw anyone in the road give him anything but perhaps they did. The rhythm of the horse and the cry of the old man mingled with the clink of milk bottles was part of the music of the morning. The notes floated upwards and slowly faded away as milkman and rag-and-bone man passed over the brow of the hill.

It wasn't only the rag-and-bone man who had a horse. There were still quite a few around in urban areas until well into the 1950s and they were an everyday sight in Penge. Bakers, milkmen and other tradesmen used them for making deliveries. You'd see them standing around patiently, heads nuzzling in their nosebags and munching quietly as they emptied their bottoms on the road with complete unembarrassment. And so it was more or less inevitable that Heather and I would call the mad woman Horsey because of the malodorous breeze she caused when she stomped furiously past us almost every time we went to Penge. She walked with enormous brisk strides and was only ever seen in one outfit – a tightly-belted, rust-coloured coat and a black beret that she pulled down all round her head to hide any hair she might have had.

'Quick! Here comes Horsey! Let's cross over,' we'd hiss as one of us nudged the other off the pavement. We always thought she could hear what we were saying because she'd turn round sharply, shake her fist and shout things we couldn't understand. And she thought nothing of stopping in the middle of the road to do this as she crossed and re-crossed it diagonally at random intervals. So we had to keep crossing it as well. It appeared she accused us of following her but it felt as if it was she who was following us. I don't think she scared Heather for a moment but she frightened me because of course I thought she was some kind of witch. And so it was that Heather found another means of torture to add to her expanding repertoire. 'It's tonight! It's tonight! It's tonight! Horsey's coming to get you tonight! Tee hee hee hee hee!'

*

If Mother Mary Agatha's words made me feel I had something to live up to, it wasn't long before I discovered that my school uniform gave me something to live down.

When I was about seven and coming home from St Winefride's on my own, I was waiting for a number 12 bus at Forest Hill and as it got darker the fog began to come down. The first number 12 that came along was full and didn't pick anyone up. The second one came and picked up one or two standing passengers but I was still a long way from the front of the queue. I began to be worried that I'd be late home. 'Promise you won't be late home or your mother will be worried.' My father said this to me almost every morning as he left home. (I had the best mother in the world. He often used to tell me so when he sat on the edge of my bed to say goodnight.) So I really *mustn't* be late. That was what increasingly filled my mind to the point of desperation. I strained my eyes to see what number bus was coming down the hill past the Horniman Museum, but it never seemed to be a number 12 and even if it was I knew I wouldn't get on it.

People in the queue started saying that the fog was holding the buses up and perhaps they'd stop running altogether but eventually another one *was* coming along and I was praying, 'Please God, please God let me get on it so Mummy won't be worried. Please let there be room.' I was about fifth in the queue by now and if enough people got off I just might manage to make it. 'Please God, please God let lots of people get off and please God, please God don't let it stop short because all the grownups behind me will push past and not let me get on.'

Well either God was listening or else it was a big bit of luck because the driver slightly overshot the stop and the platform ended up just where I was. The situation was now so serious in my mind that with only slight hesitation I took advantage of the resulting confusion and hopped onto the bus without waiting for those in front of me to go first as I should have done. I'd never, ever done anything so rude and wrong. I knew I shouldn't have done it but it was all such a scramble as other people did what they didn't normally do too and pushed onto the bus before letting people get off. I just *had* to get on it.

And all seemed well as I plonked myself down in huge relief on the three-seater nearest the platform without even glancing to see if there was a better seat somewhere else. A better seat was one next to a window, or up at the front where you could feel a bit of warmth from the engine. I didn't like the three-seaters because they were cold and they faced each other. You didn't know what to do with your eyes. If you shut them to avoid looking at the people opposite (it's rude to stare) then almost certainly one of the grownups would say pointedly something sarcastic like, 'I see someone thinks she's had a hard day!' causing a murmur of amusement at your expense. This would be followed by smug grumbles about kids not knowing what tiredness was and not knowing they were born. (Of course I knew I was born and I could tell them when so what did they mean when they said that?)

But on this occasion I was fervently grateful for my perch on a three-seater. I felt guilty about my bad manners but my heart gradually stopped thumping as I realised that everyone at the bus stop must have got on because otherwise there'd be someone standing. And if anyone *had* been standing I would have had to give up my seat to them anyway because in those days children weren't expected to occupy a seat on a bus if a grownup was standing. In a way I'd rather have had the opportunity of giving up my seat because that would have made me feel a bit better about what I'd done and would also have shown people on the bus that I really wasn't rude and I *did* have good manners – if anyone had seen me jump the queue that is.

Anyway everyone had a seat and so it hadn't mattered after all. But if I'd known there was going to be enough room I wouldn't have pushed on in the first place. And in any case I really didn't mind too much about waiting at bus stops. I wouldn't have minded not getting on that bus if I hadn't been worried about my mother worrying. I wished it would get a move on now. It seemed to be the slowest bus I'd ever been on. I couldn't wait to get home so she wouldn't be worried any more.

So I was sitting there still worrying but probably looking as if I didn't have a care in the world in contrast to the grownups around me who were always worrying about something when I felt a jab in my left shoulder and there was this woman shoving her face into mine. It was the end of the world. It all happened so quickly and yet seemed to go on for ever. She was shouting at me and addressing the whole bus at the same time and inviting everyone to look at me.

'There she is! That's the one! I saw her jump the queue! You did jump the queue didn't you? No use denying it because I know you did. I saw you. And I recognise that hat too. You go to that posh school don't you? She does! She goes to that posh school! So that's what they teach you there is it? To push past people and not think of anyone but yourself?'

I can't remember whether she got off then or not. All I can remember is the terrible sense of exposure and the shame and misery of having nowhere to hide. But as people gradually got off, a two-seater became free. I stumbled into it, thrust my burning face against the steamed-up window and tried to make them not see me. Other feelings then rushed into my heart that had nothing to do with the misery of public humiliation. A sense of injustice because the horrible woman hadn't known about my mother and so she didn't know why I'd done what I'd done. It felt as if she'd been nasty to *her* and I couldn't forgive her for that. But things far worse than injustice or muddled love for my mother came into it. Something really awful had happened to me or to the person I thought of as myself. For the first time in my life I felt furious hatred.

Well of course I knew what a certain kind of furious hatred was. Heather and I were always hating each other. We murdered each other almost every day because it was a normal and quite enjoyable way of passing the time if the grownups were out of earshot and we couldn't find anything better to do. But this was different. The feeling I had about that woman was so intense I really did want her dead. And I knew *how* I wanted her dead. She's flattened by the Golden Arrow as it thunders screaming through Penge East Station and plunges into the tunnel underneath Sydenham Hill. It's her own fault she falls off the platform. I don't push her. She just does it. Again and again and again.

Now I knew why my father said that you must never hate anyone because hating someone is like wishing them dead and you wouldn't wish anyone dead would you? Well for the first time in my life I did wish someone dead. It was the first time I realised that grownups could be hateful. It was the first time I realised that not all grownups were kindly-disposed towards me. That woman hated me because I went to a posh school. I wouldn't mind betting that I made her day. I bet she was delighted I gave her the excuse to express her class hatred, envy, resentment or whatever else it was she got off her chest that foggy afternoon.

But that's me looking at it now. Then I was a child of seven who suddenly felt an ugly stranger to herself. I wasn't good. I was terribly, terribly bad. My soul was full of sin. It wasn't yellow any more, or even mottled. It was black as the coal hole at the end of the hall. I'd fallen from grace. I don't think I thought this just because of the RI lessons, although they must have given me the means to visualise what I felt in my heart. And what I felt in my heart was that something inside me had died. It was all up with me. But I'd have to go on living. I don't know whether I'd already been told the story of Adam and Eve and their expulsion from the Garden of Eden but they could hardly have felt a greater sense of shock and loss than I did then.

✻

That was the day I discovered there was wickedness in the world, not just in other people but more importantly in myself. It was the day I reckon I lost my innocence, years before I had any understanding of sex. I wonder why it is that most people, especially Catholics, equate innocence with sexual ignorance? I find it easy enough to imagine an innocent child who knows about sexual reproduction. His innocence would lie in reasoning that since all the people he knows are good, he can trust everyone he meets to look after him – or at least to do him no harm. So his innocence has to be lost before it has a chance to prolong itself into a state of dangerous naivety.

I suppose we're prepared for wickedness by some of the fairy stories we read and which lead us most unfairly to be frightened of harmless old women who look rather strange. I must say though that I thought Little Red Riding Hood was a bit stupid not to recognise the difference between her grandmother and the wolf. He'd never have fooled me. But as I was often called Piggy at home it wasn't difficult to catch a flash of myself in a roasting pan. I think this is the fate I believed lay in wait for me if I went off with those strangers I mustn't speak to on my way to and from school.

Had I fallen into mortal sin that day when I felt such murderous hatred for that woman? It certainly felt like it but whatever grade of sin I'd committed it wasn't the kind I'd have known how to put into words and even if I could have put it into words I'm sure I wouldn't have included it in my confession. I realise now that I never even considered confessing really bad sins – partly from shame but also for the very good reason that I considered them to be my own business. I probably also reasoned that I didn't need to confess them anyway because God knew about them and I'd already repented. Not only that, but the penance I did for some sins endured for ages while I lived in perpetual dread of discovery. So having found out for myself that crime didn't pay I made up my own way of getting through confession. It became a matter of form mingled with a dash of legerdemain.

Our nearest Catholic church was St Anthony of Padua in Genoa Road, Anerley where the parish priest was bad-tempered old Father Coffey who wouldn't tolerate crying babies on the premises. Whenever my father took Heather and me to confession it was on a Saturday evening. Fortunately he wasn't moved to do so all that often, perhaps because he didn't enjoy it any more than we did. He always seemed to be in the confessional box for ages which sometimes led to unseemly sniggering between us as we tried to imagine what sins our sainted father could possibly have committed.

Ours couldn't be described as a proper Catholic home of the kind I later encountered. Catholicism only really happened at the convent and in church. My mother didn't go to church. Nor did her mother who lived with us. Only my father, Heather and I. So there were no visible signs of piety around the place. No statues of the Virgin Mary on the mantelpiece or crucifixes above the beds with last year's palm leaves folded in the shape of a cross and stuck behind Christ's agonised head. No grace before and after meals. No suggestion that we should kneel on the cold linoleum to say our prayers before hopping into bed and hugging our stone hot water bottles. Nevertheless there was no escaping confession. You had to go sometimes and you dreaded it. But then a lot of dread went on about a lot of things, as I expect it does in every childhood.

I think St Anthony's was a Victorian gothic affair but perhaps I'm wrong. To one side of it was yet another of those hideous, puzzling schools with its few square yards of forlorn asphalt masquerading as a playground. But inside the church you felt there *was* something special there among the gloom, just as you did in the chapel at St Winefride's. Some sort of mystery. A mixture of reverend whisperings, of beauty, of silence, of the smell of incense and recently snuffed candles and of the flickering red sanctuary lamp which meant that the Blessed Sacrament was in the sparkling tabernacle. It made you want to try and be holy and the first step towards that was confession. That was where you went so that you'd be in a state of grace to receive the Blessed Sacrament at Holy Communion the next time you went to mass – probably the following morning.

It wasn't that anything awful happened to you at confession. It was just the worrying business of working out a plausible list of sins which could cover your crimes and shortcomings without being specific. For example I suspect I'd have put the business of the beastly woman on the bus into the category of having had unkind thoughts about people. (That should give you some idea of my method.) Once you'd got your list together (not too many, not too few) you worried about trying to memorise it along with all the other things you had to say and that made you squirm.

Anyway, what would happen was this. You'd go into St Anthony's, dip your right hand into the stoop of holy water and make the sign of the cross. Then you'd go and kneel down towards the back of the church, shut your eyes and try to be as devout as possible while you did your preparation. The first thing you had to do was to examine your conscience. When you felt you'd done this and had got your list of sins off by heart you'd say an Act of Contrition. This was a prayer that told God you were sorry for your sins and would try not to commit them again, even though you knew you could hardly avoid committing them again without actually ceasing to breathe. Then you crept further up the church to join the people in the benches immediately outside the confessional box.

You shuffled a place nearer the door of it as each penitent came out and all the time you were going over and over what you had to say, terrified you'd dry up when you knelt down inside. Eventually your turn came and although the confessional was supposedly a place where the priest had no interest in your identity you nevertheless felt that it was terribly important that he didn't know who you were. Consequently I developed a particular way of approaching the confessional crabwise and going in more or less backwards so the priest had less opportunity to catch a glimpse of my face as I went in.

Once the door was shut behind you it was completely dark, so you'd needed to make out where the kneeler was in that brief flash of low-wattage light you caused as you went in. It was made of smooth sorbo rubber. Sometimes you could feel the dents left by the knees of the previous occupant. And their warmth too. If this happened you'd try to slide to a cold, undented bit to left or right. At about the level of your face you knew there was a wire grille behind which the priest sat. Sometimes, as your eyes got used to the dark (if you ever opened them in there that is), you saw the even deeper dark of the priest's profile. But the most usual childhood practise was to keep your eyes tight shut the whole time and just concentrate on getting it over.

> '*In nomine Patris et Filius et Spiritus Sanctus Amen.*'
> 'Bless me Father for I have sinned.'

He invited you to go ahead and once you'd got your sin-list out of the way there was a useful bit of script which went as follows:

> 'For these and all my other sins that I cannot now remember I am heartily sorry and humbly beg pardon of God and penance and absolution of you Father.'

I can't remember the whole procedure and whether you had to say the *Confiteor*. If you did then it went like this:

> I confess to Almighty God,
> to blessed Mary ever Virgin,
> to blessed Michael the Archangel,

to blessed John the Baptist,
to the holy apostles Peter and Paul,
to all the Saints, and to you Father,
that I have sinned exceedingly
in thought, word and deed:
**through my fault**
**through my fault**
**through my most grievous fault**
Therefore I beseech the blessed Mary ever Virgin,
blessed Michael the Archangel
blessed John the Baptist,
the holy Apostles Peter and Paul,
all the Saints, and you, Father,
to pray to the Lord our God for me.
Amen.

When you got to the part in **bold** you had to strike your chest, once for each line. I suppose this indicates some attenuated form of flagellation but I can't say I ever thought about it until now. And I may as well confess that I'm indebted to the internet for the above prayer which I'd completely forgotten apart from the first two lines.

Anyway I think I'm right in saying that whatever prayer you were praying in English, the priest was praying in Latin. When he'd finished he'd make the sign of the cross and give you your penance. Perhaps he'd say, 'For your penance will you please say one *Our Father* and three *Hail Marys*. Now go in peace, say a prayer for me please and God bless you.'

'Thank you Father.'

It was over! The penance was virtually nothing at all. It never was. Full of gratitude you crept into an empty bench (Catholics didn't seem to call them pews) and performed it enthusiastically together with a prayer for the priest. I found it interesting and a bit touching that priests asked you to pray for them. Did it mean that they were sinners too? And I must admit I always found those parting words of theirs consoling. I still do when I think about them.

There was one time when I'd been to confession that I really did feel as if I'd been filled with grace because I was so hugely light-hearted and happy afterwards. It was a frosty night and the star-sprinkled sky was Heaven itself. It made me skip and leap and try to touch it all the way home. I suspect my exalted state was brought on by relief at having got the wretched business of confession out of the way, combined with the imminence of Christmas. But it *felt* as if I was in a state of grace and if happiness of that kind isn't a state of grace then I don't know what is.

On the way home, or as soon as our father couldn't hear, Heather and I would whisper, 'Which ones did you tell?' This was code for, 'Which ones didn't you tell?'

So much for confession – now for mass on Sundays and Holidays of Obligation. Holidays of Obligation were feast days on which you had to attend mass. If they fell in the week then you had the day off school so there was something to be said for them. Mass, especially sung high mass, felt as if it would never end. Boredom and incomprehension wrenched yawn after yawn out of you, especially during the sermon.

All was mystery and to a large extent was meant to be. The thing about the Catholic mass, especially in those days, was that it was a theatrical performance in which the priest with his back to the congregation performed the rites required to enable the great mystery of transubstantiation to take place – for the bread and wine to be turned into the body and blood of Christ. As he raised the chalice containing the wine towards Heaven (or maybe it was the host or communion wafer that he raised) you were meant to close your eyes and bow down. While everyone was doing this, three bursts of tinkling bells came from somewhere on the sanctuary – the place behind the altar rails. One of the altar boys would be making this happen but I can't say I understood this at the time. The pretty sound seemed to come from nowhere.

After this people would queue up demurely, hands together and eyes shut, while they waited to 'receive Our Blessed Lord'. When a place became available you took your turn to kneel at the altar rails, rather dreading the prospect of sticking your tongue out. I always thought it was a horrible sight – this line of people to my right taking it in turns to stick out their tongues. It wasn't just ugly – it didn't seem respectful somehow.

There were other things to bother about as well. In those days the mass was still said in Latin and even if you had a missal with an English translation (which I hadn't) it didn't make much sense to you. All this stuff about the Lamb of God taking away the sins of the world (*Agnus Dei*). And the congregation being a flock of sheep. As a town child and a Catholic the only idea I had of sheep was derived from holy pictures and readings from the New Testament. Being compared to a sheep didn't appeal to me. They were stupid animals who got lost. Christ was the Good Shepherd who went kindly in search of people who didn't know their way around. Admittedly I didn't know my way around either but that didn't prevent me feeling resentful about the presumption that I'd go on being sheep-like all my life.

Quite apart from all the lambs and Latin, you couldn't stop your mind wandering to the question of the fast you'd had to make before you were able to receive Holy Communion. If you were going to go to Holy Communion (which you had to do, along with making your confession, 'at least once a year and that at Easter or thereabouts' as it said in the catechism) then it meant you had to go to the one at eight o'clock in the morning. This was because you would have fasted since midnight. You wouldn't have been allowed a drop of water or a crumb of food since you went to bed the night before. I thought this was to ensure that your body as well as your soul was in a fit state to receive Christ/Jesus/Our Lord/the Lamb of God/Our Blessed Lord/the Blessed Sacrament.

But fasting presented problems, the simplest being my propensity to faint if I was hungry. In addition to worrying about that, how could you not consider that the spit you swallowed or the snot you sniffed provided a far more revolting lining to the stomach than a piece of dry toast. Even thinking these things made you ashamed and led you to wonder whether you were still in a fit state to receive communion. Because thoughts like these felt like sins too unthinkably awful to mention in confession. So there was this increasing burden of guilt and complication which couldn't be removed. It could only be temporarily shoved aside – perhaps by having something special to look forward to, or by experiencing the kind of unusual, unexpected things that make children happy – such as going to sleep by firelight or waking up to find frost patterns swirling all over the bedroom windows.

Or by the comfort and quiet humour provided by my grandmother. She didn't speak quite the same as we did because she was born in Dublin. Her soft voice said things like fil'm for film and adv*er*tissed instead of advertised. Her laugh was a low, slightly husky chuckle. She reminded me of a bird, more particularly of a robin. I think this was because of the one on the front of the Cherry Blossom Boot Polish tin. Her seemingly fragile legs terminated firmly in sensible brown court shoes that had the deep shine of freshly-fallen conkers. Her most usual clothing was a carefully-pressed grey pleated skirt, white or cream blouse with its top button hidden by a cameo brooch, and a longish grey or beige cardigan. With pockets. A cardigan without pockets was no cardigan at all in her estimation. In short she wore the kind of clothes which, kept in immaculate condition, drew no attention to themselves or their wearer but which nevertheless made the requisite announcement of decency and respectability. But one thing did mark her out. She was never, ever seen inside or outside the home without a black beret on her head. This was kept in place by a hatpin of alarming length and sharpness. As long as she had this simple weapon handy she felt perfectly safe and was never frightened of anyone. She polished the furniture in the black beret, shopped in it, cooked in it and for all we knew slept in it as well.

On weekdays in the late afternoon there would usually be a comfortable hour or so by the fireplace when she and my mother enjoyed a chat over cups of tea. Quite often on these occasions her cardigan pockets bulged slightly. They held a tiny packet of cigarettes, a stubby cigarette holder and a box of Swan Vestas matches. I remember little if anything of what my mother used to say because it was my grandmother I was looking at and listening to while I kept quiet, pretending not to be there in my corner of the sofa. It was hearing her slightly foreign voice speak about Dublin and about things which happened in the unimaginably long ago past of twenty or thirty years that fascinated me. The time long before I was born, before I was thought of, before I was even a gleam in my father's eye as she used to say. Over the years the same reminiscences would come round time and again and I enjoyed them in the same way that children enjoy hearing their favourite stories over and over again. The most exciting and puzzling was the one about how they'd come to leave Dublin in 1920 at the time of the Troubles, when my mother was seven years old.

Her father, William Puckering, was an Englishman employed as a civil servant in Dublin and this was where he'd met and married my grandmother. One night he'd been working late which meant that on his way home he was out after curfew. Suddenly he heard cries of, 'That's him!' as he was set upon by some mysteriously-named thugs called Black and Tans. They shoved him up against a wall and were just about to shoot when one of them shouted, 'No it's not!' and they let him go. It shook him up so much that he decided Ireland was no place to be any more. So he took early retirement and moved his family to rural Oxfordshire where he'd been born and brought up.

As I listened and made out as much as I could from what I heard, there were sometimes things I couldn't understand because I wasn't meant to. Granny would lower her voice or hold her hand up against the side of her nose so that I couldn't do any lip-reading. But I didn't mind too much. This was the way things were. There were things that children weren't allowed to know. I was still able to enjoy her amusement, even if I didn't know what caused it. Years afterwards it didn't come as a huge surprise to find out from my mother that what had tickled my grandmother so much was quite often rather risqué. But I must have been at least fifty myself before she told me one story that caused particular mirth whenever it was alluded to. It was known as 'Sonny's Parting Shot'.

Sonny, whose real name was Clifton, was my mother's only brother and about six years older than she was. When the family lived in Dublin Sonny enjoyed a friendly enmity with an older and bigger boy called Billy Pollock. Sonny's surname of Puckering was naturally a gift to any dirty-minded boy and since most boys are dirty-minded it was almost inevitable that Sonny acquired the nickname Puck Fuck. Chalked messages incriminating Puck Fuck were liable to appear on walls anywhere in the district and even further afield in Dublin. They stayed there until the rain washed them off. Although Billy always denied it, Sonny knew the handiwork was his.

As the day drew near on which the Puckering family was due to take the boat across the Irish Sea never to return, Sonny planned his revenge. When they were clearing out their house in Upper Leeson Street he found just the raw material required – a pot of white paint and a two-inch brush. The family would have to make an early start on the day of the sailing and so Sonny had to make an even earlier one. Before anyone else was up he slipped out by the gate in the wall at the end of the garden and crept along to the one at the end of Billy's. There, secure in the knowledge he wouldn't be caught, and trusting that even with Irish rain it would take millennia to wash off, he painted his parting shot to Billy in eighteen-inch capitals – Pollock Bollock.

My mother must have been over eighty when she told me this for the first time and I don't know what surprised me more – the fact that such words were familiar to my grandmother or hearing the voice of my elderly mother saying them. Perhaps she felt liberated from former constraint by the current ubiquitous filthiness of everyday life in England.

But back then by the fireside in Sydenham such things were unimaginable. As time passed my grandmother would cup her left hand round her ear, listening for the sound of number 12 buses lurching round the corner of Lawrie Park Road. She'd raise herself slightly every time she heard one coming so that she could see if my father was on it. If he was he'd be poised ready to jump off the platform at the back before it stopped outside the telephone exchange. So then she'd say, 'Time I made myself scarce' or, 'Time I skedaddled. Here comes Himself. Let me take that cup for you Hen' and with china clinking and spoons tinkling she'd nip out of the sitting room, across the hall, into the kitchen and be out of sight in her own room before Himself even had time to put his key in the lock.

In our sort of road people kept themselves to themselves and so, apart from exchanging a few polite words while waiting for a bus, there wasn't anything in the way of social life. The houses were old, large and detached and the one in which we lived had been converted into flats. We lived on the ground floor in what was known as the garden flat and in the flat above was a family called Cotter. Their home was almost the only one apart from my own with which I was familiar. Even so, it felt like a foreign country – one that Heather and I travelled to quite often when Shiela's mother was out. They had all sorts of wonders up there. Things we didn't have down in our place. They had a spacious hall with a front door with wibbly glass in it and wibbly glass panels to either side of it and in front of each of these glass panels a tall vase stuffed with dried bull rushes stood sentinel.

The big thing about their front door was that it really was a front door. It lent eminence to them as well as to their establishment.

It was the only one of the flats to have a real one. The great big steps in the centre front of the house led up to it. Ours wasn't really a front door at all because it went in sideways under the steps and once you went in you had to turn right down a long passage. And they had a dining room which we didn't have because the equivalent room in our flat was my grandmother's bedroom. There were marvels in that dining room. Three mallards flew diagonally across one of the walls and on another was a magically-suspended display of blue and white willow-pattern plates. The idea that some people had more plates than they needed was new to me as was the idea of decorating a wall with them. And there was a collection of circular pictures with thatched cottages that stood out in relief, apparently made of painted and varnished plaster-of-Paris. And they had proper pictures as well, in proper frames – not like what we had. The only things that relieved the dingy wallpaper in our flat were mournful photographs of Killarney framed in black passe-partout.

But there were also quite a lot of things with a sinister eastern feel about them that made you shudder. Worst of all was the brass Buddha sitting cross-legged on top of the piano. Whoever the Buddha was, and why anyone should want him around with his naked belly collapsing in a cascade of flopping fat, was beyond my understanding. I'd avoid him and make for the family of elephants on the mantelpiece. They ambled along one behind the other, diminishing in size from left to right and using their trunks to hold on to the tail of the one in front.

The Cotter's sitting room was above Heather's and my bedroom and I used to encourage the alarming belief that the piano, which was immediately over my bed, would surely fall through the floor one night and kill me while I was asleep. But it felt most likely this would happen when it was hammered in the evening by Shiela's older sister Jean. She only seemed to play one piece of music and never took it from start to finish. In my ignorance I thought it was an elaborated version of:

> A frog he would a-wooing go
> Hey ho said Rowley
> Whether his mother would let him or no
> etc.

However I think now that it was a fragment snatched from a concerto by Rachmaninov. Jean used to really rumble and thunder it out. Today we'd probably say she gave it some welly.

But although the Cotter's flat had a much more prosperous feel to it than ours there was nevertheless something mildly repellent about it. It wasn't just the smell of polish mingled with Felix and the aroma from the Aladdin oil stove. It wasn't anything you could smell or see. It was something you could only sense by other means. Some kind of discomfort. You felt something was being insisted upon. A point was being made. There seemed to be anger in the high shine on the linoleum and a bossiness about the way the net curtains were controlled – stretched rigidly between 'worms' on the lower half of all the windows. There wasn't even any need for net curtains because nothing overlooked the house except ash trees and horse chestnuts. The only place you did need them was on the nasty dark side of the house where the iron fire escape went past all the parents' bedrooms. So it seems as if the nets were only there to provide something to be self-righteous about. When they hung, as they frequently did, on the washing line above the garage for all the world to see I felt glad for them as they flapped about enjoying a little freedom. But they were an annoyance to my mother and grandmother who were united in their opinion that it was common to have washing on display. It let the place down.

Another thing the Cotters had was a huge, much-indulged tabby cat called Mickey. The Felix pellets were always there in a saucer on the kitchen floor should he decide he wanted something to crunch on when he strolled in. In fact he did more than just stroll in. He was so remarkable that he used to flap the knocker on the front door when he was fed up with being outside. I didn't like Mickey. He didn't seem to be a cat so much as a person. This was probably because he was invariably referred to as Mickey

Cotter. He had a surname like the rest of us. He had a way of stopping in front of you and staring into your eyes. He looked at you as much as to say, 'So what've you been up to eh? No good at all by the looks of it.' You felt he'd start talking if he could be bothered and that he'd tell on you if he wanted to. He just disdained to do so.

I don't think my grandmother liked him much either and she certainly didn't like the smell of his fish being cooked up there and stinking the place out. As Mr Cotter was our landlord it wasn't felt possible to express annoyance directly and so hints were dropped by pointedly banging our kitchen window shut whenever it happened. But that was as far as it went and was completely ineffectual. The stink of Mickey's fish was a regular occurrence. It came about though that Mickey eventually provided my grandmother with a source of amusement. One day, over the late afternoon cup of tea she recalled a joke from her childhood.

> Oh Father I came to confess.
> And what have you come to confess my child?
> Oh Father I killed the cat.
> Oh my child you shouldn't do that.
> But Father 'twas a Protestant cat.
> Oh my child I'll forgive you for that.

So that was it! It was the Protestantism that was the trouble. Poor chap. After that she began to stop and have a quiet word with Mickey every now and then – just to let him know there were no hard feelings.

My grandmother had nothing against Protestants. After all she'd been married to one until he died suddenly during the war, not long before I was born. But what a Protestant was I had very little idea. A Protestant seemed to be anyone who wasn't a Catholic. But it wasn't even as simple as that because although Granny evidently wasn't a Protestant she clearly wasn't a Catholic either because she never went to church. She seemed to have been one once but wasn't any more.

I felt quite comfortable about this until I was told in RI that this wasn't possible. You could never stop being a Catholic. It was something you were for ever, whether you'd had the immense good fortune to have been born one or whether you'd received this precious gift through conversion by special grace from God. So if Catholics didn't go to church to hear mass and to receive the sacraments when required then they were in a state of ever-present mortal sin. Unless they repented and changed their ways then their eventual destination was certain. They would burn for ever in the eternal fires of Hell. It was as simple as that.

Religious instruction was imparted in the same way that history, geography or any other subject was – as fact. You wouldn't dream of questioning anything you were taught. The notion of enquiry or contradiction about anything told to you by an adult was one to which you had no access. Your natural assumption was that grownups always told the truth. They didn't tell lies. Only children were prone to this lamentable failing, not them. And so the certainty that nine nines made eighty-one and that the Battle of Marston Moor took place in 1644 was of the same order as what we heard about God and His One True Holy Roman and Catholic Apostolic Church.

God was made up of the Holy Trinity. He was three persons in one. These persons were separate and yet one and indivisible at the same time. First there was God the Father, then there was God the Son (who was Christ, Jesus, Our Lord, Our Blessed Lord, and the Lamb of God who takest away the sins of the world) and then there was the Holy Ghost. We were told not to worry if we couldn't understand this because, being a profound and sacred mystery, it was beyond human comprehension. The implication was that it would have been sinfully presumptuous to even try. Unthinking, unquestioning belief was all that was required. There were dark whisperings in relation to the Holy Ghost. It was said there was a sin against the Holy Ghost that was so terrible, so unforgivable that anyone who committed it would be damned for all eternity. No priest, not even the Holy Father himself, could absolve you from it.

What it was we were never told. I got hold of the idea that the sin against the Holy Ghost was to have the temerity to question the Church's teaching. I have a suspicion that the doctrine of the sin against the Holy Ghost was a clever ruse with which to frighten you, should you take it into your head to question Catholic dogma or the wisdom of Holy Mother Church. After all – who *do* you think you are?

I can't remember actually being told that only Catholics could get to Heaven and that everyone else would end up in Hell (apart from unbaptised babies who went to Limbo) but I know I must have been. In any case it was surely implicit in what you were told about St Peter and how the Church held the keys to the Kingdom of Heaven. If that was so then it meant that almost everyone you saw around you was destined for Hellfire because not many people we knew were Catholics. These people, who included quite a few of my cousins, uncles and aunts, not to mention my mother and grandmother, seemed remarkably unconcerned about what lay in store for them. They seemed to find life a laughing matter.

It felt as if it went on for years but I don't suppose it did – crying myself to sleep at night because my mother wasn't a Catholic. Instead of being able to get to Heaven with the rest of us, she would have to go to Hell and burn down there for all eternity. All I could do was pray and pray to Our Lady that she'd be converted before she died. So one day when my father sat on the side of my bed to say goodnight, I asked him whether he thought my mother would ever become a Catholic.

'Well you never know. Perhaps. Why do you ask?'

'Well if she doesn't she'll go to Hell won't she? Because only Catholics can get to Heaven.'

'I wouldn't worry yourself too much about that.' he said. 'Your mother stands a much better chance of getting into Heaven than I do. Much better than most people in fact. Time to go to sleep now.'

❋

They used to tell you it was time to go to sleep as if it was something you could just do. But of course you couldn't. Not when they were all still up and you felt left out. You weren't tired anyway. So you'd lie there for hours listening to the sound of voices (perhaps even laughter) coming from the sitting room and your grandmother busying herself with this or that in the kitchen. Then you'd hear her bedroom door click shut and you'd know she wouldn't be seen or heard again until morning. It was as if she ceased to exist during night-time hours. In fact she'd be settling down with her current library book. She always had a book on the go, the longer the better.

Like all other books she brought back from Penge Library this one would have undergone ordeal by fire. Trying not to think of the dirty hands that may have mauled its cover or of consumptives coughing between its pages she would have grasped it by the spine and flicked several times right through it while performing simultaneous additional agitation over the flames of the gas burner. Sterilisation was considered complete when the pong of hot paper and Rexine reached her nostrils at a satisfactory level of concentration.

Once she's in her room you reckon it can't be too long before Heather comes to bed. But when she doesn't and she doesn't and still she doesn't and there's all that time to get through before you can go to sleep you just can't help yourself thinking about things you don't want to think about. Like Michael.

I suppose it was a banal childhood incident. Just a doll with his head smashed to pieces after we accidentally dropped him on the concrete outside our bedroom door into the garden. But the memory keeps coming back. It was horrible to discover that his head had been empty all that time without me realising it; that his lovely eyes which opened when you picked him up and closed again when you laid him down were just blue gooseberries crudely attached to the inside of his head by wire. We tried to put him back together with Bostick but then he looked like crazy-paving. You had to accept that he couldn't come back. You wouldn't be able to play with him anymore. You'd killed him with your carelessness. So now there was something else to feel guilty about. If we'd been more careful then it wouldn't have happened. It served us right.

But feeling guilty or to blame for something was a more or less constant condition of childhood so I don't think this is why the memory keeps returning even now. I think it must be to do with the empty head. I reasoned from Michael's head to my own and was frightened that mine was as empty as his. What was inside your head anyway? On the front of your head you had your face and your face seemed to be who you were because that's how people recognised you. Behind your face was something you had your thoughts with. It was somewhere you tried to work things out. It was the place you kept memories and secrets. It was where the person was that you were talking to when the others said you were talking to yourself. It was the place that dreams came to.

Dreams. What were they? Where did they take you to? Your bed seems to be like a station waiting-room because when you go to sleep you seem to travel to another place. To actually be somewhere other than in your own bed. Somewhere totally confusing and usually frightening. It's a place you go to on your own where there's no-one to protect you and they can do whatever they like with you. They can throw you over cliffs or down bottomless black pits or they can make the bedroom curtains become giant dwarfs that turn your legs to stone as they chase you down Field End Road in Eastcote where your Aunt Dolly lives. Their massive feet shake the pavement and their snorts and grunts get closer and closer until you feel hot breath on the back of your neck and you know you're going to die. And then just as you're about to die you don't. You make it back home. You're saved. You're in your bed again. Or on the floor. Or stuck between the bed and the wall, underneath the overloaded shelf that always tips the lot on top of you whenever this happens.

Then later you realise you don't actually go anywhere at

night. You stay in your bed all the time and dreams come to you. Why do they get sent to you and who sends them anyway? When dreams come to you it's a bit like going to the pictures. But after a while you understand that it isn't like going to the pictures because your dreams are different from other people's dreams. They don't know which ones you've had and you don't know which ones they've had.

The joy of waking up lies in discovering you've survived the night. You haven't died. As the grey morning light seeps round the sides of the curtains, they become just curtains again and each scruffy piece of furniture re-emerges into familiar solidity. You know by listening to the sitting room clock that it won't be long before you'll hear your grandmother light the gas under the kettle just the other side of the wall from where you are. Then she'll go and lay the table in the other room and if it's winter she'll get the fire going too so that it'll be warmed up in there before breakfast.

But whatever dreams I had and whatever was or wasn't inside my head, it was the Michael incident that provided Heather with a perpetually foolproof method of provoking me to rage and impotent frenzy. All she had to do was pounce, grab my head in both hands, squeeze my cheeks until my mouth made a figure of eight and say with her silvery laugh, infinite patronage and air of phoney concern, 'Darling! Better hold your head – case it breaks!'

✱

'When did you last go?' This ominous question could be darted at you by either parent at any time with no warning and no apparent trigger. Anxiety seemed to lie behind it as if constipation, a word I didn't know, was life-threatening.

However, I suspect that concern about us being bunged-up sprung from my father. I doubt whether my mother would have given it a thought. Sad-looking and rather distant, she didn't seem to bother about us much as long as we kept out of her way.

It felt as though 'inner cleanliness' – something Andrews Liver Salts were said to provide – had a moral dimension to it in addition to the more obvious one relative to bodily wellbeing. It felt as if constipation was a physical manifestation of sin. What else can you think when the massive frame of your father suddenly materialises in the bedroom doorway, his nose twisted in disgust as he barks, 'Who's made a rude smell? Go and sit on the lavatory.'

It was some time before I saw the connection between making rude smells and being made to sit on the lavatory. I thought it was just a form of punishment for being disgusting – something that children were but grownups weren't. I'm pretty certain that I did time in the bathroom not just for my own disgustingness but also for Heather's. A swift declaration of innocence on her part and I was not only convicted without trial but convinced of my own guilt. So I'd go and sit in there fully-clothed on top of the closed lavatory seat and while away the time counting whether there were more black squares than white squares on the lino until someone wanted to come in and the whole business had apparently blown over (so to speak).

When did I last go? How long was it since I went? I never had the slightest idea, except that it was a very long time ago indeed. I didn't tell them that I'd sit on the lavatory without result for so long that my legs went dead and couldn't support me when I finally gave up the case as hopeless. If they'd known the truth I think it not unlikely they'd have rushed me round to Dr Allport. Perhaps they sensibly stopped bothering to ask and decided to impose a regime of weekly clear-outs instead. This was where my mother put in an unaccustomed regular appearance. Friday night was dose night. The choice of weapon was hers and it was deadly.

It was senna. She gave you a glass of it as you sat up in bed before settling down for the night. I've often wondered since whether the senna pods she got from Roland Roberts, the chemist in Penge High Street, came with any instructions. Were you really meant to pour boiling water on to them? By the time it was brought to us in thick tumblers, the resultant brew had considerately been allowed to go lukewarm so that it could be gulped down in one swig. It was the colour of tea without milk.

Although it tasted foul, I dare say there are plenty of worse-tasting liquids than infusion of senna, but as a child I couldn't imagine more acute persecution than what this evil stuff produced the following morning. By six o'clock the griping pains had begun to get your legs bicycling about the bed and they seemed to go on for hours before the time was right to make a dash for the bathroom. The teaspoon of neat Welfare orange they gave you to take away the taste of the senna was small consolation for the agony you knew was to come. I used to go to sleep praying, 'Please God let my pains come first so I can get into the bathroom before Heather. Oh please God let me be first.'

I don't remember whether I ever was. The archetypal memory is of rolling on the hall floor clutching my abdomen and clenching my buttocks and every so often struggling to my knees to hiss desperately through the keyhole, 'Hurry up Heath. Hurry up. Let me in. Let me in. I'm dying. I'm dying.' All I'd be likely to hear in reply was a gleeful 'Tee hee hee.'

❋

Because Heather's tee hee hee runs like a leitmotiv through my recollection of childhood, it was with her that I'd meant to start my letter today. I've always known that it would be difficult to catch her likeness but yesterday I thought I might be able to give you some idea by telling you the kind of things she used to do. So last night when I woke up about half past two and couldn't get back to sleep I crept downstairs to make myself a cocoa which I brought back to bed to help a stint of concentration about her. But the concentration wouldn't work. The harder I tried to track her down the more she eluded me. Instead of getting her I kept getting something which I didn't want at all and which I thought was irrelevant. I kept trying to brush it aside but it remained obstinately in front of me.

First of all it had been an image of myself sitting on the dusty rug in our bedroom. Then it moved onto the grass behind a big clump of Michaelmas daisies and this is where it stayed. In my hands is a tangled bunch of Anchor embroidery silks that I'm trying to sort out. Heather and I loved these embroidery silks because they were such pretty colours but our needlework was dreadful and once we started using them they'd get into an awful mess. This was because each silk strand was made up of six separate threads and so you not only had different colours of varying length but also strands with varying numbers of threads in them. So this messy ball of threads I'm trying to untangle is very difficult to do and the threads keep getting stuck and going into knots as I struggle with it.

So I gave up chasing Heather (I could never catch up with her anyway because she was always going to be more than five years older than me) and let my mind go into free fall. I didn't try to take it anywhere but just waited to see where it would take itself. Immediately, the embroidery silks vanished and in their place was a fragment of memory. It's a sunny summer day and there are three of us out in the garden. There's a sense of something special about it. Perhaps it's because the man I later realise is my father is there with Heather and me. At that time though I think he was just The Man. I can't see him or Heather. They're just there. She's a lot bigger than me and he's a lot bigger than either of us. Perhaps bigger than both of us put together. He's cutting the long grass with a scythe and we're meant to be raking it up. I haven't got a rake so I'm just bending over and playing at raking with my fingers. As I do so, I suddenly see the world in a new way. Upside down. And at what seems like this precise moment I discover that I exist as an individual. The familiar sound of 'Sally' turns out to be me. I exist. I'm separate from them.

So now I think I understand the significance of the embroidery silk image. In trying to talk about Heather I couldn't avoid talking about how I only emerged into some sense of who I was by reference to her – by the discovery that I wasn't part of her. And by extension that I wasn't part of the other people who lived in the flat. Until then I hadn't had a sense of being separate from them or a clear sense of them being separate from each other. I'm not sure I'd really seen them at all, any more than I'd seen myself. I was entangled with them and didn't understand about being an individual – a person.

But I don't think I managed to hold on to this knowledge. I reckon it disappeared into the surrounding darkness until I rediscovered it some time later, perhaps about the age of five when I went to school and was reminded of who I was every time I saw my full name inked inside my plimsolls. So it seems as if I was a very dim child. Oddly enough though they didn't seem to think I was. Somehow, quite early on I received the information that I was The Bright One. By listening at keyholes? That would've been entirely in character. As would my being sly enough not to get caught doing it.

As I talk to you about this now I'm having to try and ignore those potent voices from the past. The contemptuous fury of my mother's 'Who do you think you are?' (Thinking and talking about myself as I'm doing now. Oh vanity of vanities. Presumption of presumptions.) And the quiet control of my father's 'Mustn't take yourself too seriously you know. Must be able to laugh at yourself.' (When I'd been too solemn as they used to call it and not as cheerful as they would have liked?) It was my mother who said I was solemn and who kept telling me to stop scowling – something I'd no idea I was doing. In her stated opinion I was also secretive, which was certainly true and which didn't seem to be something in my favour. It was an implied fault.

And so you begin to form an idea of who you are by what they say about you. And you get other ideas on the subject from what you find in the family photograph album. When Heather was at school there were endless hours with no-one to play with and nothing to do. A great many of these were idled away rummaging inside the cupboards of a colossal sideboard in what was called the sitting room but which was also where the dining table and chairs were – squashed in behind the sofa. (To be under the table was therefore an excellent situation from which to eavesdrop on those gossipy conversations which ended with my grandmother announcing the imminent arrival of Himself.)

    Because the sideboard stood facing away from the light, against the wall between the room's two windows, it felt darker than black inside. I'd pretend it was a secret place and that I was discovering treasure that no-one else knew about. This was a difficult fantasy to keep going for long because the sideboard held just about everything that couldn't find a home elsewhere. Like dress patterns by Simplicity or Butterick which had come from Rogers in Penge and where you'd had to hang around for ages while they were being chosen. A heap of tattered knitting patterns. A quiver-full of assorted knitting needles kept together by a knotted remnant of knicker elastic. Balls of wool. The sewing box lined in pink but now of such familiarity that you couldn't pretend any more that you'd just seen it for the first time. A rectangular cash tin in dingy green, always devoid of money and divided into separate compartments, each with its own slot and into which you could pass the time by posting buttons you'd selected out of the Quality Street tin. A curiosity called a Post Office Savings tin was also empty. It wasn't difficult to work out why because there were two sets of metal teeth across its slot which made it impossible to slide out the coins on the side of a knife the way you did all the time with ordinary money boxes. To get it open you had to take it to the post office where they had a special key. (I don't think it made the journey in my lifetime.) But if you didn't get dispirited by all this, by the stack of four London Telephone Directories and the A–Z Street Atlas but pressed on through the jumble towards the centre back of the sideboard, you found something more like real treasure. Things like cases that contained never-used, silver-plated cutlery lying asleep in sunken beds of white or purple pleated satin.

    So with all that kind of stuff in the sideboard it's not surprising that it housed two items which held continual fascination for me –

a pair of long, sharp sewing scissors and a photograph album with a brown, padded leather cover. Those sessions in the sideboard constituted some of the more active moments in the days spent alone with my mother. After lunch I'd be put to bed, supposedly to recover from my exertions but in reality to get me out from underneath her feet. The curtains would be drawn to no avail and I'd just lie there killing time in any manner that occurred to me.

Then came an afternoon rest period when I found something wonderful to do. I just couldn't resist it. The scissors had been left on the chest of drawers behind the door! And there was the army blanket on Heather's bed! This blanket, which did service as a bedspread in winter, was just longing to have a fringe made on the side nearest me. So I settled down to make the scissors make one. There was something about the certitude of what those scissors did that filled me with satisfaction. Again and again they did the same thing. Their power was thrilling – almost intoxicating.

After that, whenever I was looking for something to do I'd be given the scissors and a pile of newspapers to get to work on. By the time I was five I was highly proficient at cutting round complex shapes, so much so that I was insulted by the round-ended blunt things you were given in the Kindergarten and which you couldn't possibly hurt yourself with.

❋

Now for the photograph album. I've been trying to imagine childhood without that to pore over. Suppose it hadn't been there? Suppose you lived in a world where there weren't any photographs? How would a small child get an idea of the past? What role do photographs play in developing your idea of what it means to be you? How you became you? Or how you nearly didn't become you? Photographs introduce you to a past before you came into being, a past much longer ago than last Christmas and to a world that looked different then from how it does now. So photographs introduce you to the concepts of time and change. I wonder if contemplation of the self, an awareness of one's own individuality, is possible before you become aware of the passage of time? Perhaps photographs accelerate understanding, which in their absence would only come about by more natural means in later years.

Once I became aware of the world beyond the home it seemed there were three categories of people out there – old people, grownups and children. The passage of time was limited to an awareness of the very near past and the very near future. You remembered yesterday about as clearly as the plug hole remembered the bathwater it swallowed. Tomorrow was an awfully long way ahead. Time went so slowly that it hardly seemed to pass at all. You lived in a virtually permanent present. Things had always been the same and would always be the same. Old people had always been old, grownups had always been grownups and children would always be children.

Then you start looking in the album. Most of the photographs are very small and all of them are in black and white. You do a lot of looking and wondering. Who are these unknown people? Until then I think I'd sensed people around me rather than actually seen them. I hadn't really looked at them; I'd only felt them. And I continued not really to look at them. Instead I projected the photographs onto them. They even had an effect on memories. So many of mine come to me today as if they were in black and white and had been found in the album.

I desperately wanted the pretty little girl with blonde curly hair to be me. But it wasn't. It never was. It was always Heather whenever I asked. And she seems to have had special attention because there are lots of photos of just the three of them together. I'm not there because I haven't been born yet but they don't seem bothered about this. Having asked, 'Is this me?' so often, only to be disappointed, I don't think I dared ask, 'Where's me?' in case I wasn't there at all. But I was. It turned out that I was the one with the fat face and boring hair. Well if I

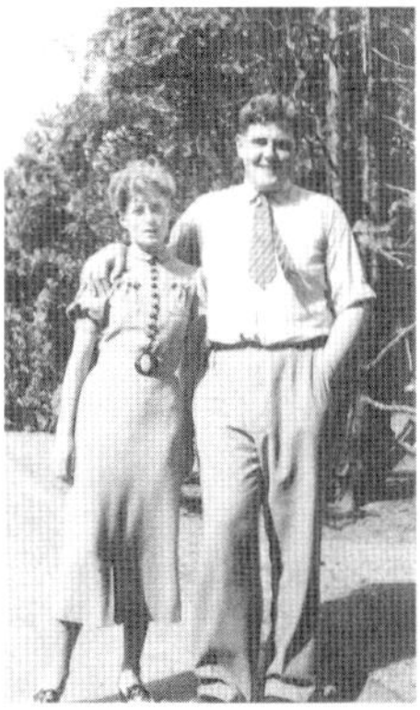
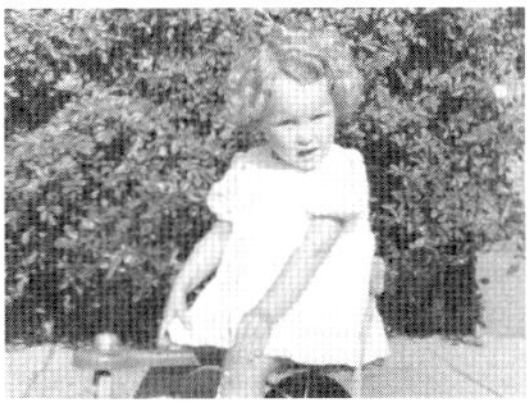
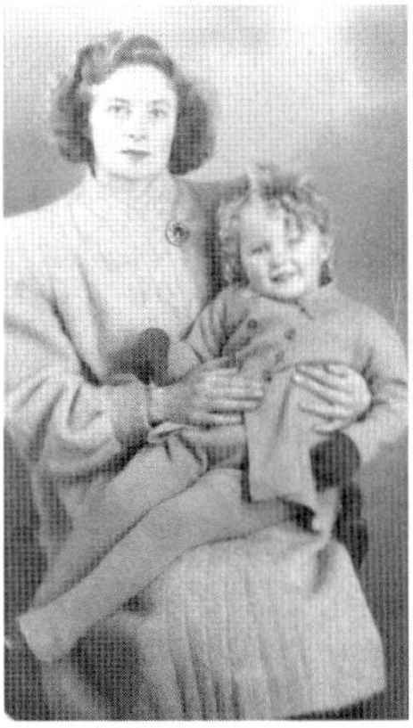
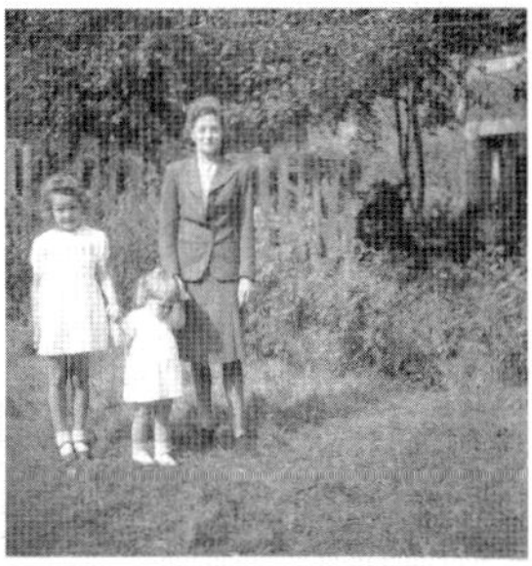
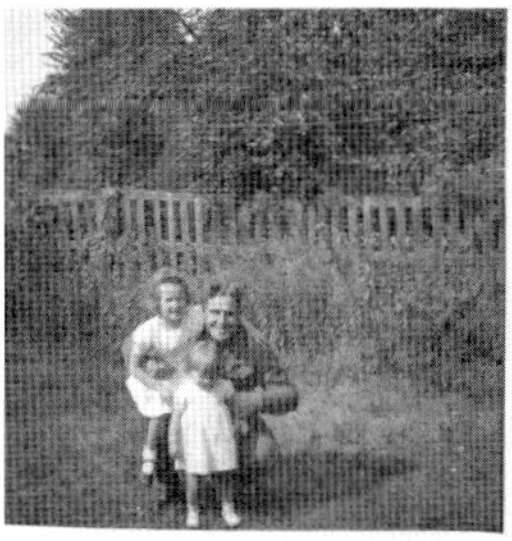
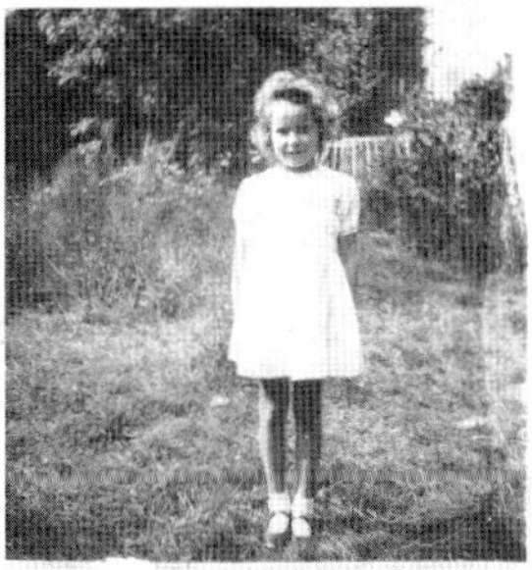
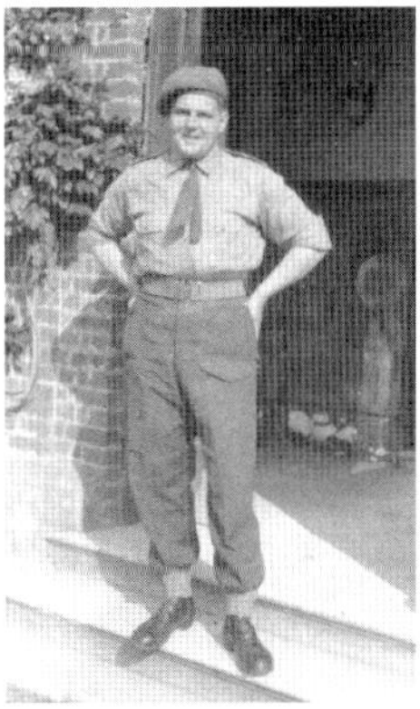
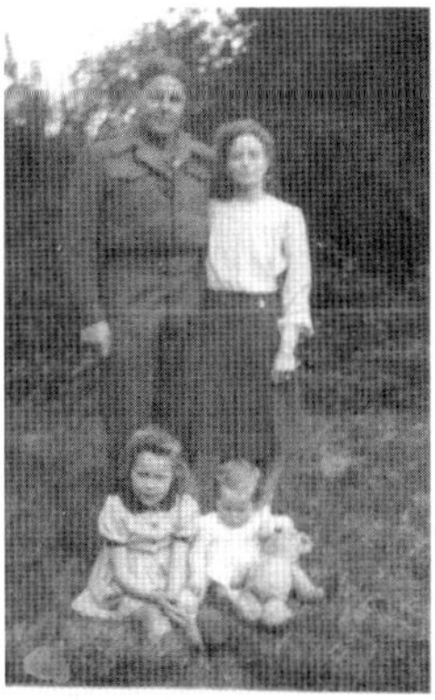
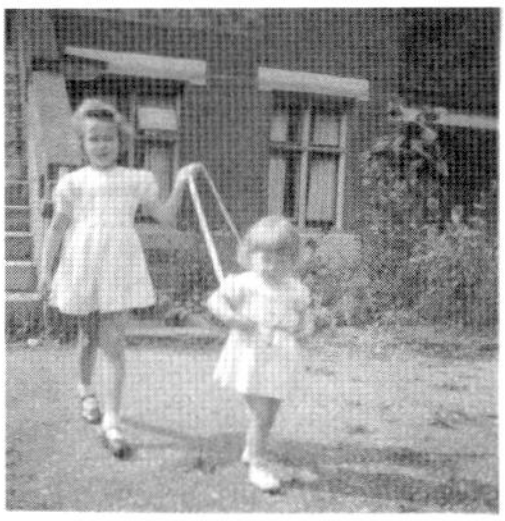
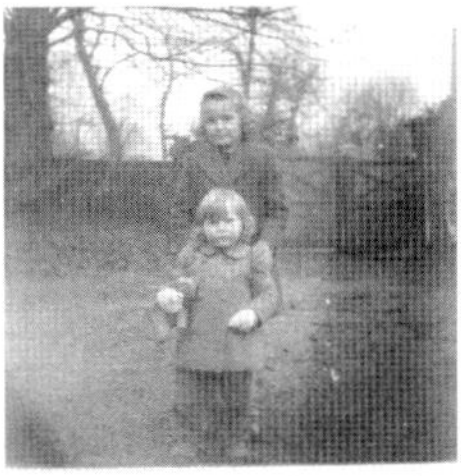
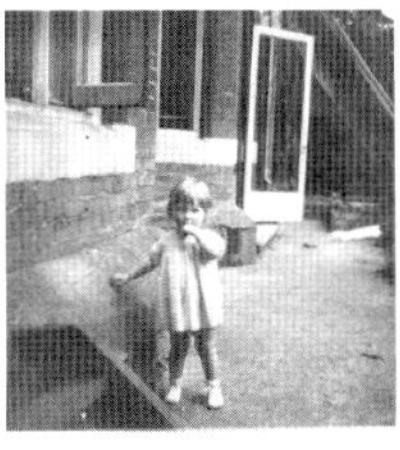
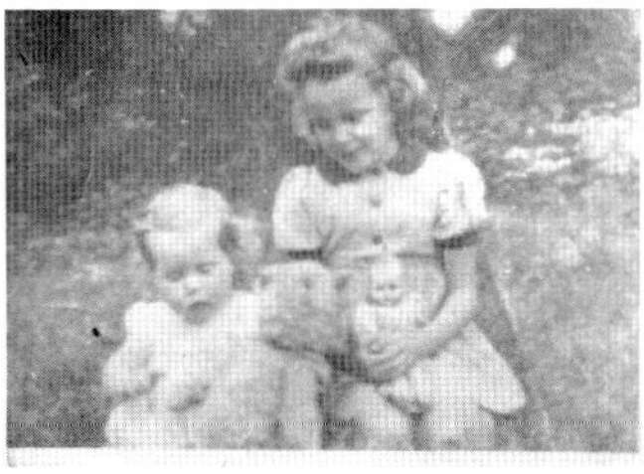
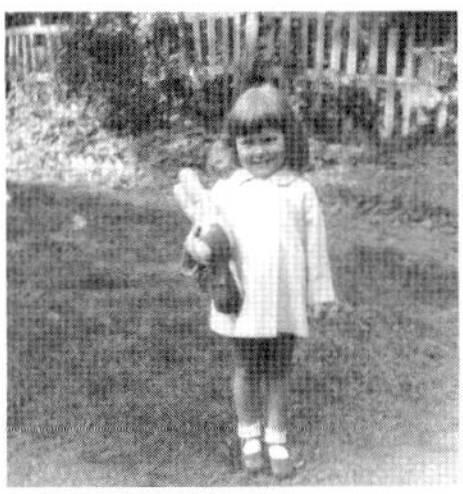

wasn't pretty at least I had the consolation of knowing my sister was. I'd boast about her prettiness and blonde curls because I suppose I thought she made up for my own shortcomings in that direction.

Then a strange and rather unpleasant thing happened. One Friday after school I'd been invited to a birthday party at a house near the fire station in Perry Vale. An additional excitement attaching to it was that Heather was going to come and collect me afterwards. It was an opportunity to show her off and I was looking forward to admiring comments. Instead of which the party girl – about whom I remember nothing at all, not even her name, – accused me of being a liar. My sister had not got blonde curly hair like I'd said she had. And it was true. Because of what she said I saw Heather as she really was for the first time. So powerful was the impression made by those photographs that I simply hadn't been able to do so before. Not only had her hair turned dark brown but she was having to wear black-rimmed National Health glasses and a brace on her teeth.

❋

During my first year at St Winefride's Heather was there too – in the final class which was known as the Upper Preparatory. Although she must have been responsible for taking me to and from the convent every day I can't remember seeing a great deal of her. But knowing she was there made things special for me. She was part of who I was. I wasn't just Sally Shervington but was Heather's Sister as well. She was one of the big girls and I knew she wouldn't let anyone be nasty to me. She'd protect me. But as I didn't encounter any nastiness she was deprived of the opportunity to express her love and loyalty in public. That is until lunchtime one particular day and the ordeal of the so-called scrambled egg. I was staring into a bowl of pale yellow wobby slosh obviously made out of powdered egg and that looked and smelled like sick. I was in a state of near paralysis, unable to believe they thought this was something I could swallow without adding some sick of my own on top of it. I expect all the other children were thinking the same but unlike them I was fortunate enough to have a saviour. The bowl went. It had gone. Heather had swooped down, whisked it away and there she was now plonking it down on Mother Mary Dymphna's desk and declaring, 'My sister is *not* going to eat *that*!' And I didn't. The muck was taken away. So Heather knew how to make herself heard. She knew how to make things happen.

But sometimes she makes things happen that I can't understand. Like when it's a sultry, overcast day with a feel of July about it. The last day of term? Heather's last day at St Winefride's perhaps? Yes I think so. There's no-one left in my building. Everyone has gone home ages ago and it's been locked up. All the convent grounds seem deserted and I'm hanging around on the edge of the meadow near the old oak wood expecting her to come from the direction of St Monica's – the big house which is where the senior part of the school is. It's very quiet everywhere.

When at last the shrill sound of girls' voices does come, it doesn't come from that direction but bursts from the other end of the meadow. There she is! Heather's coming! She and her friends are racing towards me but Heather's out in front! She's winning! She's going to get to me first! But my pride is misplaced. This isn't a game. I've misinterpreted what's going on. Those girls aren't shrieking with joy; they're shrieking with rage. They're a posse in pursuit of a criminal. They're after her blood. When they catch her, they knock her down and because they know she's blind without her glasses they pull them off and toss them into a huge bed of stinging nettles. Then they grab her by the arms and legs and counting slowly with evident relish ONE – TWO – THREE – FOUR – FIVE – SIX they hurl her on top of them. Then they bash her with tennis rackets and stamp on her panama hat. After that, perhaps feeling they've done enough but not quite, they tip the contents of her satchel on top of her.

What had she done? And what had she done on those other

occasions when she rushed into the bedroom hissing 'shoosh' and threw herself under her bed a couple of seconds before Granny burst in brandishing a tightly-rolled copy of *Picture Post* and muttering with murderous intent, 'Come on, where is she? I know she's in here so don't you be thinking of hiding the blighter either. You just come out from under there you little divil. Just you wait till I get my hands on you, you little booger (rhyming with sugar). You just wait'.

She'd probably done something like balancing one of the ten red volumes of Arthur Mee's *Children's Encyclopaedia* on top of a half-open door, or stacked the telephone directories in the hall just outside Granny's room in the hope she'd trip over them when she came out. Or perhaps she'd sneaked into the kitchen and broken into a cake that she'd just made for a special occasion – such as a visit by some of the uncles, cousins and aunts at the weekend.

Speaking about cake brings me to the subject of food in general and to a digression which I hope will give you some idea how different life was fifty or so years ago. If you were ravenous when you came home from school (and we always were) you couldn't just go and help yourself to anything. You had to wait until something was put in front of you later. Not only was there no fridge to forage in but there was precious little food in the cupboards either. It's true that in a good week there might be some digestive biscuits in the tin but you weren't allowed to take them. If you wanted something to drink then there was water from the tap. There was no such thing as a bottle of squash in our house. I wouldn't have known the stuff existed if I hadn't come across it at other people's birthday parties – although I did know about White's lemonade. But fizzy lemonade and fancy biscuits only happened at Christmas and as far as I knew simply didn't exist throughout the rest of the year.

Food had to be bought in small quantities each day. This wasn't just because there was no fridge to keep it in but because of food rationing which went on for years after the war ended in 1945. Granny wouldn't have been able to just make a cake because she felt in the mood to do so. She would have had to plan for it by saving up the coupons or points necessary to obtain the ingredients. Fresh or cooked food was kept in a safe to keep off the flies. This was a white-enamelled little cupboard with fine wire mesh in its sides and door. And in hot weather, as soon as the milk was delivered, it was brought in to stand next to it in a bowl of cold water. Muslin was then draped over the bottles so that it dangled in the water in an attempt to keep the top part of them cool too.

Perhaps there's something in the adage about the devil finding work for idle hands to do. We were certainly idle in the empty time outside school hours and in the holidays. There seemed to be vast tracts of it to squander when we weren't under any kind of supervision, even if Granny was around. In a way she seemed like an honorary child herself which meant she could be relied upon not to split on us to 'them' and get us into trouble. She was on our side.

But if she kept quiet about encyclopaedias on doors, stolen cake and stacked-up telephone directories, surely she didn't keep quiet about the spills of lighted newspaper we tried to push through her door? It didn't 'work' of course. On contact with the keyhole the flames turned into charred flakes and fell to the hall floor. But what on earth was Heather (and I with her direction) trying to do? Why do children think of doing such idiotic and potentially lethal things, with no malice intended and in the belief that it's all a great lark?

Other larks were much more innocent and only involved hoodwinking an easily-fooled child such as me, or Susan who lived in the top flat. I might have been bright in some ways but I must have been remarkably dim-witted in others. Or perhaps I was still young enough to believe in bad magic. It seemed the only way to explain the fact that however much money I posted into my red savings tin there was never anything in it. Heather claimed to be as puzzled as I was.

She got so much fun out of mystifying the gullible that she didn't always do it for obvious gain like she did when her ultimate aim was to buy buns on the way home from school. I can remember at least one occasion when she suffered for her Art. It must have been around September time. I'd already been put to bed but Heather and Susan had been allowed to go blackberrying in somewhere called the Palace grounds. The back of the houses in our road all overlooked this place. As you peered through the hedge at the bottom of the garden it looked like the deep, dark forests where unfortunate things happened in fairy tales. It was closed to the public but we used to get in there through a hole in the hedge. When he came home after the war in 1946 my father had made this so that we could come and go as we pleased. So we tended to regard the whole murky and mysterious place as our own private territory.

Anyway, you didn't have to go far to find the blackberries. They were immediately behind the hedge and went on as far as you could see. Granny was planning to use the blackberries in a pudding but when Heather came in she said they hadn't found any. There just weren't any to pick. I dropped off to sleep then but after a while I was woken by some sort of commotion. Heather was being terribly sick (of necessity in the kitchen sink rather than the lavatory because someone was having a bath) and was being given a good telling-off. It wasn't like Granny to be like that. It wasn't fair. It wasn't your fault if you were sick. Well sometimes it was. It all started as a game with no name, invented on an instant. What's happening to the blackberries? Now you see them. Now you don't. They keep disappearing. Susan picks and picks but there are never any there in the bag that Heather's carrying. Susan's look of bewilderment – the fact that she doesn't guess what's going on strikes Heather as so hilarious she just can't stop herself. So she pays the price in sick but reckons it was worth it – just to remember the expression on Susan's face.

❉

One sunny day in late afternoon I saw my father come in the

gate and walk towards the front door, effortlessly carrying a stack of big red books under one arm. These were the encyclopaedias he'd said he was going to get us. We had so few things of our own that even an obviously improving present like this one was cause for excitement. The ten volumes of Arthur Mee's *Children's Encyclopaedia* would tell us everything we needed to know.

In his introduction Arthur Mee puts it like this:

> It is an encyclopaedia of everything that comes into childhood, and by childhood it means all that period of life when the sensitive mind, the most marvellous instrument within the boundless universe, is being formed … This book is arranged so that a child can understand it. Its purpose is to give boys and girls a conception of the world they live in and of their place in it …. This book presents a simple scheme of universal knowledge which opens up a vision of the world as one great whole. It seeks to stir the mind and to awake a sense of wonder. Its purpose is to fascinate and educate … In its millions of words and its thousands of pictures it brings the mind of a child up from the beginning of the world into the midst of the thrilling age we live in.

And at the end of Volume ten he says this:

> Through all the things that are written here breathes a spirit which no dark days can conquer. This book is written from beginning to end in the faith that all is well. It believes in God and man and in our race. It believes in loving our country as the noblest country that has ever been, and in loving mankind no less. It believes that character is the greatest thing in the world, and that by teaching our children to do right, to love truth, and to cherish fine things, we can save mankind from all its troubles and build up the Kingdom of Heaven.

Well the set of encyclopaedias certainly did make an impression on me but not the kind that would have gratified the idealistic and well-intentioned Arthur Mee. Yesterday I picked up Volume One and within moments of beginning to turn its pages I fell exhausted onto a sofa, unable to put up the slightest fight against the desire for oblivion in sleep. It had brought back the sense of hopelessness it always induced in me as a child. There was the sheer physical weight of the thing for a start. Then there were those closely-crammed pages of text, the craziness of its organisation, the absurdities of its juxtapositions and judgements.

Although the mishmash of illustrations probably did open my mind to such things as the existence of other countries and cultures, their cumulative effect wasn't one of enlightenment, any more than a visit to a museum was. The random display of objects in a museum and the equally random display of objects reproduced in the books became as familiar as the photographs of Killarney on the wall, but that was as far as understanding or knowledge went. Neither encyclopaedia nor museum made any connection with the various landscapes I moved around in. Supposedly there to help you understand the world, encyclopaedia and museum crushed you with the weight of their haphazardly-accumulated parts. You couldn't put the bits together. But I wasn't consciously trying to do that anyway. I didn't really know what it was I didn't know or needed to know. I took not-knowing for granted. It was the normal state of affairs.

One day when I was about four my father lifted me through the hole in the hedge at the bottom of the garden and took me deeper into the Palace grounds than I'd ever been before. It might have been frightening without him because it wasn't long before we were confronted by a group of huge and hideous monsters wallowing in green slime in the shallows of a lake. Fortunately they weren't alive but they looked as if they could have been if someone breathed on them in the right way. He told me they were prehistoric animals but that was as far as his information went. As I gradually ventured further afield and discovered different aspects of that vast shattered landscape, the Palace grounds began to feel a bit like an encyclopaedia itself, but an encyclopaedia with most of its pages torn or missing.

One of the few things in the *Children's Encyclopaedia* that could be said to have infiltrated my brain to any extent at all was something near the beginning of Volume One. (This was probably because of the number of times I tried afresh to grasp the 'wonderful world of knowledge' by beginning at the beginning. I started again and again and again.) It spread across two pages and was entitled: THE CLOCK OF THE WORLD – THE MARCH OF LIFE DOWN THE LONG ROAD OF TIME. These days I suppose they'd call it a pie chart. It was an illustrated diagram of geological time showing the various life-forms associated with each period of the earth's history.

There were just two things which caught my attention. The first was that human beings didn't make it to earth until about one minute to midnight. The second was the similarity between the prehistoric monsters in the Palace grounds and those shown here as being on earth during the Triassic, Jurassic and Cretaceous periods; the slices of time that came before the slice that we were in – Tertiary. (Perhaps that's one of the reasons I felt there was some kind of affinity between the Palace grounds and an encyclopaedia.) So it gave you the impression that human beings were what Earth had been waiting for all that time – just like God completing His work with the creation of Adam and Eve.

Nobody seemed surprised that prehistoric monsters were there so I wasn't surprised either – any more than I was surprised by roads and bridges and railway lines. They were just there. You didn't understand it but you didn't understand anything. You just made yourself familiar with things. It seems to me that a child proceeds more by feeling than by seeking after knowledge of the encyclopaedic kind. Feeling is how they know about things. Feeling is how they learn to find their way around. Feeling is knowledge. It's their own particular kind of knowledge and it's impossible to put into words.

❋

Just a few yards to the left behind the hedge at the bottom of the garden something horrible hid among the trees. It was the skeleton of a big ruined building, open to the sky and full of iron-coloured water so dark you couldn't see how far down it went. There weren't even any walls for what was left of the roof to rest on – just an iron frame which I suppose had once been concealed with brick. A few courses of brickwork were left surrounding the huge rectangle of menacing water and on the narrow footway provided by them Heather (who did ballet) would enjoy frightening me by practicing her *entrechats*.

I still shudder when I think about that place. It appalled me. Bomb sites I took for granted but this was quite another thing. It didn't just frighten me – it worried me. Something awful had gone wrong. They'd built something that didn't work – something they didn't want any more because it was a failure. It was as depressing as a filthy exercise book which, in its pristine state, had been the object of brief optimism about the possibility of self-improvement.

There was another place in the Palace grounds where Heather could joyously exercise her power to alarm. This was quite near where the dinosaurs were. Before you got to them you went over a rickety bridge that was faintly reminiscent of the kind you see on willow-pattern plates. It was meant to go over water but there wasn't any water there – or none worth talking about. Then a few yards further on you came to a very different kind of bridge which spanned a ravine. Beyond it was a rock face and what they called the waterfall. But the waterfall was a failure too. A meagre stream slithered down the sheer cliff without a splash onto another place where there should have been water but wasn't. There was supposed to be something special about the rock face but I never knew what it was. It was made up of various layers, one of which was coal. This seemed odd because I'd never heard of coal mines in London. So now there was something else to add to the accumulating muddle inside my head.

No such problems for Heather to whom the coal seam presented creative possibilities. One day, when I thought she was on the path behind me, I turned round to find she wasn't there any more. Realising that she was playing some kind of trick on me I didn't give it much thought. I knew she'd turn up somewhere. When she did I could hardly bear to look. With her too-tight gymslip, satchel on her back and bloater shoes she was inching her way through the so-called waterfall, along a narrow slimy shelf provided by the projecting coal seam and in imminent danger of getting dashed to pieces on the rocks below. Her expedition was a triumph but she dismissed it with a casual shrug as if to say, 'Pfff – that was nothing. You just wait and see what I'll do when they give me half a chance.'

I'm trying to remember how I felt about the Palace grounds. Different things at different times I think. In the daytime it was like a world made up of very different countries all running into each other. You had to go across the avenue country if you wanted to get to the lake and prehistoric monster one and because the enormous trees down the avenue met overhead, it was very dark in there with only small puddles of sunlight on the forest floor. The avenue led you on but it led you nowhere. It just came to an end with a meandering, wobbly wall of corrugated iron. Although this had difficulty in standing up straight it still managed to stay upright enough to keep you out.

In the furthest part that we could get to from our garden and as far away as you could be from the prehistoric animals, were the remains of a lost civilisation. Balustraded stone walls stretched as far as you could see, with niches all along them and statues being strangled by ivy. A lot of the statues had toppled off and lay broken among the brambles and you could see more of them lying around when you looked through the enormous swirls of barbed wire. The barbed wire stopped you getting to the enormously wide steps that would have let you explore deeper into the mysteries of this particular country. Heather always wanted to go in there but I wasn't keen. Notices said DANGER KEEP OUT. There were unexploded bombs in there left over from the war.

Although the Palace grounds seemed to be made up of contrasting countries all running into one another it also felt like somewhere that had no ending. When I lay in bed at night and thought about it spread out there in the dark, beyond what I thought of as the forest behind our garden, it seemed to dissolve into blackness and go on for ever the way the sea does when you look towards the horizon. I suppose this was because the jagged barrier of corrugated iron and barbed wire prevented us from discovering its furthest limit. It was a whole world. A world we couldn't get to the other side of. A perplexing, disturbing and even frightening parallel universe.

As I've told you before, I used to be sent to bed hours before there was any chance of being able to go off to sleep. So if I hadn't got anything particular to worry about I'd lie there listening to the trains. To the clunk rumble rumble clunk, rumble rumble clunk as they went over the bridge I knew would fall down. To the singing sound made by the ones on a different line – the one that went over the high brick bridge where Sydenham turned into Penge. To the sudden cut-off scream of the Night Ferry as it plunged into the tunnel underneath Sydenham Hill. And on frosty nights to the electric crackle and flash made by the trains and which lit up our bedroom. All the time I could hear the trains running I didn't feel alone and so the dark world beyond the bedroom was still the familiar world of everyday life. But once they'd stopped and everyone had gone to sleep except me, the silence transformed everything. What whirled around inside my head and what lay spread beyond the end of the garden seemed to become one and the same thing.

Rather like the way the prehistoric monsters in the Palace grounds became linked in my mind with pictures in Arthur Mee's encyclopaedia, so the inside of my head and the world which had dissolved into darkness became confounded with other images and words to be found at the beginning of Chapter One, Volume One. Fascinating though the following extract may be I don't think it's calculated to help a child get a good night's sleep.

> The big ball we live on, with its mountains, and rivers, and seas, and plants and animals, is only a speck in the vast infinity of space. It is surrounded by millions of suns and planets born untold ages before the Earth came into being, which have now burnt out and ceased to spin. In comparison with its own Sun, the Earth is a tiny thing, and if it were a little nearer that shining star it would be drawn into one of its fiery whirlpools and devoured like a daisy in a prairie fire. And there are many suns in space millions of times as large as ours. Besides suns and planets, too, there are tremendous clouds of glowing substance known as nebulae, so huge that the Earth in the middle of one of them would be like a pea in the Pacific Ocean. In space itself the Earth is quite lost. Think of the width, and breadth, and height of space!

Personally I'd have preferred to think of no such thing but I couldn't help it because of the illustrations. One of them, entitled FROM SUCH A CLOUD OF FIRE CAME EARTH, shows the nebula of Andromeda 'as seen through the big telescope at the Yerkes Observatory in Chicago'. It's possible to pass over this one without too much interest or concern because it just looks like a starry sky but four pages on there's one of a different kidney. This one's entitled THE PROCESSION OF THE WORLDS.

It's a realistically rendered view of the solar system from outer space but there, at the foot of the page and out on the very edge of space, are a small boy and girl. It looks as if he's wearing a diminutive version of his father's dressing gown and she's demurely buttoned into her nightgown as they perch on what looks suspiciously like a cloud made of rock, and gaze with equanimity towards the sun surrounded by its planets. Earth floats away above their heads. Top left on Earth, the British Isles are represented by a couple of minute smudges. Those two small figures all alone out there in space made me shiver. The picture seemed to conjure up my own sense of vulnerability as well as those dreams in which I was tossed about into nothingness and chaos. Or perhaps it was pictures like these that induced nightmares in the first place. But I don't think so.

How was knowledge supposed to be deepened by the inclusion of these implausibly cute children? One of the causes of the miserable muddle inside my head was surely the muddle that was Arthur Mee himself and his encyclopaedia. The hefty tomes were too much for a small child even to hold and yet in all of them were sections devoted to items that would supposedly benefit and amuse the very young. When my father read them to me at bedtime I pretended I was enjoying them because I didn't like to admit that I didn't enjoy what I was apparently supposed to enjoy. And I didn't want to hurt his feelings. He thought he was giving me pleasure.

He surely must have read me the execrable piece of so-called poetry entitled THE SHUT-EYE TRAIN which was accompanied by a sickeningly sentimental illustration. I only mention it here because of what I've said before about dreams seeming to be a form of travel. The picture, which is entitled OH THE SIGHTS THAT THEY WILL SEE, swarms with rather goofy-looking toddlers in their night clothes as they rush towards a row of lighted windows. By an open door, beckoning, stands an old woman of dubious appeal for children. Wearing apron, cap and gown she holds a lighted candle in one hand and a bell in the other. She looks like nanny, witch and schoolteacher all in one. There's a full moon low in the sky and layers of mist swirl above everyone. However, on closer examination this turns out not to be mist but steam from the engine that's going to pull the Shut-Eye Train. It's on its way to Shut-Eye Town where 'everything is passing fair and golden dreams await us there.' The first stanza goes like this:

> Come, my little one with me!
> There are wondrous sights to see
> As evening shadows fall,
> In your pretty cap and gown.
> Don't detain
> The Shut-Eye train –
> "Ting-a-ling!" the bell it goeth,
> "Toot-toot" the whistle bloweth,
> And we hear the warning call:
> All aboard the Shut-Eye train.

The unreliability of Arthur Mee's critical judgement can be gauged in his encomium of the poet.

> The poetry of Eugene Field is the quaintest and prettiest ever written for the entertainment of children, and the Shut-Eye Train is one of the most charming of them all.

But it's the fundamental dishonesty of the poem's content that makes me cross. In order to present the pleasing fiction that dreaming is a wholly enjoyable experience, nightmares – which are surely suffered by every child – are never mentioned. And the idea of the steam train as a benign form of transport to the Land of Nod strikes me as particularly inappropriate. This is because I can remember the terror that consumed me when the Golden Arrow shot through Penge East and how the vibrations from the shaken platform passed right through me from foot to head. Bone-crushing and bloody death was just a few feet away. It was the killing power of the thing. Even more horrible though than being on the platform when it went through, was being on the footbridge that went over the railway line. It was such a flimsy structure that there were gaps between the boards on the floor. So you could see the glint of rails before they were suddenly obliterated by the top of the train as it shot screaming underneath you and shook you up and down.

As it was with nightmares so it was with what used to be called the facts of life. Nicely brought up children were kept in ignorance of sex (I didn't even know the word) and so it had no place in Arthur Mee. In his 'wonderful world of knowledge' photographs of famous statues such as Michelangelo's David have a misty look about them in the genital region where anatomical detail has been rigorously suppressed. But apart from the omission of facts about sexual reproduction for which it would be unrealistic and unfair to blame him, I now know that Mee's 7,384 pages omit just about everything I needed to know if I'd known then what it was that I needed to know – namely enough history to understand the mysterious complexity of the landscape that surrounded me and through which I made my way. But throughout my childhood and into adolescence I was under the misapprehension that everything I'd ever need to know could be found within the oppressing ten red volumes of Arthur Mee's encyclopaedia.

My parents apparently realised that in one important respect this couldn't be the case and when I was about twelve a fat new book suddenly appeared among the scruffy and meagre collection in the bookcase. It was called *The Family Health Encyclopaedia*. Its arrival wasn't commented upon and I supposed that my mother needed it for some reason. It was over forty years before I discovered this was where our parents expected us to find out about the facts of life, more coyly referred to in those days as 'the birds and the bees'. It was certainly delved into furtively while they were at the pictures on a Saturday night but I found more in it to horrify than inform – like the shiny plates of the human body which revealed the internal organs reproduced in brilliant colour.

It certainly didn't enlighten you about what men actually had. You knew they had something that hung on them and they wee'd standing up instead of sitting down like girls did. But they had something else as well because I'd seen pictures of ancient statues in a peculiar old book of photographs called *Life and Movement*. This was another volume given undue attention when the parents were out. Nobody seemed to know where it had come from or whose it had been. Or at least no-one was owning up. Its apparent purpose was to celebrate the beauty of the human body but sometimes the men had a bunch of something between their thighs and some of them had leaves sprouting there. I seem to remember too that there was one of Hercules with what appeared to be the contents of the Augean stables spread out around his feet. And there was that nasty statue of Laocoon and his sons being crushed by snakes. So the associations with what it was that made a man a man weren't very pleasant.

And I could never forget that silly ditty (if that's what you'd call it) about little girls being made of sugar and spice and all things nice (obviously not true in my case) whereas little boys were made of slugs and snails and puppy dogs' tails. I spent so much of my childhood whiling away time in the garden that I was well-acquainted with the revoltingness of slugs and snails. And I didn't like the look of what I'd seen wobbling on a dog's bottom underneath his shamelessly upright tail as he trotted along in front of us down Penge High Street one morning. I thought it very odd that his female owner had put a tartan coat on his back. Why did a dog need to wear clothes? And if she

# ART TREASURES FROM OLD GREECE

A COPY OF THE STATUE OF THE SATYR BY PRAXITELES

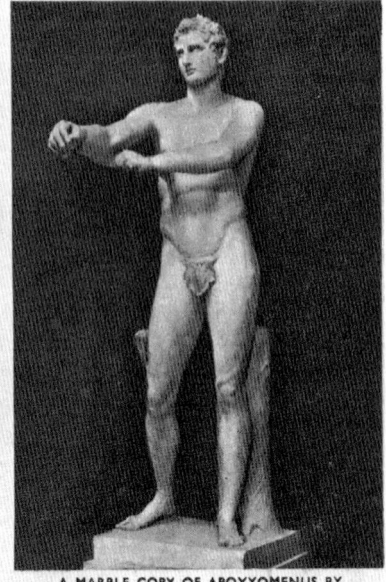

A MARBLE COPY OF APOXYOMENUS BY LYSIPPUS IN THE VATICAN

A MARBLE STATUE OF HERMES, BY PRAXITELES, FOUND AT OLYMPIA

AN EARLY COPY OF A STATUE OF HERMES BY THE SCHOOL OF PRAXITELES

did want to dress him up you'd have thought a pair of trousers would have been more appropriate instead of letting him go around being rude like that. I felt embarrassed for her as well as for the dog but also of course for myself. You felt dirty even being curious about it and in a way you didn't really want to know anything at all about it. You'd rather close your mind to it. You sensed fear and shame and horror and sin.

❊

If my own experience is anything to go by then the anxieties of childhood can take several different forms. Apprehension. Worry. Guilt. Dread. Fear. Horror. Terror. An ordinary child surely experiences all of these. What strikes me now when I recall my early years is the extent to which I kept these things to myself. I can only assume that's what all children do. The only exception in my case was when I let my father know I was worried (though worry was hardly the word) that my mother would burn in Hell for all eternity because she wasn't a Catholic.

It didn't occur to me to burst into tears or otherwise let on that crossing over that flimsy-feeling footbridge with the ever-present threat of a train roaring underneath made my legs shake so much that it was difficult to put one in front of the other to get to the other side. I suppose I didn't show any fear because I wasn't expected to feel any. As nobody else was making a fuss about it, as nobody else was frightened, this seemed to tell you that there was nothing for you to be frightened of yourself. In this sort of instance, being frightened was something I was vaguely ashamed of. And yet surely fear of that kind is entirely normal and understandable. One might even say it's natural in the face of something as unnatural and monstrous as a clanking, screaming, smoke-belching express train.

I hope you don't think I'm asking you to feel sorry for me, because I'm not. In fact to find myself the object of pity or patronage has always infuriated me. Perhaps it's because I was the baby of the family and therefore liable to be the object of merriment whenever I said or did things that showed I didn't know or understand what everyone else knew or understood. Being laughed at was something that made me want to cry and if we started to cry my father would tell us to stop blubbering or leave the room. Only babies cried. It was contemptible. So very early on I sensed the safest thing to do was to keep quiet. Don't let on. Don't give yourself away. Don't let them see your foolish terror. Don't give them a chance to laugh at you. In those days grownups appeared to have very little, if any, insight into the mind of a child. It's as if they'd entirely forgotten what it was like to be one. In my parents' case a good example is provided by a visit to the pantomime one Christmas, probably in 1947 when I was four.

Remembering how desperately hard-up my parents were it makes me sad now to think of them somehow finding the money to take us out for what was meant to be a treat. It was at the Penge Empire, later the Essoldo Cinema, and was the first time I'd ever been to a theatre or seen any kind of live performance. To start with it all seemed very exciting because we had a box close to the stage and this made you feel rather special. But I wonder if I'd still remember that evening if it weren't for the horror that hit me when a sudden explosion at the corner of the stage near us blew the wicked witch to pieces. I threw myself on the floor and stayed there for the rest of the evening. No-one seemed to notice.

How could people just carry on as if nothing had happened? How could they laugh about someone, even a witch, being blown to pieces? I remain convinced about the pieces – that I saw her black dress and pointy hat (and by extension her) blasted to bits. Perhaps this was a special effect of some kind or maybe the bang coincided with a smoke bomb exploding and the blue cloud it left behind enabled the witch to nip unseen into the wings. But as far as I was concerned we'd actually seen her killed in the most horrible way and everyone else thought this was very funny.

As we walked home in the dark afterwards I expect they

said, 'Did you enjoy that Sally?' and that I said, 'Yes'. I'd have known it was what they wanted me to say. Or else it was what I wanted them to hear because it was what I knew they wanted me to say. Later that night Heather said to come into bed with her because she could tell I was crying. When I told her why she explained it hadn't been real about the witch. It was just pretend. Make-believe. The witch wasn't a real witch and she hadn't been killed. Nobody had been killed. This was very comforting but I still didn't understand why it was funny to pretend to blow somebody to pieces. Any more than I understood why nobody seemed to find it horrible when the Guy was burnt on bonfire night. I only remember us having one Guy Fawkes night and this was put on by Shiela's father. Earlier that day I'd wandered down the garden to where the bonfire was stacked up as high as the apple tree and on top of it was what looked like a large doll dressed in blue-and-white striped pyjamas. I liked the look of him. He looked like someone I could be friends with. I knew he wasn't real but at the same time he was alive in his own way, the way just about everything is alive to a small child. I couldn't look when they lit the fire underneath him.

Later on at St Winefride's, when the nuns taught you about Guy Fawkes and his dastardly plot to blow up the Houses of Parliament they conveniently forgot to mention that it was a Catholic plot against a Protestant monarchy. And when they taught you about the Civil War it was obvious that you were meant to be on the side of the Catholic Cavaliers and against the Protestant Roundheads. It was easy to oblige, because the Cavaliers with their long hair and fancy clothes were so much nicer to look at than the Roundheads.

Battle of Marston Moor 1644. The convenient rhyme provided by four and moor is why this has stayed in my head since I was ten and being taught by sweet, snaggle-toothed Mother Mary Ambrose in my final year at St Winefride's. But without looking it up, I couldn't tell you which side won. The Roundheads I expect. That's all I ever learnt about the Civil War during my schooldays. It never came up again. Nothing of much interest or relevance ever did come up. So don't believe everything you might hear about education having gone to the dogs since the demise of the grammar school. I spent seven years at one but the experience left me profoundly ignorant through very little fault of my own.

✻

It's a bright, breezy May morning that smells of hawthorn and warm earth. The scents of May always remind me of St Winefride's – probably because of the beauty of its grounds at this time of year and also because May was the month of Mary. So it seems an appropriate time to tell you something about her.

The Blessed Virgin Mary and Mother of God was generally referred to by the nuns simply as Our Lady. Their order was called The Ladies of Mary because she was the special object of their veneration. Our Lady's gentle eyes gazed down at you from statues and holy pictures without actually meeting yours. Enclosed in her own mystery she wasn't actively engaged in seeking out the secrets of your heart, but she was always there if you needed her. She was your friend and she was your mother as well as God's mother. If you were in trouble she'd have a word with Him; intercede for you as it was called. Your sins didn't make her angry because she was incapable of anger. She was full of infinite pity and understanding. But your sins did make her sad and because you didn't want to make Our Lady sad you tried to be good.

Although Our Lady listened to the sorrows of the whole world she was closely associated with happiness. She was *Causa nostrae Laetitiae* – Cause of our Joy – and the daily hymns sung in her honour were invariably jaunty and bright. Mary had a great many names and sometimes these were recited in a litany. After each of her names was invoked, a nun with an exquisitely pure voice would sing the response *Ora pro nobis* (Pray for us). I'm having to look in a book to find the names now but here are some of them:

> Lily among Thorns
> Rose ever Flowering
> Tower of Ivory
> Spotless Dove
> Mary Immaculate Star of the Sea

And in May we used to sing a hymn to her that went:

> O Mary we crown you with blossoms today
> Queen of the Angels and Queen of the May

Queen of the Angels and Queen of the May – I thought those were the loveliest of all her names. And that hymn had the loveliest tune too.

So Mary was associated with flowers, purity and all forms of beauty. That was why her house, school, chapel, grounds and grotto had to be kept in perfect order and cleanliness. If a floor was being polished it was being polished for her. When a table was laid it was laid with the same care that Our Lady herself would have put into it. Mary was all around and could be sensed in perfection of all kinds – in the high shine on the old floor tiles along the corridor leading down to the beeswax-smelling refectory, in the scent of wallflowers, lily-of-the-valley and lilac in May, and perhaps most of all in the high blue skies of summer. Blue was her colour and she was up there in the sky. We knew this was so because the nuns had told us. They told us that Our Lady didn't die and get buried like other people. She was assumed into Heaven. She just floated up there when it was time for her to leave the earth. This was because she was the Mother of God and presumably it happened on a summer day since the feast of her Assumption was, and still is, August 15.

Mary was nearly always dressed in blue and white, and in the prettiest pictures of her she's standing on top of the clouds or on top of the world with a crown of stars around her head. The nuns didn't dress like her though. As part of their pursuit of holiness they wore clothes designed to eradicate vanity and mortify the flesh. The only visible parts of a nun were her hands and about three-quarters of her face. Her head was firmly encased in some kind of armature which was covered in shoulder length black material and the top half of her forehead was clamped behind a starched white band. I know there are specific words for these garments but if I ever knew them I've forgotten them now. Her long-sleeved habit went to within an inch of the floor and was made of heavy, black fabric that must have been horrible to wear in hot weather. But the long, blue floating panels before and behind her that fell from just below shoulder level lent elegance to her appearance. As she glided along a corridor with the head-up-shoulders-back carriage appropriate to a lady, these panels imparted a particular grace to her movement.

The Ladies of Mary emulated the perfection of Our Lady and taught us that all girls should do the same. It was a long time before I understood the impossibility inherent in such an aspiration. Until I became vaguely aware of the 'facts of life' I presumed that emulating Our Lady just meant trying to be free of sin and being neat, tidy, polite, upright and well-behaved. This was probably because at the end of each term's school report there was a section considered more important than any other. This was the one in which your appearance, behaviour, politeness and deportment were assessed.

✽

A few years ago I bought a book called *The People in the Playground* which is about the way children pass (or used to pass) their time during break at junior school. For over twenty years its author, Iona Opie, watched and listened with the dispassionate curiosity appropriate to the natural historian. The particular school she observed was evidently not dissimilar from the kind that used to puzzle me as a child and which filled me with such horrified fascination. It was very much the average school with a tarmac playground and built to a standard Board of Education design soon after the Education Act of 1870. I could hardly credit some of its content because nothing could have been further removed from my own childhood experience. Here's an extract:

> (One of his friends turned and shooed away two 8-year-old girls who had crept up. 'Go away, you shouldn't be listening, you're too young.')
> Two months later, all went well,
> Four months later, belly began to swell.
> Nine months later, belly went pop.
> Out come a baby with a nine-inch cock.

It was recited in all seriousness; not to shock, but as information in which I was known to be interested. He would no more have smirked during the telling than would Miss Dean-Smith the folksong scholar have done while discussing one of the bawdy songs she studied.

In a similar spirit another boy offered Iona Opie this bit of rhyme:

> Mary had a little lamb,
> She also had a duck.
> She put them on the mantelpiece
> To see if they would fuck.

The next time I went to visit my elderly parents I told my mother about the book and expressed my astonishment about the sexual knowledge the children apparently had, the four-letter words with which they were familiar and my puzzlement over the fact that I never came across anything like it in my own childhood. 'Why do you think we sent you to the convent?' she said.

So it seems that instilling Roman Catholicism into us was the least important factor in our schooling. While our parents certainly believed in the importance of education, they believed even more in the necessity for correct speech, good deportment, politeness at all times and sexual ignorance. Yet there we were as six- or seven-year-olds using words such as 'conception', 'womb' and 'incarnation' on a daily basis. You couldn't get away from things to do with the body. You couldn't get away from reminders about death either. Not a day passed without saying the 'Hail Mary' several times. It used to go like this, and I suppose it still does:

> Hail Mary full of grace! The Lord is with thee. Blessed art thou amongst women and blessed is the fruit of thy womb, Jesus. Holy Mary, Mother of God, pray for us sinners now and at the hour of our death. Amen.

You had to bow your head as you said Jesus.

Since the whole business of being a child was about unquestioningly doing as you were told, it was easy enough to learn things like this without giving the slightest consideration to their content or meaning. For instance I didn't know that 'hail' was a form of greeting – only that it was hard, cold stuff that fell out of the sky sometimes and stung your face. Of course I had no idea what a womb was either and (because I was unaware of the significance of the comma after womb) didn't know whether the fruit (apple? orange? cherries?) belonged to Mary or to Jesus.

I didn't realise until years later just how much flesh and blood was inherent in Catholicism. For example when you went to Holy Communion you were supposedly consuming the actual body and blood of Christ – an idea which makes me feel distinctly queasy. One could go further and say that the Catholic Church was obsessed with sex. Holiness was hardly attainable without sexlessness. And it was probably the very denial of sexuality, the repression of sex and its identification with sin that rendered it so insistently present.

Perhaps the most significant and frequently used of Our Lady's names was The Immaculate Conception. If any of us had had the intelligence or temerity to ask what conception meant I wonder how the nuns would have dealt with it? But I expect they'd already forestalled the question by telling us that what it meant was that Mary alone was born without the stain of Original Sin which everyone else inherits from Adam and Eve. So conception became synonymous with birth and was not its necessary precursor.

Something similar happened with the word 'virgin'. A virgin we were told was a woman who was pure in thought, word and deed. Although it would naturally have been a grievous sin to allow yourself to formulate the thought, I expect I vaguely imagined that Mary was pure in deed because she didn't make rude smells, have cheesy feet or pick her nose even when there wasn't anyone around to catch her doing it.

And then there was the feast of Christ's Circumcision. This was on January 1 and was another of the Holidays of Obligation when you had to hear Mass. What was being celebrated was apparently His presentation at the Temple by Mary and Joseph when He was just seven days old. I always sensed something a bit uncomfortable and not quite right about this particular feast day. Perhaps I'm just imagining the reticence surrounding it. But perhaps not. Anyway, I suppose it was just as well that it took place during the school holidays.

❋

After using the word 'reticence' the other day when I was writing to you, I found it stayed in my mind. This is almost certainly because more than any other word it sums up the ethos that surrounded me as a child – which is what I'm trying to explain to you – and which is almost unimaginable now. In many ways reticence was an aspect of good manners in those days. You didn't ask personal questions or expect to be asked them. You dressed neatly and without ostentation so that you didn't draw attention to yourself. You protected your privacy and respected that of others. When you spoke, you spoke quietly. You didn't speak about yourself or about other people.

You didn't speak about money.

Most of all though you didn't speak about ill-health or other bodily matters. If anything was going on in that department of the adult world then it was the older or bolder child who had his or her ear pressed against the closed door. Perhaps this is what Heather had done. Because something had happened. Although we weren't in disgrace we might as well have been because we had to spend a lot of time in our bedroom being very quiet. When I whispered why, Heather said it was because of me and what I'd done. I didn't know I'd done anything.

Then Heather isn't there and it's more silent than ever. She must be at school and that's why my father tells me that I'll have to open the door when the doctor comes. He tells me to keep a lookout for her arrival by kneeling on a chair by the sitting room window. As soon as I see her coming I'm to run down the hall and stand on the stool he's left there so that I can reach up and let her in.

Well I stay obediently at my post until eventually a small black car stops outside, a door slams and the rickety gate is swung open by a sturdy party in a grey two-piece costume. On her head is something not unlike an upside down saucepan. Well it's got a handle or something sticking out the side. Perhaps it's a feather but I don't think so. Anyway this must be her. This must be the doctor. I must let her in. She's already knocking irritably for the second time before I manage to complete my task. However, before letting her in I've been told to ask her if she's the doctor. So I do and her brusque riposte takes me by surprise. 'Who d'y think I am?' she snorts, sweeping me aside. In spite of her rudeness I follow her down the passageway and across the hall to my mother's bedroom where she shuts the door in my face.

Another fragment of memory seems to belong to this time. It's afternoon and my mother is sitting in her armchair gazing towards the window. Tears are running down her face. I go up to her and say, 'What's the matter Mummy?' I want to comfort her and make things better but she doesn't look at me. Just gives my hand a slight squeeze while at the same time moving it in a direction that indicates she wants me to run away. It was more than forty years before I understood what had been going on and where I came into the story. I won't tell you about it now though because the sense I eventually managed to make of things doesn't belong here. It belongs later on.

*

When I was seven and started going to school on my own, my parents gave me certain tips on survival. Among other things they told me not to talk to any nasty men and if anyone came up to me and said my mummy was round the corner then I wasn't to believe them. I was to run away – even if the person who came up to me was a woman. I hadn't the faintest idea what a man or a woman would want with me but I didn't give the matter any further thought. Then one day as I'd just come through the subway under the railway line at Forest Hill, a woman approached me with the very words I'd been warned about. So I said, 'No she isn't' and completely unconcerned just carried on walking towards the bus stop. I'd forgotten all about it by the time I got home and never told anyone it had happened.

Precisely because of its unattachment to feeling of any kind it strikes me as odd that I still recall it, because as I reflect on my early childhood the fragments of memory which stand out are invariably associated with strong feelings of some kind, or a complex of sensitivities and emotions. Very often it was probably because I found myself in trouble for reasons I didn't understand.

Like when it's a sunny summer morning and we're at the bus stop outside where we live. It's a weekday and it must be the school holidays. My father has the day off so he can take us to London. I'm full of anticipation because there's bound to be a treat of some kind. If we're lucky perhaps he'll take us again to Ludgate Gardens and what I'll ask for is a chocolate ice cream sundae with a Pompadour wafer stuck in it and an orange squash with a straw. Impatient to be off, I fix my attention on the corner of the road around which I'm willing one of those familiar red double-deckers to come at every moment.

Instead of a bus comes a man with a wide-brimmed hat on the back of his head, slowly pedalling his bicycle up the hill. When he's a few yards away I see he's a black man (probably the first black person I'd ever seen because there weren't many around in those days) and that he's smiling broadly at us. He seems to know us but I'm fairly certain we don't know him. Anyway it's impossible not to smile back and surely it would be bad manners not to. His singsong voice says, 'Morrrrrrrrnin' Sunshiiiiine' in Heather's direction as he cycles lazily past without a backward glance. Naturally she smiles back and says, 'Good morning.'

For less than a second I can entertain the idea that this pleasant encounter bodes well for the rest of the day but the smiley black man can't be much more than two yards beyond the bus stop before I realise Heather's in huge trouble. My father's hissing, 'Don't you ever do anything like that again. You must never …' What's she done wrong? She was only being polite, the way we were told to be. And if she's done something wrong by saying good morning then I must have done something wrong too just by smiling. So we're both in trouble and the day's ruined before it's begun.

When the bus comes along we get on in silence and go upstairs. Presumably we haven't been forbidden to speak but it seems a dangerous idea and so I don't chance it. When you're in trouble you feel your parents don't like you and so you just keep out of their way until they don't seem to mind you again. But there's no getting off the bus. We've got to go through with the day – with him being kind to us when we don't deserve it just because he's promised to take us out and he never breaks a promise. I don't know about Heather but I'd rather give up on the whole thing and disappear down the end of the garden to sit on the swing – so that I can forget everything I don't want to remember.

✻

There was something about my father that made you feel he wasn't quite like other men. Conspicuously well-built and upright, you just couldn't miss him. He stood out in a crowd. This could either be a source of pride or embarrassment, although embarrassment had no part in my feelings about him until I was in my teens, with the possible exception of when he took us swimming at Beckenham Baths and wore his ancient, lightly moth-holed black all-in-one swimming costume. But even then he still had an aura of distinction about him. Consequently some kind of distinction seemed to be conferred on us by having him as a father. Something we had to live up to.

We didn't understand what it was he did for a living but whatever it was he went to the Old Bailey to do it. He often used to take us there, which is why we went to nearby Ludgate Gardens. I don't know what image, if any, Ludgate Gardens may have summoned up in your mind. Somewhere with grass, flowers and the tinkle of running water perhaps. Well nothing could be further from reality. The place we knew as Ludgate Gardens was on the edge of a huge bomb site – a tiny space made cheerful with pots of scarlet geraniums and where in good weather the tables bloomed with bright sunshades among the ruins.

So as the train clanked and squealed and groaned its way into Holborn Viaduct station you'd look hopefully for the bright umbrellas. And you'd look up at the gilded figure of the woman on top of Old Bailey's dome. Blindfolded and carrying a pair of scales she represented impartial Justice. All we knew was that when people got into trouble with the police they had to go to the Old Bailey and might get sent to prison. Heather and I somehow picked up the idea that if ever we got into any trouble with the police, or indeed into any other kind of trouble, then our father would lose his job. So although he wasn't a policeman it felt rather as if he was. In fact he was a probation officer, an occupation he took up after the war.

Getting the idea that he was some kind of policeman wasn't difficult. One afternoon he and I were walking somewhere near Dulwich when we came across two boys with catapults. He strolled up to them and said, 'I'll have those please. You can pick them up this evening at Catford Police Station.' As we walked away from them the boys gobbed (my father's word) at his retreating back. When I asked why he'd confiscated the catapults he replied simply, 'Because catapults are nasty things.' Once we were round the corner he tossed them over a hedge. Feeling rather sorry for the boys and a bit shocked that my father had lied to them I protested meekly, 'But you said they could pick the catapults up at Catford Police Station.' 'Oh those boys won't go anywhere near a police station. Not unless someone drags them there by the scruff of the neck.' Evidently he recognised them as the kind of boys he had under supervision.

In spite of this particular bit of high-handedness my father was a warm, observant, compassionate man with a deep interest in people. It was obvious that they responded to this. They confided in him, told him their problems and often asked for his help. People knew instinctively that he was someone they could trust. And you knew you could too. You knew he loved you because of the things he did for you and because he said he did and you knew you loved him back but the trouble was that you couldn't really feel it because at the same time that you knew you were safe with him you were also scared of him. He was such a big man. When he suddenly appeared in the bedroom doorway you automatically tried to hide what you were doing in case it was wrong or pretended to be doing something that you reckoned would be safe – like colouring-in or reading.

✻

It didn't occur to you to ask questions about the world around you. There was too much of it to know where to start. Any knowledge you had of it was limited to certain levels of familiarity that enabled you to find your way around. The only ways you did this by yourself was on foot or by bus. You lived in a vast, largely alien world through small parts of which you learnt to thread your way. In the process, you got very strong feelings about the rightness or wrongness of different roads and different number buses and different houses. As far as roads were concerned, some invited you to go along them while others told you that you weren't welcome. Some roads did neither because they didn't care one way or the other. The ones that felt like that were the ones you went along most frequently.

Crampton Road didn't fit into any of these categories though. It was familiar because we often went along it to get to Penge East station but it nevertheless had a breath of hostility about it. Perhaps it was the ugly-sounding name that said, 'This isn't your place and you can only come down here because you're going to the station. If you weren't going to the station I wouldn't let you.' Like the other back streets in Penge its houses were all stuck together in straight rows facing each other with very small front gardens. Their chunky walls with pillared gateways looked too big for them. Before you got to them though you went past the newsagent on the corner and then Mr and Mrs Quick's tiny shop that was a bit like a cave and smelt of salt and soap.

One day, just as my father and I had walked past Quick's, there were two women standing with their arms folded gossiping up ahead on the pavement. They looked almost identical in their wrap-around aprons, slippers with fluffy edges and hair in curlers clamped under hairnets. Before we reached them my father said I'd better walk in front of him. While I was doing so I heard him say good morning. 'Do you know those ladies?' I asked. When he said he didn't I asked him why he'd said good morning to them. 'Just being polite.'

Did I glance over my shoulder and see the look they exchanged which said, 'oodzeethinkeeiz? Mister 'igh'n'mighty?' Or did I not look back in case I saw it? I don't know. But at the time I was presumably older than seven because my understanding that people who didn't know you at all could hate you, not because of who you were but because of what you represented, had begun that foggy afternoon on the bus coming home from St Winefride's. It was reinforced a year or so later as I made my way there one autumn morning.

It was a bright, frosty day and so I'd taken the route I liked best. This meant only taking the number 12 a couple of stops as far as Cobbs Corner. Getting off there not only saved some bus money but also gave you plenty of time to saunter down Silverdale (a road that invited you to go along it because it had a pretty name as well as silver birch trees on either side) and then along the winding path across Mayow Park. In there you could sniff in the nutty smell of oak trees and look out for acorn cups and pounce on the occasional brightly-coloured leaf that had been missed by the park-keeper's broom. Anyway, on this particular day I'd crossed over it and come out of one of the green iron gates onto Mayow Road. In front of me lay the joyful sight of pavements deep in dry chestnut leaves to kick my way through right up to the school entrance.

I've hardly started doing this when I hear a girl shout from the other side of the road, 'There she is! Come on let's get 'er'. They're on me in a moment, she and this boy both about the same age as me who apparently go to some sort of school over there. After shoving me up against the iron railings they go to work in silence with feet and fists. I'm puzzled about what it is I've done to deserve their hatred when as far as I know I've never seen them before in my life. So after trying without much success to land a few bruises on their shins in return I say, 'What are you paying me back for? I haven't done anything to you. And anyway two against one's not fair.'

The girl replies by dragging the nail of her index finger down my face before pinging my hat elastic under my chin, then ripping the whole thing off and flinging it into the road. It's a brown flat-crowned object that flies rather well when expertly propelled the way she does it. 'Snob, snob, stinking little snob. You go to that posh school up there and my mum says that your *mummy 'n' daddy* (sneeringly) pay ten bob a week to send you there. My Nan says so too.' This outburst seems to leave her not knowing what to do next. A short pause is then followed by some desultory kicks and punches before the incident fizzles out. The girl and boy seem to evaporate.

Even so, after I've rescued my hat and continued on my way I'm careful not to explore my legs for bruises in case my attackers have their eyes on my retreating back. I don't want them thinking I'm a cry baby. Nor do I want to give them the satisfaction of knowing they've managed to upset me enough to make me want to cry even though I don't let myself. It isn't because the scratches and bruises hurt. Nor is it anything to do with a sense of injustice. It's the surge of fiercely protective love you feel towards your parents when someone dares to be scornful about them.

Even if school uniform wasn't intended to invite attack or abuse it certainly marked you out. And it was meant to. A uniform made it easy to spot pupils behaving badly in public places. Also, in my day convent schoolgirls over the age of eleven were considered virtually undressed without a hat. You'd get called out in assembly for that and be kept in detention every night for a week. The same thing would happen if you were caught eating in the street. The latter crime was probably the more heinous.

To go back just once again to incidents involving school uniform, there was a third one which seems to belong here even though it was devoid of verbal or physical attack. Well it wasn't so much an incident as a moment of sad discovery. After I left St Winefride's at the age of eleven I went on to a convent grammar school in Croydon which was also run by the Ladies of Mary. To get there you went by train from Penge West and after a couple of stations you got out and changed at Norwood Junction. In those days the carriages were divided into compartments, each holding perhaps six passengers facing forwards and six backwards. During the rush hour there was very little room to put your feet on the floor without treading on those of the person opposite. And the trains were often so overcrowded that half a dozen other people might be standing and trying to put their feet on any chink of floor they could find between those that belonged to people lucky enough to be sitting down.

Anyway, one morning I had to be at school early for netball practice. This meant catching a train much earlier than I'd ever done before. I'd been told always to go into a Ladies Only compartment, thus avoiding (or so the theory went) any nasty men. When the train came in though there was something different about it. It wasn't just that I couldn't see a Ladies Only compartment. It was that the compartments of all the carriages were full of men. Unfamiliar looking men. There didn't seem to be any women anywhere. It looked like a Men Only train – except there was no such thing. The idea of squeezing into one of the compartments was a bit embarrassing but I'd have to brave it. I spotted one that looked as if it had a spare seat if the people in there moved up a bit. So I opened the door and after struggling not to stand on anyone's feet or bash them with my satchel or netball as I pulled it shut I managed to perch in a small space grudgingly made available for me.

Nobody gave me the ghost of a smile as they usually did. The tentative one I gave the man opposite was soon frozen away by the blank gaze he gave me before closing his eyes. I was an outsider and an unwelcome one at that. That's what it felt like. As I cast furtive glances to right and left I was astonished by what I saw. The ten or twelve men in that compartment were in a kind of uniform too. I can't remember the details but what stuck in my mind, or the impression I got, was that they were all very small, all very old, and that they all wore flat caps. The other thing they had in common was their huge black boots which seemed quite out of scale with the rest of them.

I had got on what was known as a workmen's train – one of those that ran at particular times with specially reduced fares for low-paid working men. There was total silence between them and if the lack of expression on their faces, the emptiness of their eyes and the air of exhaustion suggested by their sagging shoulders didn't tell of resignation with their lot, then it spoke of utter hopelessness about where they were having to go today, tomorrow, the day after that and the day after that for ever. They seemed so completely lacking in vitality that I sometimes wonder what kind of impression Lady Godiva herself might have made had she insinuated herself amongst them. I imagine them giving her a brief glance and thinking 'woman, long-haired, naked' before closing their eyes for the last precious moments they can call their own until the journey home at night.

I was obviously very far from being Lady Godiva but I was every bit as out of place in that compartment as she would have been. A glance at my school uniform had inevitably registered me in their eyes as a rich kid and a snob. Or so I've always believed. Even though I was neither I found their prejudice perfectly understandable. We were doing the feudal system at school and it seemed to me that these were the kind of men who would have been serfs back in the twelfth and thirteenth centuries. It made you wonder whether things had really changed all that much since.

*

It's breakfast time one morning in winter and I'm about three and a half. My chair's against the wall so that I can't tip it backwards. This is the wall that's got the four photographs of Killarney framed in black passe-partout on it. They're somewhere above my head. My mother is sitting on the side of the table that's to my left and my father on the one to my right. Behind him is a window through which a white light shines on my mother's face. We're very close together because the flaps on the table haven't been pulled out. I'm hugely pleased to see a bowl of porridge in front of me that's got brown sugar on it as well as the top of the milk to make it utterly perfect. I express my delight by rocking my chair against the wall but I've only managed about three rocks when my father snaps with awful sternness, 'Stop that!' Shocked by this unprecedented outburst and not knowing what I've done wrong I glance through blurred eyes at my mother. Perhaps I'm hoping for some kind of explanation or to find out whether she's cross with me as well. It would be unbearable if she was. But apart from sad eyes her face is devoid of expression as she looks straight at him and says quietly, 'She was only being happy.'

With those five words she did much more than defend my right to be happy. She let me know that they weren't. As parents they were scrupulous in their avoidance of arguments when Heather and I were around. There were never any rows at home. What there was instead was an atmosphere. Without realising what you were doing you instinctively sniffed it out by listening intently whenever you crossed the threshold, especially after you'd been out for any length of time. Perhaps you'd only been messing about doing nothing in particular in the wilderness at the bottom of the garden or been down to Woolworth's to spend your pocket money. Nevertheless it was always possible the wind had changed direction while you were out.

It could be a bad sign if the sitting room door was closed. So you'd creep up and put your ear to it, trying to make out what kind of tones you could hear; whether they were speaking normally or had deliberately lowered their voices. You didn't really want to hear what they were saying. All you were trying to find out was whether you were in trouble or not. As long as you didn't hear them say your name you could start breathing again. And if you heard any hints of good humour you could skip off in relief about the immediate future. You could get on with being happy.

You could sense darkness around the edge of everything even though on the face of it there was nothing wrong – something bad about the adult world which was horrible as Hell. But whatever it was, you tried not to acknowledge the dark. Instead you kept your eye on the sunlit garden beyond.

❋

'Don't talk to any nasty men!' Quite often this was called out when you pulled the front door shut as you left home. It was said in much the same way as any other injunction designed to ensure that you came back intact. Nothing unduly alarmist. Just a reminder to keep your wits about you – like they might remind you to look both ways before crossing the road.

Nasty men would of course be strangers. Your father, uncles and other familiar males weren't nasty in spite of whatever it was that made them men and whatever it was that men did which you didn't know about, didn't want to know about but couldn't help puzzling about in virtually unconscious but ever-present fear.

But God was a man, Jesus was a man and priests were men. And there was the Pope as well, St Peter's representative on earth and apparently some kind of saint in his own right. Framed black-and-white photographs of His Holiness, the bespectacled Pope Pius the XII, could be encountered but easily ignored on walls of classroom or corridor. The company he kept was considerably more colourful and pleasant to look at than he was – fat cherubs the colour of pink marshmallows, the deep red glow of the Sacred Heart of Jesus, the golden wings of the Angel Gabriel and the heavenly blue sky that surrounds Mary at the time of her Assumption.

So priests and popes were men but not men as other men were men. Like the nuns, they didn't marry and so were holier than other men because they kept themselves apart from women. In their capacity as priests they didn't really count as men and were allowed into the convent to say mass and to hear confessions. They were more than allowed in though; they were reverenced. It was a bit like expecting God to lunch. He was admitted into rooms where no ordinary man could enter and he was allowed into places where no woman, even a nun, was permitted to tread – like the sanctuary, the holy place behind the altar rails where the Blessed Sacrament was kept in the tabernacle.

If you couldn't keep your mind on the holy business in hand, as was frequently the case, you wondered how the altar linen stayed so immaculate, how the big brass candlesticks always gleamed and how the polished floor managed to shine in perpetuity without any apparent intervention by the nuns. It was some sort of miracle. But miracles were an everyday fact of Catholic life. And mysteries. There were lots of those. That was the way it was. Mysteries were in the air you breathed. Mysteries were the very stuff of which Catholicism was made up. They were at the heart of everything.

❋

Before the war … during the war … after the war … since the war … because of the war. Almost every sentence uttered in grownup conversation seemed to contain one of these phrases. Very soon after I began to become aware of my existence in about 1946 I knew that a war had just ended and that the man who had come to live with us and who was apparently my father had been away for a long time fighting in it. Bomb sites and war-damaged buildings were part of the everyday landscape, especially in Penge.

I don't remember the moment he came home for good and suppose there was just a gradual realisation that his presence was permanent. However, I feel certain that my earliest memory is of seeing him for the first time. This would have been after the war was over but before he was demobbed. He couldn't just come home from Germany once the fighting stopped but had to stay on there for about a year and a half to take part in its administration. I didn't understand this for years. I suppose I vaguely imagined that war was just a kind of deadly game that went on for a long time until it stopped and everyone came off the field. I had no idea of the devastation it left behind and that millions of people were homeless and starving as a result of it.

My first conscious sighting of my father seems exactly like a tiny black-and-white photograph. It's hard to believe that it wasn't in the album along with all the other snaps I came to know so well. Perhaps it seems like a photograph because my memory is of a static image. I see him in profile as he stands outside the front door waiting for it to be opened.

So he hadn't got a key. It's as if he was just a visitor. I can't help wondering now why no-one had seen his approach. You'd have thought someone would have been on the look-out so they could rush to open the door before he reached it wouldn't you? But perhaps they didn't know what time to expect him. Or perhaps he'd managed to find some way of being earlier than he'd said because he wanted to give us a surprise.

It was late on a winter's afternoon and the centre light was on in the sitting room where we were – perhaps because my mother was knitting or doing some smocking. So the contrast between the inside world and the outside one would have resulted in a monochrome image in the window frame, an image of the top half of a big man in army uniform. That's probably why I see it as a photograph. In the darkening sky behind him, too big for me to see from where I was at the time, was the black skeleton of the horse chestnut tree near the front gate. Something I *could* see though was the big cardboard box he had under one arm. The oldest I could have been was two and a half but I might have been only two and a quarter.

Sometimes you think you really do remember something but on reflection you realise that you're probably animating things you've been told by parents or grandparents. You've made them part of the contents of your head. Over the years you fit together what you remember with what they've told you and come up with something rather like a film of yourself as a small child.

I can see my two-year old self summon the courage or curiosity to open the sitting room door as quietly as possible and pop my head round it. The man is in the armchair near the window. He gives me a gentle smile. I don't smile back – just go on looking. He holds out his hands with the palms upward as if he's carrying something very carefully. But there's nothing in them. Then he says something with his eyes that tells me he's asking me for something and there's nothing to be afraid of. I realise what he means and set out across the room to climb on his knee.

I suppose I must have run away in shyness after I'd first seen him at the front door and he was probably at home for a couple of hours or more before I came out of hiding. All I'm sure I remember is peeping round the door. My father remembers my solemn appraisal of him and my mother remembers (approvingly) that I didn't make any fuss about the rough texture of his uniform. I have a feeling that when eventually I did turn up to see him, everyone in the room stopped talking. There was a quiet sense of occasion. Something had been accomplished.

It's often said that one's earliest memory carries particular significance; that there's a reason why you remember that specific moment. I certainly believe this is the case with mine. The significant memory is of the soldier outside the door on a winter afternoon. Of a man waiting to be let into the world of women.

✻

Inside that box under my father's arm was a Japanese dolls' tea set for Heather and a white furry dog for me. I wanted the tea set to be mine and not the dog because you couldn't really do anything with a dog the way you'd be able to with the tea set. And he wasn't dainty and pretty like the tea set was. But I understood perfectly well that the dog was an appropriate present for me because I was a baby and Heather wasn't; that it had been chosen for me because I couldn't break it or hurt myself on it. (Had I already acquired my reputation for clumsiness?) His fur felt nice and soft but his head didn't move and his legs wouldn't work. I can still feel the hardness and rigidity of his body. Just like a dead dog in fact and there's not much you can do with one of those. But I managed to pretend I wasn't disappointed because I didn't want to hurt my father's feelings; or those of the dog.

It feels as if it's the same afternoon that Heather and I are playing with the tea set and I'm astonished to see that she's got two wine gums – those sweets that stick your teeth together. One's green and the other's orange. She gives the green one to me and as there's only one thing I can think of doing with a sweet I put it in my mouth. I've hardly had a chance to give it a lick before Heather wrenches my jaws apart and fishes it out. 'You're not meant to *eat* it Fatty.' I don't understand why not (she knew about sweet rationing and I didn't) but I do understand that I've blundered. The first blunder I'm aware of making. I've blundered because I'm a baby. I'm THE BABY and always will be. I'll never know what's going on the way the others do. It's as if there's a game going on in which you're taking part but no-one has thought it necessary to tell you what the rules are. You're just meant to know. Not knowing the rules means you often say things that make them laugh. They say they aren't laughing at you but only at what you've said. You don't see the distinction and you're quite right not to. There isn't one.

In later life they told me about the time the family was playing 'I Spy' to pass the time on a train journey. It was before I had any idea about letters and the sounds they make so I don't know how it came about that I was taking part in it. Perhaps I asked for a turn. Anyway, I said, 'I spy with my little eye something beginning with C'. And then it went something like this:

'Car?'
'No.'
'Chimney?'
'No'.
'Crane?'
'No.'
'Carriage?'
'No.'
'Crow?'
'No.'
'Camera?'
'No.'
'We give up Sally. What can you spy with your little eye that begins with C?
'Window.'

It's as easy to understand the laughter that followed this conclusion as it is to imagine the mortification of children who inadvertently cause hilarity in such a way. Just because they don't consciously remember such events doesn't mean they haven't been affected by them. A series of tiny incidents like this can, I feel sure, lead a child to decide that the safest way to proceed in life is to keep your eyes and ears open and your mouth shut. That way you lessen the risk of being laughed at for a fool and are less likely in general to put your foot in it. That's certainly what I did.

I suppose that when my father came home with the box under his arm it could have been Christmas 1945. It doesn't feel as if it was Christmas but I know he was on leave from the army then. He told me that on Christmas day that year he came across two German prisoners-of-war in the road outside and invited them in. My mother recalled that they wouldn't accept sugar in their tea until they'd seen her put it in her own cup and then drink from it. They were suspicious that it might be poisoned.

It must have been rather an awkward business altogether because even if the adults hadn't been almost wholly ignorant of each other's language, what on earth could they have talked about without embarrassment? This is where children can come in useful. When I told one of the Germans that something I was holding was mine, he smiled and managed to explain that they had the same word in German – *mein*. Perhaps I was telling him that the dog was mine.

I don't remember the dog's eventual disappearance but it doesn't take much imagination to work out what happened to him. My mother paid scant regard to the notion that children had any right to personal property. The dog probably went the same way as the white rabbit that had been made for me by Aunt Dolly. He was a very basic rabbit but much-loved by me because he was plain and soft and had become comfortingly grubby. But above all he'd been made for me. He was *mine*. Or so I thought. Then one day when I couldn't find him on the shelf where I knew I'd left him I asked my mother where he was. Her light-hearted reply was that she'd just given him to the dustman. I cried privately but almost certainly audibly about this and so perhaps when she decided the time had come to do in the dog as well she was a little more considerate of my feelings.

Another time I discovered that something I'd been given didn't belong to me was at the end of a seaside holiday. Although we probably went to Brighton or Hastings every summer for the odd day we very seldom went away for a proper holiday. In fact I think we only had two, both of which were spent in a caravan on the Essex coast somewhere near Clacton. I don't think I'd ever been so thrilled by anything in my life. I was entranced by this miniature home. If it rained, as it surely did day after day, I don't remember it. My abiding memory is of utter joy as I swung my bucket and spade on our way towards the sea in the sunny freshness of a summer morning. You couldn't see the sea straight away because the road sloped upwards as it ran between rustling fields of golden corn edged with poppies and cornflowers. The combination of that never-before-encountered beauty with the knowledge that when you reached the top of the slope the sparkling sea would be spread out in front of you was everything I could ever wish for.

I was very sad when the first of these holidays came to an end but was comforted to think that I would at least still have my bucket and spade. My father had bought them for me on the first morning from the shop just over the road from the caravan site – the sort of shop that still exists in seaside towns and which are crammed with shrimping nets, beach balls, inflatable toys and acidic, tooth-rotting pink rock. The bucket and spade had been my friends the whole fortnight and most intimately involved in all my delight but when the caravan had been sorted out and locked up, my mother caught sight of me holding them. Snatching them out of my hand and flinging them under the caravan she snapped, 'Oh for goodness sake! You can't take that rubbish with you on the train. Leave it behind for the next children.'

As things turned out, that bucket could have come in very handy on the homeward journey. Although we had seats on the train, it was very over-crowded and the corridor was crammed with passengers and luggage. As I'd had too much sun on the back of my neck the previous day it wasn't long before I whispered, 'I'm going to be sick.' My mother somehow managed to bundle me out and shove me past all the obstructions so that I got to the lavatory just in time.

When we'd been back in the carriage for a while she made the horrifying discovery that she'd left her handbag there. Not feeling inclined to undertake the struggle a second time she said to my father, 'Oh well it doesn't really matter. There's nothing in it anyway.' 'Only our train tickets' he muttered'. The expression in his eyes was one of controlled alarm and the feeling was passed on to me. While she was gone in search of the handbag and which to everyone's relief she did manage to recover, my father began to fashion that day's newspaper into a three-cornered hat. When I asked Heather what he was doing this for she said, 'He's not making a hat Piggy. He's making something for you to sick in.'

When my mother said there was nothing in her handbag you knew she meant that there wasn't any money in it worth talking about. There would only have been a few coppers in case we needed to 'spend a penny' as it was called in those days. Ladies lavatories on railway stations had a hefty kind of brass box attached to the outside of the doors into which you posted a penny which enabled you to open them. When you went in, the door slammed behind you with a resounding clunk. They were unpleasantly disinfectant-smelly places and as it was believed you could catch something very nasty from public lavatory seats (there was some kind of notice about diseases on the back of the door) you were told to go without sitting on them. I never mastered the art of this and invariably only succeeded in peeing into my already suspect knickers.

But to return to the lack of content in my mother's handbag, which was rather like a tiny maroon Art Deco suitcase. There would have been a handkerchief or two, a comb missing some of its teeth, the cheapest of mirrors, a bottle of aspirin, perhaps a small tin of Nivea and, almost certainly, the worn down stub of a lipstick that had been passed on to her by her glamorous, unmarried sister Eileen.

I don't know what it was like in other households but in ours we learned that it was considered vulgar to discuss money. Perhaps this was because we didn't have any. I can't remember a time when money, or more precisely the lack of money, wasn't an ever-present source of anxiety to my parents and consequently to me. It wasn't something they actually told you about but you couldn't help knowing. And you couldn't help feeling that you were in some way responsible for this state of affairs. You cost them money they could ill afford to spend and, conscious of their worries, you felt sorry for them as well as to blame.

❋

All four rooms in the flat had 1930s fireplaces covered in mottled, glazed tiles of indeterminate colour. Centre stage on the one in Heather's and my bedroom was an extension to the wireless that was in the sitting room. The fireplace was stepped down at each side and on one of the steps on the right-hand side I used to keep my tin money box. It was a red, oval-shaped thing meant to resemble a post box. There was never very much in it but I was quite good at saving the odd threepences and sixpences that came my way. As I've already told you, the way you got the money out was to slide a knife in the slot. This was a perfectly simple operation and didn't take long, but one day my mother burst into the bedroom, grabbed my money box and in a quite frenzied manner set about it with a tin opener. No permission asked. No explanation or apology given. No restitution ever made.

So now that made two people in the family who thought my money was theirs for the taking. I didn't trust money boxes after that. I don't think it would have occurred to me to tell my father about this outrage, any more than it ever occurred to me (or Heather) to let on about our mother's prodigious bouts of explosive and destructive anger that sometimes erupted when he was safely out of the house playing cricket. I'm still puzzled why my mother was suddenly so desperate to get hold of a couple of shillings. I know my parents were appallingly hard up but were things really as bad as that? I suppose they must have been. Even so I knew my father wouldn't have done what she'd done. He was a respecter of people, even if the person in question was only a child. But come to think of it he must have known, because he would have asked what had happened to the money box. So I suppose it must have been because of this that he suddenly said to me one day, 'Come on. Let's go down and open a Post Office Savings Account for you.' After that I used to enjoy going down to the post office in Penge to deposit the tiniest amounts and to see the counter clerk write in my book and then stamp it with the place and date.

✽

The idea of a mother being a housewife was quite unknown to me. My mother was just my mother. She wasn't anything except herself. I suppose that if anyone was a housewife at our place it was my grandmother. It wasn't until I went on to Coloma and made friends with girls whose mothers presided over immaculately furnished and shining chalet bungalows with diamond-paned windows in Shirley that I realised some people thought things were a bit odd with my family. I began to be defensive about my parents. I sensed a kindly pity directed towards me because my mother went out to work. In those days though, well-spoken women who held down office jobs didn't say they went out to work; they went to business. I suppose this was to distinguish themselves from women who did manual work in bakeries, laundries, factories and shops.

I felt a distinct but rather puzzled dislike of two mothers who clearly didn't go to business. They looked too young and carefree to be mothers anyway but apparently they were. They were on a huge hoarding that carried an advertisement for Persil just by the railway bridge that was nearest to the flat. In those days before commercial television and colour supplements this was one of the few kinds of advertisement you were likely to encounter. It was something to look at while you waited for the bus.

As I recall, bottom right is a boy in a grey shirt with a slightly lost expression on his face underneath his school cap which is all askew. To his right, a beatifically smiling boy with his cap on straight and wearing a gleaming white shirt is regarded with smug satisfaction by the two smirking, girlish women. They whisper behind their hands and (insincerely) intimate pity for the boy in the grey shirt. They're sniggering about his mother because she doesn't know what they know – that Persil washes whiter. I was sorry for the boy in the grey shirt. Not so much because his shirt wasn't as clean as it might have been but because his mother was being looked down on.

Which isn't to say I wouldn't have loved it if my mother

had been the housewifely sort, had I known such a phenomenon existed. Perhaps she would have enjoyed domesticity if they'd had more money and hadn't had to live in a rented flat. As things were, you took it for granted that the sheets on your bed were perilously close to becoming rags. You inconsiderately and somewhat guiltily helped them on their way. This was when your big toe found a small hole and encouraged you to make it bigger so that it could go on to make a satisfying ripping sound as it split the sheet from top to bottom. So it served you right that you then had to put up with the unpleasant scratchiness of blanket next to your skin. You took it for granted too that you only seemed to have one pair of serviceable knickers to your name and that if you didn't swill them out yourself then nobody else would. I can't think of any other reason I would have needed to drape them overnight across the plate rack on top of the gas cooker so they'd be dry by morning. Actually I don't think they ever were dry by morning. I just had to put them on, bacon-smelling and still damp.

Apart from the kitchen sink there were no facilities for doing washing at home. No coppers, washing machines or dryers. Sheets, towels, tablecloths and shirts were sent to the New Era laundry round the corner and came back each time noticeably worse for the experience. All other washing had to be wrung out by hand and hung on the line underneath the crab apple tree in the hope that it would get dry eventually.

Very often it was the state of our clothes (few as they were) that triggered my mother's frenzied rage. Suddenly she'd become aware of hems hanging off, loops broken inside blazers, buttons missing and stains on skirts. One day, in a fit of maniacal fury about the condition of our school coats she caused an immensely heavy mirror-cum-coat rack to come crashing to the hall floor. Naturally we accepted the blame for all these things. Naturally we didn't split on her but pretended to my father that we didn't know how the mirror-cum-coat rack fell off the wall – it just did. Naturally it didn't occur to us that she was in any way to blame herself. It was our fault she was unhappy and the only thing to do was to make ourselves scarce until the storm had passed.

❋

I don't know how truthful it is to say that even in those days I had a sense that things hadn't always been like this. I think I had, and have still, a shadowy recollection of easygoing peacefulness in the time before everything changed. I think that even if I can't consciously remember this previous existence it makes sense to speak of the emotional imprint it left behind. If I piece together what I remember with what I learnt later I don't think I'll be very far from understanding what was going on. What had happened was that everything changed for ever when my father came home for good from Schleswig-Holstein in 1946. He'd been away for six years which was twice as long as he'd been married when he enlisted in 1940 at the age of twenty-six. What was going on was what social historians refer to as post-war readjustment.

My father had had nothing to do with the move to our present home in 1943 when my mother was expecting me. He would have been in training with tanks and artillery for D-Day – somewhere like Salisbury Plain or the Yorkshire Moors. She'd long been accustomed to making her own decisions and managing everything by herself, in the same way that most women made decisions and managed everything by themselves during the war. As an elderly lady told me once, 'The war made women of us dear – it did really.'

People tended to move around a lot during the war, especially those who lived in or near London. In its early stages, my father and mother set up home with my mother's parents in a rented house at Hayes in Kent. Perhaps this was when my father was about to join up and knew he'd be going away. However, once the bombs began to fall my grandfather, whose brothers had both been killed in the First World War and who was afraid of gas attacks, decided that he wanted to live in the country. My grandmother wouldn't go with him because she didn't want to be separated from her son and three daughters who all lived in London. Also, she rather enjoyed the excitement generated by war – just as she enjoyed a thumping good thunderstorm. I expect too, that she wanted to go on being useful to my mother who had Heather to look after. So my grandfather went to lodge with a baker and his wife in rural Oxfordshire and my mother and grandmother moved into a small upstairs flat at Kirkdale in Sydenham.

Like so many other people, my mother left London from time to time to stay with relatives who lived away from where the bombs were falling. Before I was born she went with Heather to St Albans for several weeks and also to Cornwall, both rather dismal experiences I gather. But mostly she just stayed where she was. Heather and I were conspicuous by our presence because almost all children had been evacuated – something my mother considered unthinkable. She said she received quite a few disapproving comments about this from strangers in the street.

As we weren't living in central London, staying put probably seemed as good a thing to do as anything even though several houses nearby had been demolished by bombs in September 1940. But soon after the start of the Normandy landings on 6 June 1944 Hitler began launching his V1s from the Pas de Calais. My father, who at that time was a captain in the Guards Armoured Division, wasn't scheduled to embark until D-Day plus Eight and so the first V1s must have arrived before he'd even crossed the Channel. Whether he knew about them at that time I don't know but he'd certainly have been worried if he'd known that a disproportionate number of them were to fall in places like Penge and Croydon rather than in central London and that the consequent death and destruction was to be as bad as the worst days of the Blitz. The V1s were pilotless aeroplanes which zoomed over day and night and crashed roaring to earth when they ran out of fuel. People christened them doodlebugs or buzz bombs.

So this was evidently what drove my mother to take Heather and me to Weston-super-mare by train, leaving Granny on her own in the flat. She and Mr Powell who lived next door, were the only people left in the neighbourhood and became quite friendly as they helped each other out with this and that. Even so, nothing could tempt my grandmother to accept his invitation to treat his comfortably-set-up cellar as an air raid shelter. Her preference was for swift obliteration above ground rather than slow suffocation beneath it.

✻

The stamps on my identity card show that we arrived in Weston-super-mare on 12 July and came home on 11 October when it must have seemed the danger was largely over. What my mother wouldn't have known about, because it wasn't reported in the press, was the arrival of the first V2 on 8 September. The size and speed of the V2s made them the most destructive weapon known at that time. Apparently they travelled so fast that you couldn't hear them before they exploded. By the time they did, you were either dead or not. As with the V1s, a disproportionate number fell in south London especially between November 1944 and March 1945. It was in March that a V2 demolished another of the houses in our road, just a few doors up from us, killing all its occupants.

A couple of years or so before that, when my mother was still living with Heather and my grandmother at Kirkdale, a policeman called to tell them that my grandfather had died. So Granny set off alone by public transport to do what needed to be done. It must have been the simplest of funerals he had in the parish church at Alverscot with at best only half a dozen mourners present. Even my mother couldn't be there.

My grandmother always believed that his stroke was caused by shock and sorrow. The baker and his wife were a kindly couple who were getting on in years and had no children. Then not long after my grandfather went to live with them they were overjoyed by the unexpected arrival of a baby girl. A few months later this apparently healthy child suddenly died and my gentle grandfather died a couple of days later. No headstone was ever put up and forty years on, the only way we could identify his grave was because it was beside that of the little girl.

My grandfather's civil service pension died with him and so my grandmother was left penniless at the age of about fifty-two. As this was before the advent of the Welfare State, she was dependent on one of her daughters for a home. So it was fortunate she already had one with my mother. Married at sixteen, she'd never been in paid employment in her life. The only thing she knew how to do was cook and so she began to do so outside the home in the kitchen of a nearby residential hotel and later at a small private school in Beckenham.

So, if I reflect on the virtually unremembered first three years of my life it isn't too difficult to imagine what they were like. In spite of the prevalence of air raid sirens, bombs and rockets or the occasional low-flying fighter-plane the days would have been generally peaceful. The only male voices around would have come out of the wireless. The soft voices of my mother and grandmother would have been discussing the news perhaps or wondering how to put together an appetising meal out of the unpromising ingredients they'd been able to obtain that day after hours of queuing at the shops. Perhaps they reminisced about Dublin or talked about the latest film they'd seen. But I doubt whether a great deal of talking went on at all, particularly after the blackout curtains were drawn. Their pursuits would have been quiet ones like reading, or sewing while listening to the wireless.

The struggle to remain decently dressed during this period of drastic shortage meant a great deal of make-do-and-mend as it was called. The tissue-like paper of dress patterns might end up as lavatory paper. Woollen garments might be unravelled and re-knitted into something else. Old curtains might be turned into dresses or skirts. Indeed when the war was over and my father enquired after the whereabouts of his cricket whites he found they only had one leg. The other had been cut off and turned into a summer coat for me.

※

Until well after the war my cot was in the parental bedroom and so it seems quite likely that I felt I had a special relationship with my mother because we would have had that room to ourselves for over three years before my father returned. I have three clear memories of being in the cot.

The first one is in daytime. Morning. I'm holding a cellophane bag that makes marvellous crinkling sounds when you squash it. Inside are some mothballs that I'm sniffing and about to lick. My mother snatches the bag away, thrusts it at my grandmother and gives her a good telling off for having given it to me to play with. I feel sorry for Granny because she was only being nice. Perhaps it was having heard her being told off that subsequently made her seem more like one of us than one of them.

It's daytime too in the second memory. Afternoon. The sun slants across the eau-de-Nil eiderdown on the double bed. And there's a rainbow on the ceiling where its rays bounce off the cut glass stopper of an empty scent bottle on the dressing table. I'm pleased to see that I have my mother's company. She's in bed – so she must be ill; but she doesn't look ill because she's sitting up and making something out of gauze and cotton wool.

In the third memory the room's black. It's the middle of the night and it's terrifying. I'll tell you about that later.

I only remember seeing my mother in bed on that one occasion and yet in my early years I was always anxious about her state of health and worried that she might die. She was certainly left tired, thin and anaemic by the war and in this she was by no means alone. Like almost all mothers everywhere she'd given her children most of the nutritional food that was available and gone without herself. She didn't seem very firmly attached to this world. The expression in her eyes said she was either in another one or that she wished she was. For years I felt an anguished longing for her which went unfulfilled. I suspect that very often it's the far-from-perfect mother who inspires the deepest feelings in her children. Devoted mothers tend to get taken for granted.

Something I take for granted is that much of life's poignancy springs from the fact that children never really know their parents and parents never really know their children. Perhaps it's not fitting that they should. Yet just occasionally an aged parent comes up with an astounding outbreak of honesty. What I'm thinking of now is a moment, twenty or so years ago when my mother was about seventy and my parents had been a model of married contentment for decades. My father must have been away somewhere and we were on our own. Quite unexpectedly she burst out about her feelings towards him just after the war. They were a mixture of hostility and resentment. Whereas she was tired, under-nourished and worn down by the dreariness of war on the home front, the good food and exercise he'd had during his years of training and later on the battlefield had left him at a peak of health and fitness. She felt affronted by this. Also, his experience as an officer had increased his confidence. He'd become accustomed to giving orders and expecting everyone to jump into line. Chucking his weight about in other words.

On the same occasion she said what she'd sometimes said a touch bitterly before: 'You and Heather were cowed as children.' My dictionary defines this ugly word as intimidated or frightened but both of these synonyms seem too strong to describe the effect my father's presence had on us – too unfair to the person I know him to be. Yet what else but fear and intimidation could account for the fact that it seemed natural to be terrified of getting into trouble, natural to be a bit sly and deceitful in order to avoid the risk of this and natural to feel it was dangerous ever to let on about what went on inside your head. What can you be frightened of in a household where there's not the slightest threat of even the mildest physical punishment? I suppose it's the unsmiling face and chilly voice that comes in your direction when you do something wrong. What you're frightened of is that they don't love you any more, or won't love you any more, which to a small child is to be under sentence of death. You don't know this and yet in a way you do. Perhaps you could say this knowledge belongs in the category of things you unknowingly know. You often know something without knowing you know it.

❋

I don't know how old I was when I became aware of the other grandmother. Grandmother Shervington just seemed to appear one day, perhaps when I was about four or five. It turned out that she was living round the corner in Thicket Road at some sort of shabby guest house for the elderly. Years later when I asked my mother why she'd moved into such a seedy place, her acerbic reply was, 'Oh she wasn't there long. Just long enough to find out she wasn't going to live with us. She thought she could push my mother out.'

This grandmother was quite different from the other one who worked so hard on our behalf. This one, in spite of being short and slightly stout, had something a bit regal about her. Perhaps it was the way she sat straight-backed in the best armchair, took it for granted that she'd be waited upon and had a propensity to make pronouncements. She was a good looking woman with immense charm and her silver hair which swept softly away from her face was kept in place with the merest whisper of white hairnet. Her Irish ancestry probably accounted for the charm. I don't know about the good looks.

Her principal garments were always black, as was customary with people of her age in those days. Perhaps that's why the only item of clothing I can recall is the dead animal she draped round her neck. I don't know what these things were called but apparently the animal was a fox. This garment, if you could call it that, was one of the few things I didn't accept uncritically as a child. I gazed with distaste at its pointy head and black beady eyes and wondered what it was doing there (I still do). On the floor beside her was a capacious black leather handbag which held among other things her cigarettes (Players Navy Cut), a small bottle of whisky (for medicinal purposes of course), spectacles and her current piece of knitting or crochet. Her hands were seldom idle but the rest of her body frequently was. This was said to be because of weak knees and if anyone was entitled to have weak knees she certainly was. She'd not only given birth to ten children (six boys and four girls) but had nursed them successfully through even the most serious of illnesses. Then, almost as soon as the youngest had grown up she found herself nursing her husband who was dying of cancer in his mid-sixties.

After his death she gave up the tenancy of the family home in Wembley and seems to have then led a peripatetic existence as she worked her way around the family expecting to make a home with one or other of her children. In this pursuit she even went as far as Australia, intending to stay for the rest of her life with her son George. Approaching the voyage as if it were a luxury cruise, she kitted herself out with clothes of doubtful utility in the outback. It didn't take her long to get through the considerable sum of money that my grandfather had put by for her support and to become a financial worry to her hard-up children. It must have been not long after the failure of the Australian venture that I became aware of her.

I realise now that I know very little about my grandparents and I expect most people would say the same. Grandmother Shervington was born Ellen Murphy in 1878 at Liverpool where so many of the Irish settled. In spite of her common maiden name I suppose it wouldn't be too difficult to find out a few things about her but it hardly seems worth the effort. It wouldn't tell me what she thought and felt about the world in which she found herself. It wouldn't tell me who she was.

It occurs to me that if only my grandmothers had been told

the life stories of their own grandmothers then we could find ourselves back in the early 1800s – quite some time before the Irish Famine of the 1840s which perhaps propelled great-grandfather Murphy to take the boat to England in search of a better life.

At the time of the Easter Rising of 1916 my other grandmother was still living in Dublin with her husband and children but I don't recall her ever speaking about it. Tracing *her* roots might be rather more difficult because in addition to having begun life with the equally commonplace Irish name of Clancy she said she didn't know the year, month or day of her birth. All my mother can tell me about her is that she was brought up by a grandmother and was one of four children. Her sister Alice was a nun and her sister Susan a children's nurse. Her only brother Jack, like so many other Irish people, set sail for the United States. He was never heard of again.

Temperamentally, I've always felt more affinity with my mother's family than with my father's. Perhaps this is why I'm interested in the smallest fragments of quite ordinary information that she's dropped from time to time about her father and mother. Like them going off for bicycle rides together in the

Oxfordshire countryside and coming back with bunches of wildflowers to put on the window sill. How when they were both desperate for something to read they'd be driven to rip a book or magazine to pieces. One of them would read a page, tear it out and pass it over to the other. And how my grandmother fixed up a rudimentary dark room under the stairs to develop and print her own photographs.

It's probably not a good idea to think too much about the infinite number of chances on which your existence depends; of all those things which had to happen in precisely the way they did happen so that you managed to get born and begin the process of becoming the entity you think of as yourself. Nevertheless I'll mention a couple of them.

An obvious one is the Irish Troubles. If it hadn't been for them then my mother's family wouldn't have come to England and so I wouldn't be here and neither would you. A less obvious one is Granny's interest in photography. This was picked up by Sonny who later began working at Kodak in Wembley. As this meant doing night shifts the family moved from Bayswater to be near him. It wasn't a popular move with his sisters but Granny was anxious he was fed properly. So if she hadn't worried about Sonny's stomach they wouldn't have moved to Wembley where my father's family lived and so my parents would never have met on Alperton station and I wouldn't be here and neither would you. But that's enough of that.

Although I'm telling you something about four of your sixteen great-great-grandparents I can't say I share the current enthusiasm for genealogy as such. I'd only be interested if diaries or letters had come down to me – something personal that gave you some idea of what a particular person had been like. All that's come my way is a mass of photographs from my mother-in-law. Looking at those of long since dead, unidentified and elaborately dressed little girls taken at the seaside in Edwardian times just makes me feel sad. Although Heather and I are dressed more appropriately when this photograph was taken forty or so years later it's essentially the same image. Perhaps it's the fact they were taken at the seaside that prompts the thought that an individual life amounts to little more than a single wave slowly swelling to break on the shore before being sucked back where it came from. It's this idea that helps me grasp the immensity of geological time and the insignificance of human beings. Maybe you think this is a dreary thought but there are moments when I find it quite consoling.

Yet perhaps I shouldn't have been so dismissive about genealogy. I've recently looked inside a painstaking piece of work done by my father's brother Rupert many years ago and have found it rather interesting. From at least 1650 generations of our branch of Shervingtons lived in or near Stratford-on-Avon. They seem to have been of yeoman stock but once the canal system was put in place two generations of them became boatmen. This meant that their many children were born at various places along the waterway network. Then when canals were superseded by the railways they seem to have naturally progressed to an association with them. My grandfather, like his father before him, was employed by a firm called Stephenson Clark & Co – ship and railway wagon owners and coal factors in the City of London. Their job was to chase delayed wagons in transit, to redirect loaded wagons of coal as required, to ensure that empty wagons were returned promptly to the collieries and to arrange the repair of 'crippled' wagons. So these were useful, middling sort of people and one of the perks they enjoyed was a virtually unlimited supply of free coal. And incidentally they can be seen to have played their part in the massive rise in population. My grandfather was one of eleven children and then, as you know, went on to father ten of his own.

※

After the Puckering family came to England in 1920 they moved home several times. It seemed to appeal to Granny, perhaps because it was the nearest she got to travelling or having a holiday. It was a change of scene and it was easy to do in those days because rented property was readily available. Apparently it took her no time at all to transform the new place into a home but the isolated and somewhat primitive cottage they first went to in 1920 wasn't to her liking. So they moved to Chipping Norton and then to Oxford before going on to Bayswater in London about 1927.

By contrast, the other grandmother lived her entire married life in Wembley. But then as I've said she walked away from it almost as soon as she'd buried her husband there and she too went on the move – in search of someone to live with. Where she differed completely from my mother's mother was in her assumption that she could be a welcome and revered guest in the home of some one or other of her children. It's surely understandable if she considered herself retired and reckoned it was time that someone looked after *her* for a change. The trouble was that her sense of who she was and what was due to her caused friction wherever she went. A ripple of mirth ran round the family at her indignation when her son Douglas had the effrontery to tell her that it was time she took a back seat.

After her failure to push the other grandmother out of the flat, she spent perhaps three or four years in an old people's home in Croydon during the early 1950s. This is where I mainly remember her. Sitting in the grounds on a summer's day near the shade of a Cedar of Lebanon she managed an effortless impression as mistress of a substantial country house. But her residence came to an abrupt end when my father received a telephone call from the matron. Grandmother had been expelled. Apparently she'd caused such annoyance and/or offence that it was, according to the matron, imperative that she be collected. *At once*. What she'd done to deserve this I don't know. The only thing she owned up to was having (quite rightly in her opinion) drawn attention to the insanitary state of the drains.

The other grandmother ran into trouble of a different sort when she must have been in her mid-forties and they were living in Wembley. My grandfather left her. He moved out and went into lodgings nearby. His removal may have been prompted by the fact that Granny had taken a liking to sherry. Or maybe she took a liking to sherry because he'd moved out. I don't know. But the terms on which they were reunited a year or so later suggest the real reason for his departure – namely her dedication to looking after four adult children who were still living at home. They all worked different hours of the day and night but whatever time they turned up she was ready to serve them a freshly-cooked meal.

My grandfather apparently told her that if she wanted him to live with her again then this would have to stop. And so it did very quickly. The expedient employed was simple. The parents just moved out and let their offspring get on with it. Eileen, Sonny, Dolly and my mother were left to pay the bills and look after themselves. The bills probably weren't much of a problem but none of them had the slightest experience of running a home and no interest in it either. In a very short time, according to my mother, they were living in squalor. They quite literally didn't know how to boil an egg. This wasn't a state of affairs that would have been allowed by Grandmother Shervington, for whom daughters were of far less consequence than sons and whom she tended to treat as unpaid servants on those occasions when she just happened to have her feet up.

Anyway, from then on throughout the thirties until the outbreak of the Second World War my mother's parents lived wherever Granny's fancy led them – at one time to Winchester where my grandfather had a sister with the amazing name of Fruzhanna and to various places-on-sea in Essex and elsewhere.

It pleases me to think that neither set of grandparents can have been prone to bigotry because in both cases an Irish Catholic woman had married an English Protestant. Maybe where my father's parents were concerned this lack of bigotry was enhanced by the English family's hostility to their marriage in the first place. Grandmother Shervington's being Irish was quite bad enough but I believe it was her Roman Catholicism that caused particular disgust. My grandparents' distance from the Shervington family became virtual estrangement after my grandfather himself became a Catholic.

In spite of strong adherence to his new faith, the family of ten adult children he left behind when he died in 1940 didn't smell of sanctity. Quite the reverse. Whether he'd overdone it or underdone it with them where religion was concerned, more than half his children ceased to be Catholic at all. (One of the sons married a Russian Jew whose family had fled persecution and the likelihood of death to find initial refuge in the East End of London.) I suspect that even my father, affectionately known as St Peter, was sometimes less than zealous in his religious observance. This must have been so because he married my mother at a register office. Consequently, as far as the Catholic Church was concerned there had been no wedding at all and he was living in sin (mortal). As this upset his parents, he and my mother were married again – this time in church. No photograph exists of either wedding but it was easy to imagine how lovely my mother must have looked in a dress made out of the white lace I found fragments of in the top drawer of her dressing table.

Even if the grandparents themselves led blameless lives, several of their ten children found it was more than they could manage once they grew up. Quite a lot of mortal sinning went on, some of it conveniently overlooked. For example one Sunday afternoon at Beckenham Cricket Club I was delighted to find a new uncle in one of the deckchairs. As I'd never heard of him before I sensed something a bit irregular between him and one of my aunts. I later discovered that this irregularity (he was married) had begun back in the 1930s and only ended with his death over forty years later. My grandmother evidently enjoyed his company and didn't seem to disapprove of the arrangement. The breadth of her moral tolerance in this case might have had something to do with his Rolls Royce.

So with relatives like that, it's not surprising that when I made my First Holy Communion in 1950 it didn't cause much of a stir – the kind of stir it would have done in a better class of Catholic family like the one I eventually married into. I wasn't given any pearly-covered prayer books with pages edged in gold, holy pictures, or rosaries made of silver and semi-precious stones. But my mother stayed up all night to finish my dress with which I was perfectly pleased until I saw what the other girls were wearing. Then I wished mine was long and frothy like a wedding dress or at least a bit more like a party frock. And I wished my veil didn't look quite so much like the old net curtain it probably was.

Anyway, the last thing we were meant to be thinking about was our appearance. We were meant to be thinking about the wonderful thing that was going to happen to us that day, the day Mother Mary Ambrose had prepared us for and which she said would be the happiest one we could ever have. This was because throughout our whole lives we would never be closer to God than on the day we received Our Blessed Lord for the first time. We would be filled with overwhelming joy. I can't say I felt anything of the kind myself but I *was* impressed with what came afterwards. This was a breakfast of soft-boiled eggs with toast soldiers followed by ice cream and chocolate fingers. That day's great revelation was that you could eat party food in the morning and not just in the afternoon.

When breakfast was over we all had to go outside to have our photograph taken. This was the result. Not much sign of overwhelming joy, especially in the front row second from the left. That poor boy's brow was always furrowed like that. I used to wonder what it was that made him so unhappy. I still do. And I can still feel the ferocious rigidity of his body as he shoved me away when I was once foolish enough to touch his arm in a friendly way.

*

Our flat was in one of the tall detached houses which still follow the curve of Crystal Palace Park Road in SE26. Solidly built of red brick in about 1880, I couldn't imagine a time when they hadn't been there along with all the other features of the local landscape. They were of similar design to one another and of no particular charm, yet considered as a whole they were impressive and you felt there was something special about living there. You felt too that even though they shared family features, each one looked at you in a different way. The further up the hill you went the smaller the front gardens became until they were virtually non-existent. The houses there seemed especially stern – as if they were looking down on you and weren't on speaking terms with each other either. A lot of them had enamel plates screwed to the gatepost saying, 'No Callers. No Hawkers. No Circulars.'

    Although the houses down our way didn't seem hostile they all felt secretive except ours. You knew people were there but you didn't really know them. You didn't see people going in or out much and there wasn't anything in the way of social life. Polite words exchanged at the bus stop was about as friendly as it got. Familiarity or nosiness was thwarted anyhow by dark front gardens crammed with sprawling shrubberies and lanky trees struggling towards the light. The only people I could snoop on were the next-door neighbours – both elderly couples who had their big houses all to themselves.

On the right-hand side you don't need to snoop anyway. This is where Mr Powell and Mrs Parkinson live and work in gentle harmony to keep their garden perfect. They must be quite happy for you to see them because there are plenty of places where you can have a good peep. One of the prettiest views is between the blue hydrangeas near the crab apple tree. I marvel at the garden's order and beauty and wish ours was the same. And I think how wonderful it would be to have a balcony like theirs where they can sit overlooking it while sharing a pot of tea in the late afternoon sun.

Things are very different on the other side. Here the close-boarded fence tells you that you aren't meant to see anything. But there's nothing to stop you putting an eye to various small holes in it and making less pleasant but more interesting observations about our other neighbours. Everything in there is overgrown and neglected. Tiny Mr Brower, always in crumpled black suit and Homburg hat, trails about aimlessly for hours in the long grass, out of sight from the house and talking to himself all the time. Sometimes he cries. When it's time for him to come in, Mrs Brower's dumpy figure appears on the veranda to call out, 'Toby, Toby, Toby, Toby, Toby, Toby, Toby' before vanishing inside. It sounds just as if she's calling a cat. Once, on a warm sunny day she puts a caged parrot outside. She talks to it and offers it something on a spoon from a bowl she's holding. It looks like custard. When he's had enough she licks the spoon he's been eating off and finishes the stuff up herself. It makes me feel sick but I know it serves me right for being a Nosey Parker.

※

Beauty wasn't a word I remember hearing in my childhood. It didn't seem to be something most adults bothered about, which was just as well because there was very little of it around. Or perhaps there was very little of it around because most adults didn't bother about it.

When I began to take in my surroundings I think I thought there were two distinct worlds – the hard, brick-built, traffic-noisy one in front of the house and the soft, tree-filled, quiet one behind. They seemed about the same size and equally natural. I think I presumed things had always been like that. Roads, railways, lamp posts, bus stops, bridges and shops in one. Trees, grass, flowers, bees, butterflies and birds in the other. But it can't have been very long before I realised there was an awful lot more of the world in front than there was of the one behind.

The immediate neighbourhood contained an obvious contrast. If you ran down the road and round the corner you were in the shabby ordinariness of Penge High Street with road upon road of terraced houses leading off it and barely a tree in sight. But if you ran up the road and off to the right you were in Sydenham with large gardens and winding tree-lined roads of handsome three- or four-storeyed detached houses.

As you went further afield by bus it became more confusing. You couldn't tell where one place ended and another began. Penge, Anerley, Norwood, Croydon, Sydenham, Forest Hill, Peckham Rye, Camberwell – the places all ran into each other. There weren't any gaps between them. It went on and on and on. In practise it was the bus stops that were the only places that mattered. They marked a spot and had a name. So you could get yourself around without any sense of geography and very little curiosity as long as you knew those names. I didn't even connect them to what they were named after – Woodman, Crooked Billet, Robin Hood, Pawlene Arms, Regal, King's Hall, Penge Empire. To me they just marked a spot on the pavement which was either nearer home or further from it.

So all you did was learn how to get yourself to the few places you ever went. Sometimes though you got bored enough (or adventurous enough) to discover there were different ways of arriving at the same place. Every so often while dawdling home from St Winefride's I might dare to dash down a strange road not knowing where I'd end up. Once, after tearing down standoffish Venner Road in case anyone challenged my right to go along it, I felt an explorer's sense of achievement to find myself breathless and astonished at Penge East Station. By that time the bridge over the railway was an old friend and I could have hugged it.

The world of bus routes and railway lines felt heavy and monotonous but because it became so familiar I didn't dislike it. I was at home in the bits of it I knew. But within this world there were certain things that induced what I can only describe as yearning. I couldn't have said what the object of that yearning was because those things that caught my attention didn't satisfy it. They merely hinted at the existence of something I longed for but which possibly didn't exist. So it was mixed up with sadness. A feeling that I'd never find what I wanted because it just wasn't there. Maybe it had been there once but wasn't any more.

There was an elaborate building in Penge that brought this on, perhaps because it looked as if it might have been a Tudor palace. And whenever we travelled by borrowed car through a certain part of Dulwich it felt like a pocket of the past; a country survival from more gracious times. Perhaps this is why I see it in my mind's eye whenever I read about Elizabeth Bennett's visit to Hunsford in *Pride and Prejudice*. And the church of St John the Evangelist in Penge felt as if it ought to have been surrounded by fields because it looked as if it belonged in the country. I reckoned the reason these buildings were lovely was because they'd been built a long time ago. They were made up of complicated shapes and had all kinds of decoration on them. They weren't just blocks of brick with windows and doors cut out of them. When they'd been built, people had known how to make beautiful things but they didn't any more. Now they just made prefabs which they put up where bombs had blown up what had been there before.

There was another side to my yearning and this too was to do with beauty – the beauty of the natural world. But what was the natural world? How much was there and where was it? Was it there at all? I knew the nature they kept in parks wasn't natural, however pleasant the parks themselves might be. The ones I liked were those that seemed natural because they were mostly trees and grass. The ones I loathed had signs saying KEEP OFF THE GRASS and things like floral clocks and carpet-bedding. Cut out of the grass that you had to keep off were beds filled with regiments of violently-coloured flowers. The park I have in mind now is the recreation ground in Penge which is where I got my first sighting of such a place. I don't suppose I was more than five but I never willingly went in there again. I couldn't understand how anyone could feel anything but revulsion at the sight of a bed filled with row upon row of lipstick-crimson salvias. I still can't. The shape of the plants added to the spiteful effect. It was painful to be in a place like that because it was the exact opposite of the natural place where I wanted to be. I couldn't have told you what I meant by a natural place because I'd never seen one but it surely would have had meadows full of wild flowers with whispering trees all around and no buildings for miles except a tiny cottage with smoke coming out of the chimney even on a summer day.

So I had to make do with make-believe. There was a place not far from home that worked quite well. If you went through the hedge at the end of the garden, past the dark pond where dragonflies zoomed around and half way up the slope towards the cricket field you could daydream there in the long grass.

*Forest Hill Station*

*Cobbs Corner*

*Venner Road*

Once you were lying down you couldn't see anything except trees and sky. And you weren't just out of sight but out of earshot too in a way that wasn't possible even at the end of the garden.

This natural world I longed for was probably an idea made up from various sources. Perhaps a watercolour illustration in one of the few books we had. Fields, trees, hedgerows and streams glimpsed through a train window. What I yearned for was of course an imaginary place that had nothing to do with the reality of country life about which I knew nothing. It didn't have any flies, cowpats or pigsties in it. And yet now I come to think of it, it's just as likely that it wasn't an imaginary place at all so much as somewhere suggested by the meadow that we loved to play in during the summer term at St Winefride's.

The nearest I ever came to somewhere else like this was during a picnic we went on one day near Sevenoaks. All I remember of this outing is sitting on a grassy slope, replete with happiness because it's a sunny day and cucumber sandwiches are about to come my way. They're being taken out of a greaseproof paper package when I spot a splash of blue at the bottom of the slope and dash towards it. It's a sprinkling of wild flowers I've never seen before.

I think I restrained myself from picking them until we were ready to go home, but pick them I must. I wonder why human beings have such an apparently instinctive urge to take possession of anything beautiful when possession almost invariably results in its destruction. Even before we were half way home the little blue flowers whose name I didn't know had lost all sign of life. I grieved bitterly about their senseless death and when we got home I hopelessly tried to make it up to them by putting them in water. Before I went to bed I looked in my *Observer Book of Wild Flowers* and found out they'd been harebells.

Then next morning I woke up to find a miracle had happened. Inside the Shippham's Paste jar the harebells had all come back to life and were as lovely as when I'd first seen them. I looked and looked at their dainty, drooping heads and felt I'd been forgiven.

✻

Just as there came a time when the bridge at Penge East didn't frighten me any more, so it came about that night time didn't either. I began to enjoy lying awake in the dark when everyone else was asleep and listening to owls hoot. It was as if I had the world to myself. I often fancied I heard something that people weren't meant to hear. I'd sit up and strain my ears. Silence made a sound. Listening to that sound told me there was something out there. The something-that-was-out-there seemed to breathe.

According to its various moods it made the weather do different things. I liked its wild moods best. This was when it made the wind smack the window panes and suck out the curtains and made dry leaves scamper frantically for shelter. Something was being said and I was intent on making out what it was. People would say it was just the wind blowing some leaves around but I knew better. The roaring wind and chattering leaves were thrilled by what they were doing – by what they were being made to do by something else. I didn't have a name for this something else. I just thought of it as It.

The most marvellous thing about It was that it didn't care

whether you'd been good or bad. If you felt full of sin and dread (like I did for ages in case I got found out for forging my father's signature on a school report) it could help you forget. But it couldn't do this unless you were on your own, like I was one snowy February day when it was starting to get dark. As soon as I got home I'd rushed out to make a slide on the concrete outside the bedroom door. It was a really good one and I whizzed and whizzed in exhilaration as anxious blackbirds called through the fading light and you could only see by the snow. I went on and on so long that eventually I seemed to lose myself altogether, to become one with all creation and to be where I was meant to be. When at last I had to go indoors, I found the necessary readjustment almost painful. Of course the shabby comforts of home were welcome on a winter's evening but I felt as if I'd shut the door on something that might never happen again. Perhaps it had been a special moment that I'd just been lucky enough to catch. In any case, whatever it was that happened to me out there, my enjoyment in it and memory of it remained a source of private consolation. It was something I wouldn't have put into words even if I could have done.

With so little incident in my childhood and so much time to squander, perhaps it's not surprising that the weather was a huge source of interest and excitement. Perhaps it was the presence in our bedroom of a door straight into the garden that encouraged this. I could just turn the key and go out, even if I was still in my pyjamas. I could have gone out in the middle of the night if I'd been brave enough but as soon as I woke up I'd jump out of bed to see what It was making the weather do. Sometimes you couldn't see out at all because it had been so cold during the night that the glass was covered in swirling frost patterns. The ice was so thick that hawing on it wasn't enough to melt it. You had to use your tongue to make a spy hole. When you did, your tongue stuck and felt as if it had been burnt. If there was a hint of sun then the tops of the trees in the Palace grounds would be a misty pink. I'd get outside as soon as I could and just stand there for a few moments feeling it seep into me and letting it take my breath away.

One winter morning I almost did stop breathing. When I woke up it was still dark and I thought it was the middle of the night. For some reason the curtains hadn't been closed the previous evening and there was this wide, golden stripe across the bottom of my bed that had never been there before. I leant forward to find out what made it and saw an immense amber moon low in the sky behind the black outlines of trees beyond the garden. I couldn't look at it enough and I looked so long and hard that I began to think I was seeing things. I saw the moon move. I watched the shining amber disc slide silently out of sight and felt that a secret had been shared with me. There seemed to be something special about night time and very early morning.

Most of all it was the dawn chorus that made me feel that what happened when people were asleep was some kind of secret being kept from them. I'm not talking here about the bit of twittering that happens at first light and which passes for a dawn chorus these days. This was something quite different and probably close to extinction now. What I heard then in London was the age old sound of an English wood in spring. Complete with the call of the cuckoo it was and still is the most perfect combination of sounds I've ever heard and overwhelmingly beautiful. It wasn't so much a chorus as a vocal orchestra. It felt as if the birds were survivals from long ago when everything was fresh and beautiful before people came into the world and mucked it up. Then suddenly they'd stop. It had all gone and there was a dead emptiness out there. It was as if they didn't go on because they knew people would be around soon. Trains would start running and the first number 12 bus would squeal to a halt outside the front gate.

✸

The kind of feelings aroused in me by the elements were probably the kind you were meant to get in church, but which I never did. For me, joy in the natural world was all to do with beauty, wonder and a sense of freedom and nothing whatever to do with sin, shame and a sense of constraint. The secret knowledge that It was there provided consolation and hope.

 In later years as a teenager struggling to avoid mortal sin by trying to believe the unbelievable and tolerate the intolerable I hit on the idea that God was in everything and that what I'd thought of as It was in fact God. I didn't really want to associate my private joy in the natural world with a God who was obsessed with sin, guilt and mortification and so I discarded the idea without mentioning it to anyone. This was just as well because if I'd dared to air my views during religious instruction I'd have been lashed by the venomous fury of Miss Reed's tongue. Much later I discovered that what I'd briefly considered as a way of combining my private experience with the teachings of Holy Mother Church was a heretical idea called pantheism. I'd only been at Coloma a week or two when something happened to confirm my belief that if you wanted to survive it was essential to keep quiet. To get into trouble was the worst thing I could think of and it soon became apparent that you could get into the most awful trouble just for asking questions. Not that it occurred to me to speak up, but it did to a girl called Jo during an RI lesson taken by Miss Reed.

She wasn't especially plain and if she'd worn a little make-up Miss Reed could perhaps have been passably attractive. But I suppose that would have been vain and therefore a sin in her book because God wasn't concerned with outward appearance but only with inward grace. The outward appearance in this case was a shiny face the colour of porridge, topped with darkish bobbed hair that often looked in need of a wash.

I don't remember Jo's question but I do remember that she asked it in a spirit of genuine enquiry. It was to do with Catholic doctrine (about which there is much to enquire) and was something I'd wondered about myself. So I was interested to hear what the answer would be. The answer, if it could be called that, was a frenzied verbal assault on Jo which went something like this:

'And just *who* do you think you are Josephine-whatever-you-name-is? I've been watching you. You think you're so *clever* don't you? Well you're *not* clever. I'll tell you what you are. You're *stupid*. What you are is *nothing*. NOTHING, NOTHING, NOTHING. No more than a speck of dust. A scrap of insolence who dares to question the wisdom of the Church Fathers. The wisdom of two thousand years.' She kept on and on and every lesson after this Miss Reed's eyes flicked in Jo's direction, on the look-out for an excuse to pounce. Not that she needed one really. If no facial expression provided one then she'd pounce anyway. A face devoid of expression could be deemed equally insolent. You knew Miss Reed needed a focus for her fury. A victim. Someone to torture. If she hadn't found one in Jo then she'd have found one in someone else.

We sat in silence because there was nothing else we could do. There was no redress against persecution of that kind because as a child you were automatically in the wrong. If you got told off then it must have been your own fault. Perhaps the woman deserved pity. Maybe she was a victim herself – at the mercy of a tyrannical old mother she was having to look after. Or perhaps

Jo's question threatened to undermine her faith, a faith without which she'd no longer know where she belonged or who she was. Anyway, whatever it was all about, you'd learned that to exercise your mind in freedom was yet another sin to add to the list of ones you had no intention of mentioning in confession.

Nothing in the nature of thought was called for either in Miss Hoolahan's RI class – only endurance of boredom so deep that your eyes watered and your jaw ached with the effort of stifling your yawns. Still, at least when *she* droned on and on it was about everything on earth except Catholic doctrine and for that one could only be grateful. In contrast to the likes of Miss Reed she seemed to believe that a woman's appearance told you about the state of her soul. A messy one was the outward sign of inward deficiency whereas a neat one was the expression of virtue. And it wasn't just your appearance that mattered. It was your general demeanour – the whole way you carried yourself. It was the way you held your head up and your shoulders back. It was the way you spoke in low tones and never shrieked with laughter. It was the way you walked down the street. In everything you did, even unto the manner in which you stepped on or off a bus, it should be apparent to everyone that you had the distinction of being a CATHOLIC girl.

Quite what she meant about this last one I had no idea and unfortunately Miss Hoolahan didn't think fit to show us how she stepped off a bus herself. I mentioned the mystery to a non-Catholic friend called Shirley and by doing so provided her with an ever-ready source of merriment. Her sky-blue eyes would brim with tears of laughter whenever she visualised her Catholic friends getting on or off buses with their knees clamped together.

When Miss Hoolahan went on about the importance of wearing gloves and the necessity of keeping your clothes clean and in good repair I was more conscious than ever of how far short of acceptability I fell in this direction. I slithered my savagely-gnawed nails under the desk and hoped she wouldn't catch sight of the gold safety pins holding up my hem. Actually I don't think she even knew I was there. I don't think she really saw me or anyone else in the over-crowded room. She was too wrapped up in herself. We were just a captive audience. Ostentatiously well-groomed herself, she presumably wanted us to make the connection between her own appearance and the superior state of grace she must therefore enjoy. Her self-satisfaction with what she'd managed to achieve with the meagre materials at her disposal was much in evidence. As was her apparent belief that her brother, the sure-to-be-canonized Jesuit priest about whom she regaled us weekly, added significantly to the glory that shone upon her.

One day she began class with head bent reverently towards a gold fountain pen. With elbows resting lightly on the edge of her desk she held it with great delicacy between perfectly-manicured index fingers and invited us to gaze upon it. There was a minute's silence as we did so. It was, she then explained apologetically, too precious for her to pass amongst us but she wanted us to share her joy by letting us at least look at it. For it was infinitely precious to her. This was a pen of peculiar distinction. This was a pen given to her by her brother. This was a pen she could never permit anyone else to touch. This was a pen she would never let out of her sight. This was a pen she'd be holding when her soul finally left her body as she took her last breath.

❋

On my last day at St Winefride's Mother Mary Ambrose had tears in her eyes when she said goodbye to us all. One by one she gave us a slim blue paperback book. It was, she told us, the story of a very special saint – a little girl called Maria Goretti who was the same age as us when she was martyred and whose especial holiness we should all strive to emulate.

It didn't sound like the sort of book I wanted to read but as I sauntered in a sweetly sad mood out of the school gates for the last time I was glad to have a keepsake from St Winefride's and from Mother Mary Ambrose in particular. I was in no hurry to get home and so as soon as I got into Mayow Park I threw myself down on the grass to start reading it. I wasn't there long though because I didn't get very far with it – probably no further than where Maria says, 'Mother, when will I make my First Communion? I can no longer live without Jesus.' I didn't spare her another thought and never looked inside the book again. I don't know what happened to it.

I didn't know what happened to Maria Goretti either and so the other day I thought it was time I found out about her. This didn't take long on the internet but it did make me wonder how the author of the blue book told Maria's story without risking the corruption of the innocently ignorant minds it was intended to improve. Personally I wouldn't describe Maria's story as improving at all but I'll give you a brief resumé of it so that you can make up your own mind about this. It will also give you some idea of the ethos in which I grew up which would have been unimaginable to my daughters, let alone to you.

Maria Goretti was a pious, illiterate Italian girl. In the summer of 1902 when she was only eleven she found herself the object of eighteen-year-old Allessandro Serenelli's lust. Furious that she fights him off he threatens to kill her unless she gives into him. Eventually, after trying to choke her into submission, he stabs her fourteen times. Having successfully defended her virginity she dies of her wounds two days later. Before she dies she forgives Allessandro and asks God to forgive him too. For many years, while serving a long prison sentence for the crime, Allessandro shows no remorse. Then one day in his cell he has a vision of a young girl in a garden, wearing a white dress. She's gathering lilies. When she brings fourteen of them to place in his arms, he realises that she's Maria. As he takes them from her each lily is transformed into a still white flame.

Maria Goretti was canonized in 1950, just four years before the blue book was given to me. The ceremony was attended by 250,000 people including Maria's mother. Pope Pius XII said that the story of a simple girl could be looked upon with admiration and respect. 'Parents can learn from her story how to raise their God-given children in virtue, courage and holiness; they can learn to train them in the Catholic faith so that, when put to the test, God's grace will support them and they will come through undefeated, unscathed and untarnished ... From Maria's story carefree children and young people with their zest for life can learn not to be led astray by attractive pleasures which are not only ephemeral and empty but also sinful ...'

Quite how a girl's natural revulsion at the prospect of rape can be seen as the repudiation of an attractive pleasure is beyond my understanding. I know that at any age I'd have fought to the death to avoid being raped. I'd have put up a fight on my own behalf without any pretension to holiness. I certainly wouldn't have needed to know the name of Jesus and nor, I'm sure, would any other woman in that predicament. If Maria Goretti was indeed holy then surely it was because she forgave her murderer. And generally speaking I'd have thought a woman might be considered holy who successfully denies her longing for illicit sex. But as far as the Catholic Church was concerned this woman would still be in sin because the thought was as bad as the deed. So she might as well have done the deed anyway. She was damned either way.

And if she was married then sex was a duty she had to perform whether she wanted to or not. She was obliged to bring as many souls into the world as it pleased God to give her and no unnatural means of limiting their number was permitted. Under pain of mortal sin. In the case of obstetric emergency where it was a question of whom to save – her or her child – then it was God's will that she should die in place of the child. Once she'd lost her virginity she'd stopped being a Child of Mary and become a Daughter of Eve. She got what she deserved.

But years before this dismal stuff was being dumped on me I was being prepared at St Winefride's to sit for what the nuns referred to as The Scholarship. This was another reason for my being there. If you passed then you gained a free place at a grammar school. If you failed then you either went to a secondary modern one (where common children went) or your parents went on paying fees for private education. I knew my own parents would go on paying fees for me however difficult it was for them but I also knew they were saving up to put down a deposit on a house. (The leases on all the houses in Crystal Palace Park Road were running out.) So although they didn't put me under any kind of pressure I wanted to pass not just for my sake but also for theirs.

Which scholarship examination you took depended on where you lived, as did where you took it, and because I was deemed to live in Kent I had to take the Kent examination. This was reputedly more difficult to pass than the London County Council one which was to be taken by everyone else in my class but I'd been so well drilled in what to expect when I turned over the examination papers that I wasn't at all bothered about what lay ahead. I was quite looking forward to it.

Further excitement was added to the whole business when I woke up on the big day to find that it had snowed heavily during the night. I was surprised and touched when my mother told me to put on her snow boots and fussed about whether I'd be warm enough. It was such a special occasion that she must have taken the day off work to come with me to the door of the school in Penge where I had to sit the examination. I'd never seen it before because it was down a road I'd never been.

It turned out to be another of those places purporting to be schools which didn't look like schools to me. Inside was worse than I could have imagined. I was shocked not just by its hideousness but by the fact that children had to go there day after day. The walls inside were brick painted in dingy, chipped green and cream paint, icy draughts came at you from all directions, the desktops had all been carved up by penknives and the lavatory was outside in the playground. That was the worst thing. I'd have crossed my legs until I burst rather than go in there.

Although my performance at school was in no way outstanding, I'd always got on well enough and brought home acceptable reports. I don't think I was competitive. I didn't aspire to be top of the class, perhaps because this situation was always occupied by the aptly named Maureen Head. She was first with everything. No-one could compete with her brilliance and her parents complained about the schoolwork being far too easy for her. She needed stretching they said.

Then one morning at assembly, a few weeks after we'd all taken The Scholarship, her brilliance went into partial eclipse. After we'd said prayers and sung a hymn to Our Lady, Mother Mary Ambrose told us all to sit down. She made one or two announcements of the usual kind and then went on to tell us she'd received some wonderful news by first post that day. This wonderful news was that Sally Shervington had been awarded a rare A pass in the Kent Scholarship. What this meant was that Sally could take up a place in any high school or grammar school of her parents' choice without even having to go for an interview.

So with that satisfying success, the summer months of 1954 must have been some of the happiest of my life. I don't remember them though. All I remember is a pleasant sense of imminent change, and expectation about what lay ahead. It must have been the first time I had a glimmer of ambition. A sense of something waiting for me. A future in which I'd stand out and do wonderful things. I'd be top of the class in everything, frightfully good at shinning up ropes in the gymnasium and terribly popular with everyone. And I'd tell people to stop calling me Sally because Sally wasn't my real name and I didn't like it. I was going to be Sarah from now on. Sally was a baby's name.

The only day I do remember was the day of the class outing to some unremarkable bit of seaside on the Kent coast. I recall my disappointment on finding out that valuable time was going to be wasted on the outward journey. It transpired that when we stopped half-way, it wasn't just so that we could be excused but so that we could visit the shrine of Our Lady at Hartley. I felt I'd been cheated out of valuable time at the seaside but when I went inside the little church, knelt down and gazed at its decoration of shining gold and silver hearts placed there by people whose prayers had been answered, I suddenly found that I had a heartfelt one of my own to offer up. 'Dear Our Lady, please don't let there be another war.'

✽

In spite of my ignorance of world affairs (and, indeed, of everything else) fear of war in the 1950s was perfectly reasonable. This was the time of the Cold War, when Russia was a deadly enemy. I couldn't understand why anyone should be our enemy. We didn't start wars did we? Britain was a good nation. It was other people who started wars. People like the Germans. Anyway, when you went to the cinema, the newsreels invariably featured good British soldiers fighting wicked ones in the Far East or somewhere. Or they showed bad business in the Middle East which, then as now, was always riven with conflict, and somewhere else that Britain was mysteriously involved. You heard all about this on the wireless too. So even if you didn't understand anything about it, you knew the world was full of danger in spite of things looking safe enough in your own part of it. The bongs of Big Ben striking the hour before a news bulletin always felt enormously reassuring. As the bongs rippled outwards round the room they seemed to speak of order, authority and things under control. Big Ben seemed to be at the centre of everything. Big Ben felt like the heart of the nation.

I'm trying to think how you got an idea of where you belonged in the larger world; how you acquired a sense of being British and how being British was part of who you were. Well there was Arthur Mee for a start, but failing him there were maps and atlases abounding which showed vast swathes of the world's surface coloured in pink. The pink areas indicated the expanse of the British Empire. So you became imbued with a quiet pride in belonging to the top nation. It was just part of the air you breathed and was confirmed and consolidated by the knowledge that we'd won the war against the Germans. No-one thought to tell you that in order to do this we'd had rather a lot of help from Uncle Sam, that all the atlases were out of date and that the collapse of the British Empire was far advanced.

I think it likely I wasn't aware of the Empire at all until my first year at Coloma, because one day I was surprised to see all my friends from Shirley in Girl Guide uniforms. Apparently they were allowed to wear them to school because it was Empire Day. As I admired and marvelled at all the badges they'd gained and neatly sewn on their blouses I didn't let on that I'd no idea Girl Guides existed. I only knew about Boy Scouts and that was because they used to come round in Bob-a-Job week.

But when my father was a boy he couldn't have helped knowing about the Empire simply because of where he lived. If you remember this was in Wembley. He was born there in 1914 a few months before the start of the First World War and so he was ten or eleven when the British Empire Exhibition of 1924-1925 took place in Wembley Park. Whether he was in the Great Boy Scout Jamboree I've no idea. I doubt it somehow and it rather looks as if the only part he played was as an ear of corn bending from side to side with thousands of others in simulation of a wind-blown Canadian prairie. The memory of this absurdity always makes him laugh, as does the recollection of the exhibition filling him with longing to become a Mountie (someone in the Royal Canadian Mounted Police). But this wasn't to be and when he became superintendent of six hundred special constables in London at the age of twenty-two there was, alas, no horse to go with the job.

But if the Empire Exhibition had little or no effect on my father's future, the same couldn't be said for his older brother George. It was here he learnt about something called The Big Brother Movement under whose auspices he could get an assisted passage to Australia to work in agriculture. In order to get his father's permission he had to promise two things: to write to his mother every week and not to marry before he was thirty. Keeping both promises, he worked immensely hard at farming, raised a large family and never came back to England.

England and Britain were more or less synonymous in my mind. From the way Mother Mary Ambrose taught us about national flags and emblems and how the component parts of the British Isles had come together, it seemed to be a friendly business and rather generous of England to let Scotland, Wales and Ireland come in with us. Arthur Mee's confidence that ours was the noblest nation the world had ever seen was evidently widespread and taken for granted. It was also taken for granted that Britain's nobility was made manifest through the character and behaviour of its individual heroes. I know for certain that my sense of Britishness and the idea that there was such a thing as a national character came to me strongly but subliminally through films I watched in the 1950s. I've more or less forgotten them now but I know they did their work.

However, cinema-going wasn't a prominent part of my life whereas listening to the wireless was. It was a major component of indoor life. Whatever was on in the sitting room came to Heather's and my ears through the extension that our father had rigged up on the mantelpiece in our room. We woke up with the wireless and went to bed with it too. If the bongs of Big Ben hadn't stirred us into obvious life in the morning then he'd crack a big knuckle on the bedroom door and call out, 'Wakey wakey girls! Rise and shine! Breakfast's in five minutes so chop chop.' If it was a freezing morning with ice on the inside of the windows then a single bar of electric fire might be allowed for a few minutes so that you could warm up your underwear before hurrying into it. (Although heating up my knickers wasn't always a good idea.)

I listened to (or heard) all sorts of programmes I didn't much like. One of these was *Top of the Form* which was on once a week at half past seven in the evening. Once Heather had become allowed to stay up much later than me, then various blandishments were employed by my father to get me into bed. He'd say things like, 'Now if you're a good girl and hurry up and get washed and into your pyjamas you can listen to *Top of the Form* in bed.' He presented the offer as if it was a real treat and so I tried to experience it as such. But oh dear reader, if I'm honest, how I loathed it. It made me squirm.

Opposing teams from different schools took part in a general knowledge quiz. A man and a woman took turns asking the questions. The man sounded rather pleasant but I took a dislike to the woman, who was called Joan somebody-or-other. I particularly disliked her because if an unwary child began to say, 'Is it … ?' she would always make a retort like, 'I'm asking the questions Janet – not you. It's for you to give me the answers.' I thought it was astounding that the children knew any of them because my own stock of knowledge didn't go much beyond the facts that Paris was the capital of France and that Henry VIII had six wives. Perhaps my poor father, who was under the misapprehension that I was clever, thought I was able to enjoy myself by pitting my wits against those of the contestants.

Obviously this wasn't the case but leaving this shaming shortcoming on one side, what I hated most was the way the grownups addressed the children as 'boys and girls' and the way the two teams ecstatically hip-hip-hoorayed each other at the end of the programme. I can't explain why these things made my skin crawl but I know they made me feel that I'd got no alternative but to be a somewhat sulky outsider. I was already an outsider at the public library in Beckenham. The female in charge there became identified in my mind with the one on *Top of the Form*. Therefore I was convinced the librarian must be called Joan (a hard, unforgiving name) and that her wireless counterpart must look just like her. Eyes watery blue with inbuilt accusatory cast. Hair in sandy plaits anchored on top by combs. Olive green costume of oppressive respectability.

I don't even know why I went to the library. I suppose my father took me in from time to time, just for something to do. Or perhaps we went there after we'd come out of the swimming baths. When it came to reading matter he didn't seem to have any suggestions so I'd grab two or three books at random, lug them home on the 227 bus and never even open them. I just didn't like them. I hated their institutional smell and the way they all looked the same. The feeling of failure associated with the borrowed books I didn't read and my lack of enthusiasm to borrow any more meant that I never returned them on time. The longer I left it, the longer I left it until it became ever more impossible to even consider a visit. But in the end there was no escape and you had to go through with it, probably during the school holidays by which time the books were about two months overdue.

An astonishing sight met me on one of these dismal occasions. When I went in, the librarian wasn't at her desk but I could hear her voice. So I looked around and there she was in the far corner of the room, sitting on a chair with a semicircle of cross-legged, eagerly-listening children at her feet. It was obviously some kind of club she ran and everyone looked frightfully pleased with themselves. Very cosy it looked. Very exclusive. So not for the likes of me. She made this quite clear when she came over to deal with the books I'd brought back. She made sure to tell me off loud and clear so the goody-goodies had the enjoyment of savouring my humiliation.

✻

It's a long time since I've been able to write anything to you. Almost a year I think. Perhaps I might have been able to find the time but I know I couldn't have found the heart. This was because of my father who died last May at the age of ninety-three. Until he was nearly ninety he could still put me in mind of a mighty oak tree and for his sake I'd always hoped that he'd be felled by the merciful lightning-strike of something sudden like a stroke. Instead of which we had to watch his increasing enfeeblement and see his life reduced to the slowest of slow shuffles between bedroom, bathroom and armchair. I'm glad I didn't know it then, but by comparison with what came next, these were the good times. What came next was a nursing home and unhappiness too awful to recall. Even so he was still asking after you all until a few days before he died.

The trouble is that now it's rather difficult to get back into my stride. I've dropped the threads of my story – if a story is what it is. And in any case story is rather a slippery word. 'Don't tell stories!' was an expression you heard often in my childhood. Perhaps you still hear it in yours – or will do when you're older. (When I began to write there was only Bella but now there are Nelly and Jos as well.) 'Don't tell stories' meant 'Don't tell lies.' I can't remember being accused of telling stories (oh yes I can – once when I was about four – but not in so many words even then. More of that later perhaps.) but of course I told them.

The ones that stick in my mind are the gratuitous ones – sudden unaccountable fabrications. Like the time I came home from a girl's birthday party (which seemed to have taken place in some kind of cosy underground bunker) and burst into tears for reasons I didn't and still don't understand. So I immediately sought to cover up or explain this by saying they'd been unkind to me. I said the jelly was disgusting and that they'd made me eat it up. They'd said that if I didn't eat up all my jelly then I couldn't have any birthday cake. They'd never said anything of the sort of course and the jelly wasn't at all disgusting. In fact they couldn't have been kinder to me. Perhaps that was the trouble. I just can't remember. But what I do remember is feeling ashamed of having traduced this innocent family. Kelly I think their name was. And because I was ashamed I almost persuaded myself to believe my own story. But at least nobody ever knew I'd told that lie and nobody got hurt because of it. It was a different matter that time when I was about four.

My mother came into the bedroom where I was playing on my own and smilingly gave me two squares of chocolate wrapped in silver paper. You can't imagine what that meant in those days when there was so little of anything around. Chocolate was the rarest of rare treats and instead of eating it herself she was giving it to me. I didn't even have to share it with Heather. It felt like a declaration of love. And loving her as I did and longing for her to love me, I couldn't bear to eat it. It was much, much more than chocolate. It was treasure. Of course I licked around the edges a bit until the squares lost their corners but for ages and ages I kept it hidden away so that I could hold it secretly whenever I got the chance. Until I lost it.

Then suddenly there it was again. It turned up in the pocket of a coat I'd just put on. Yet even though I was spellbound at its miraculous reappearance I had to lob it frantically out of the bedroom window when I realised that my mother was about to open the door.

I felt wretched about it, but for some reason it never occurred to me to go out afterwards and retrieve it. It was as if it was beyond recovery. So a few days later when she came in from the garden with it held out in the palm of her hand I went beetroot-red and pretended I'd got no idea how it got there. I wouldn't/couldn't tell her why I hadn't eaten it and why I'd thrown it away. So then she did something I would have loved her to do in normal circumstances but simply couldn't bear on this occasion. She sat me on her knee. I felt agonised as she gently tried to get to the bottom of things. In the end she gave up and with sadness in her voice told me to run away. What she must have thought was exactly what I hadn't wanted her to think. That I had spurned her love. That I hadn't appreciated what she'd given me. As I'd stood there with the just-rediscovered chocolate it in my hand I'd known that this is what she'd think if she saw me with it still uneaten. So that's why I'd hurled it through the window.

✻

Hurling food out of a window brings to mind a very different incident that happened many years later when I was about twelve and on my way home from Coloma. Twelve year old girls were still children then and I was no exception. I hardly gave a thought to my appearance and if I was aware of it at all I think I'd only have been conscious of disappointment at my inability to be anything other than scruffy.
After I got off the train at Norwood Junction I used to plonk

myself and my satchel down on a bench near the booking office and talk to an Indian porter while I waited for another train to take me on to Penge West. His skin was quite pale so perhaps he was only half Indian. Perhaps he wasn't Indian at all. Anyway I always thought of him as the Indian porter. He was small and had a rather sweet face that for some reason reminded me of a mouse. He used to ask me about my day at school and about this and that and I'd prattle away as naturally as if he were an uncle. Then when my train came in he'd close the door after me, I'd let down the window by its leather strap and we'd go on talking until the train moved off. He'd wave to me and I'd lean out of the window and wave back to him until the station was out of sight. I don't know how long this went on for but it was a pleasant fixture in my private life between school and home.

Until one Friday evening when it came to an abrupt end. I'd got into the train for Penge and let down the window as usual. He was smiling up at me and holding out a small packet. A present. He told me it was two biscuits. These would probably have been quite welcome in normal circumstances but as soon as I'd thanked him they turned to poison in the bag. Because still smiling up at me he followed their gift with the fatal words, 'Do you realise how pretty you are?'

No I did not. The only thing I realised was that his interest in me wasn't avuncular after all. Pretty or not my face blazed with shame. And so, I'm certain, did the rest of me. What he'd said had nothing to do with my face. It had to do with other, unseen, unsavoury places covered by my clothing, particularly by my knickers. Somehow I managed to go through the usual waving routine and then the second the train was round the bed I hurled the foul, contaminating packet as far as I could over the side of the bridge and onto the road below. I don't think I ever set eyes on him again because after that I waited for the Penge train as far as possible down the platform.

✻

I'm sure the Indian porter wasn't any kind of pervert. I can't believe he meant me any harm and I feel rather sad about him now. But there were plenty of perverts around and I seem to have had an unhappy propensity to attract their attention. These were the nasty men I'd been warned about. These were the men who tried to press you into accepting a lift in their car or came up to you pretending to be a friend of your father and saying what a spoilsport you were not going down to the park with them. They didn't bother me too much though because I never saw them again. They were just pests, but even so they were obviously up to no good.

The one that did bother me was the one I thought of as the Polish man whom I saw almost every day on the train. Like me he got on at East Croydon and off at Norwood Junction. He never took any notice of me but I could easily have picked him out in an identity parade. He was stockily built with an aquiline nose and blonde hair swept back from his forehead. I'm pretty sure he worked on the railways because he used to walk out of the barrier at Norwood without presenting any sort of ticket.

But he must have been watching me because it became apparent that he knew I had a habit of sticking my head out of the train window between Croydon and Norwood. I used to do this because I enjoyed the sensation of the wind rushing into my face. One day he got into the compartment next to the Ladies Only that I was in and when I stuck my head out I found his face staring into mine with his hair streaming in my direction. Embarrassed, I thrust my head back in. Perhaps he liked sticking his head out of train windows too but it seemed odd that he wanted to have the wind on the back of it instead of the front. At Norwood, with every hair in place, he got out, slammed his door shut and strode to the barrier as usual without a glance at me.

I thought it was odd but didn't give the matter another thought and I've no idea how long afterwards it was that when I leant out of the window I saw a pair of large hands agitating something floppy like a uncooked sausage. My head shot back in horror and seconds later we were in Norwood where everything was as it always was. The Polish man got out, again with every hair in place, and made for the exit as normal. I couldn't believe it had happened and yet I knew it had. I wasn't even sure I knew what I'd seen. I just knew I shouldn't have seen it. And I didn't want to have seen it. It didn't occur to me to tell anyone. I didn't have the words for it. And I felt to blame. What he'd done made me feel filthy. As if I was the one who'd done something wrong.

Perhaps men like this take such absurd risks because they're sexually inadequate and desperate to find a means of exciting themselves into activity. Perhaps some try to do it by talking dirty. I imagine this is what was going on during the incident which I now think of laughingly as a newspaper column under the headline: OUTRAGE AT EAST CROYDON.

Sun streams through the opaque window of the ladies' waiting room, making me squint as I stand in front of the giant mirror combing out my hair prior to putting it up again in a pony tail and retying my ribbon. It's possible I've even got a tiny bit of rouge to put on that I've pinched from Heather's drawer. This modest prettifying has become a daily event while waiting for Nick and Paddy's train to arrive. They're friends from the John Fisher School further down the line and I always look forward to seeing them. It seems I've moved on a fraction since the biscuit-hurling occasion.

I invariably have the ladies' waiting room to myself and very few people ever come into the main waiting room either. So I'm instantly apprehensive when I hear rattle of glass in rackety door followed by unhurried but deliberate steps in my direction. It's what I thought it might be. A man. My hands freeze in mid-air as I stare at him staring at me. It would be bad enough if he'd simply looked in at the door but he's done more than that. He's had the outrageous nerve to step right over the threshold. Our encounter, which is over in moments, ends like this.

He: Would you like to be touched up?
Me: No thank you.

Departure of man. Rattle of glass in rackety door. I'm alone again and can resume my activities while pondering on what he said. Perhaps he hadn't meant what I'd thought he'd meant. I'd thought he was referring to cosmetics. This was because my mother's sister Eileen had a habit of peering critically into the mirror of her Helena Rubinstein powder compact and saying something like, 'I must just touch up my countenance. I can't go home looking like this.'

A few minutes later I'm disturbed again. This time by two plump, breathless women bearing string bags bulging with groceries.

'Has a man been in here dear?'

'Yes.'

'Did he say anything to you?'

'Yes'.

And in my innocence, without prompting, I go on to tell them precisely what. Sharp intake of breath by one. Suppressed shriek from the other. Then they spring into action. Simultaneously they assault the rattling, rackety door, struggle as they both try to shove themselves through first and go out leaving it wide open. They waddle off as fast as bulk and baggage permit and call back to me, 'We're going to get the stationmaster dear. Yes, stay where you are love. Don't move. We'll be back in a mo.'

Well I don't want to stay where I am and I've no intention of doing so if I can possibly help it. I don't want to miss the John Fisher boys. Luckily for me, just when it sounds as if official feet are beginning to clatter down the slope towards me, the train pulls in. As usual, Paddy's already got his door open and I spring in. He bangs it shut behind me and the train moves off.

✻

Needless to say I said nothing about this at home. With regard to bodily matters I'd long since known that my parents were too embarrassed, frightened or disgusted to give me a straight answer to a straight question. When I was about nine we were given some homework to do about mammals. The dictionary said that a mammal was an animal that suckled its young. I was sitting at the dining room table while my mother sat sewing by the fireside. 'What does suckle mean?' I asked. 'I don't know,' she said. 'Look it up in the dictionary.' So I did and therefore made the connection with my mother's concealed bosoms and why she pretended she didn't know the meaning of the word. At about the same age I asked my father why it was that unmarried women didn't have babies. 'Well they do sometimes' he said 'but it's not very usual.' And one day when I was alone in the flat with him the telephone rang. I answered it and a man's voice said, 'Do you know anything about the facts of life?' I said yes which wasn't true, realised it was a dirty man and put the receiver down. When I told my father what the man had said he went a bit pink and replied, 'Well you know dear, men do tend to get a bit silly in the spring.'

Looking back on what I've written it seems as if my curiosity was limited to matters sexual. I really can't remember asking questions about anything else. I never for a moment wondered why the moon looked so huge going down behind the trees. I was too busy being full of wonder at its beauty. As far as I was concerned it simply *was* huge on that particular winter morning. If someone had told me this wasn't so, that it just looked as if it was and I could find it all explained on such and such a page in Arthur Mee, I wouldn't have wanted to know. I don't know what I wanted to know or what I wanted to be taught. I just know I wasn't being taught anything of any interest or relevance to me. Any windows onto joy through learning and discovery remained firmly blacked out.

It feels as if a great break in my life happened when I left St Winefride's. This is because my career at Coloma turned out to be such an immense disappointment in every respect. First there was the ugliness of it and the dreariness of its surroundings. It was a huge, several-storeyed slab of a place in dirty brick, crammed into a too-small site with no gardens or fields to play in, surrounded by high walls topped with broken glass. A distinct air of the penal institution clung to it. Perhaps it had indeed been one in a previous incarnation before the nuns took it over. A workhouse perhaps.

For as long as I could remember, school had been a place I'd always been glad to go to. A place where I belonged. A place where I knew everyone and everyone knew me. I didn't know anyone at Coloma but I presumed it would be the same for all the girls. But on that first morning in the grossly-overcrowded form room that was to be mine for the next year it became apparent that the majority of the girls in 1C had been friends for years. They'd all come from the same school. Somehow I divined that their parents hadn't had to pay fees to send them there in order to gain a place at grammar school by passing The Scholarship. When I quite naturally said something to my new acquaintances about us all having passed The Scholarship I was stared at with astonishment. They soon put me straight about my blunder. None of us had passed a Scholarship. What we'd passed was something very common called the Eleven plus.

So that was one of three things clarified before I went home that day. The second was the unsettling realisation that my well-spoken new friends had all been pupils at their local council school – the safely suburban equivalent of the ones that had so appalled my senses in Penge. The third was that if I wanted to keep the friends I was in the process of making then I'd better not use the expression 'council school'. It was to be many years later that I myself encountered the equally laughable snobbery of the public school product towards the grammar school one.

Apart from being the only one to have come from a private school, there were other things which seemed to set me apart and make me feel like the odd one out. Quite ordinary things I suppose. Like the fact that I'd never played netball before and thus was swiftly unmasked as a complete idiot for not having a clue about its rules. Like the shabby old flat I lived in with no friends nearby, which was miles away from their cosy semis and enviably sociable existence. And like the less ordinary thing which I've mentioned before, that my mother went out to work.

Precisely what she did I don't know but she did it five and a half days a week in a civil service department near London Bridge.

An ironic consequence of Coloma's status as a grammar school was that its Catholic pupils were in the minority. Not many of the girls I went through school with were Catholics and indeed my closest friend was proud of the fact that her parents, as highly intelligent non-believers, had never seen fit to have her christened at all. This bothered me quite a bit on her behalf and consequently I tried to prove the error of their ways by parroting a passage from the Catechism. The look of polite pity on her face as she turned away to get on with her work probably planted the first seed of doubt in my mind; the beginning of trying to think things out for myself.

I recently found around the house a battered copy of *Catechism of Christian Doctrine (Revised edition 1954)*. It's the exact counterpart of the one from which I'd been quoting that day. I found it among my mother-in-law's effects and kept it for its possible future interest as a historical document. So I might as well use it as such now by quoting its final question and answer.

> 370  After your night prayers what should you do?
> After my night prayers I should observe due modesty in going to bed; occupy myself with thoughts of death; and endeavour to compose myself to rest at the foot of the Cross, and give my last thoughts to my crucified Saviour.

Looking back on that eternity in secondary school it feels the same as it felt at the time – like being in prison. And just like a prison it achieved as little for its inmates as prisons generally do. Innocent of any crime, our apparent purpose as pupils was to pass examinations. No greater enemy of education could ever have been devised.

You put up with it all though because you had to and because you had no idea things could be otherwise. You unconsciously made the reasonable assumption that what they were teaching you was something you really ought to know. And so from various syllabuses imposed on me along the way I gained the inescapable impression that history was something that happened somewhere else a long time ago. History hadn't happened in the twentieth century, had nothing to do with anyone in my family (no-one famous in it) and above all it had no connection with the suburban world in which I lived. If it wasn't in the school textbook or in the encyclopaedia then it wasn't history.

And as for literature (however you might define the word) – I never imagined it could still be going on; that people were still writing. Because literature had all been done quite a long time ago as well. It wasn't done anymore because the world wasn't the same as it was when Wordsworth and Keats and people like that wrote about its beauty. It was a different world now with cars, tarmacked roads, railways, ugly buildings, bridges and bombsites covering it up. Where was the world of Jane Austen and John Constable? Why was everything so spoiled? Something awful had happened.

It's true I'm exaggerating a bit because I remember Eliot's *Wasteland* was on the A-level syllabus but the subject of his poem seems to prove my point. It confirmed what I felt myself; that we were living in a damaged time, in a blasted world that was very far removed from the one inhabited by the romantic poets. And yet the romantic poets hadn't lived so very long ago. Whatever it was that severed their world from ours seemed to have happened very quickly.

❋

I'd discovered Jane Austen for myself among the few books we had at home and fortunately the pleasure I was beginning to find in her was never ruined by study or examination. I didn't know about John Constable because of anything I'd been taught at school either. I don't know how I became familiar with reproductions of his work but perhaps I'd seen them on birthday cards or the top of someone's biscuit tin. Eventually though, when I was about fourteen, I acquired a coloured postcard of one of his paintings which summed up everything beautiful for which I longed.

I've already tried to give you some idea about the absence of visual stimulus in my childhood and how very difficult it was to make chance discoveries or make any sense out of anything. But I think it's worth mentioning again because there are so many readily-available sources of knowledge now that the difference between then and the present day is unimaginable. And if you can be bothered to read these letters when you're grown up in twenty or so years time, who knows how much further things will have changed by then? Anyway, things being as they are, it only took me a few seconds just now to find that much-loved image displayed on the website of the National Gallery. It's called *The Cornfield*.

It's just possible that I'd seen the original when my parents took us up to Trafalgar Square one day by the number 12 bus. But I don't think I could have done because if I had, I'm certain they would have had to tear me away from it. As it is I only remember a few moments about this outing and it was altogether a bemusing business because it was obvious that they knew no more about paintings than I did. All that was being established was that such a place as the National Gallery existed. We were being introduced to it rather in the same spirit that we'd been introduced to Beckenham library. It was up to us to make of it what we would. They were just doing the best they could for us. Well you can't ask more than that from your parents and it was certainly better than nothing.

Most of the time we were there I felt the familiar overwhelming hopelessness. A combination of not understanding what was special about the pictures and why on earth they'd been painted in the first place. There seemed to be all sorts of rather rude ones with virtually undressed pink women being chased by men or monsters in unrealistic landscapes. It was embarrassing going past them in my parents' company. When I had a sly glance at their titles I found they purported to illustrate Greek or Roman myths. And then of course there were the religious paintings, many of which looked liked enormous versions of the little holy pictures I was so familiar with and which were, for obvious reasons, quite devoid of appeal.

Then suddenly there was a picture that leapt out of the wall at me. This wasn't because of its vaguely familiar urban subject matter but because of the way in which it was painted. With very free brushwork and joyful blobs of colour the artist had brought an everyday scene to vivid life. Better than life. It was a cityscape at night and the roads and pavements were all wet with lights reflecting in them. It could have been somewhere I knew. So places you knew could be worth painting! That was something worth knowing. Years later I went back to find it and discovered it was *The Boulevard Montmartre at Night* by the French Impressionist Camille Pissarro. I only mention this because of an interesting coincidence. Many years later still, I found out that during the 1870s Pissarro, who by that time was one of my favourite painters, had lived in our area and painted numerous pictures of the newly-built suburban landscapes of Penge, Anerley, Sydenham and Norwood.

❋

It's mid-February now and the weather's been so perfect for nearly a week that I can hardly bear to miss any of it by being indoors. Sometimes you get such wonderful weather you feel you don't know what to do with it. The sun was just beginning to melt the frost when I went out this morning to stroll beside the stream in the field opposite. There was warmth on my back and coolness in my face. In the bluish distance up on the downs I think I could hear larks singing. Closer to home a great tit was going see-saw, see-saw, see-saw. Slightly further away the rooks were making a mighty racket as they cawed and squawked, rising and falling around their old nesting sites in the lime trees along the main road through the village.

If it weren't for the frost it would have been a difficult squelch in the field because we've had such an enormous quantity of rain in recent weeks. One happy consequence for birds is the lake on top of the garage. In the weeping pear behind it, sparrows and blue tits queue up to go for a lengthy splash. Only four in at a time seems to be the rule they enforce between themselves.

It was at this time of year and on just such days as today that as a teenager I'd repossess my soul by walking in a remnant of countryside on my way home from school. By this time we'd moved further out from London to a new semi-detached house in a place called Bickley, near Bromley in Kent, and I travelled there by bus. I'd get off the 119 at Hayes to miss out on Bromley and the onward ride by 94 so that I could walk more or less straight, over a stile or two, across the fields in the direction of home. No-one ever knew I did this, which was an important part of its charm. There wasn't anyone at home now when I got in. Granny hadn't made the move with us and so I'd got plenty of time to get rid of the muddy evidence.

I'd assumed that this modest but life-saving piece of countryside had long since been built over because you could feel the threat hanging over it even then. It was all that separated the 1930s semis of Hayes from the big detached houses along Bromley Common. However, when I looked at Google Earth just now I found to my surprise that it's still there. But for how much longer I wonder? And it makes me sad to think of my own involvement in the concreting of England. The three houses in which I've lived during my married life were all built between 1966 and 1971 and they've all played their part in the relentless suburbanisation of the countryside.

I frequently wonder about the effect surroundings have on you and think it's worth while occasionally to try and imagine what sort of person you'd have been if you'd grown up in a completely different environment. Let's suppose I spent the forties and fifties growing up here in this Hampshire village of Bishop's Sutton and that my father was an agricultural worker – an occupation for which he would have been physically and

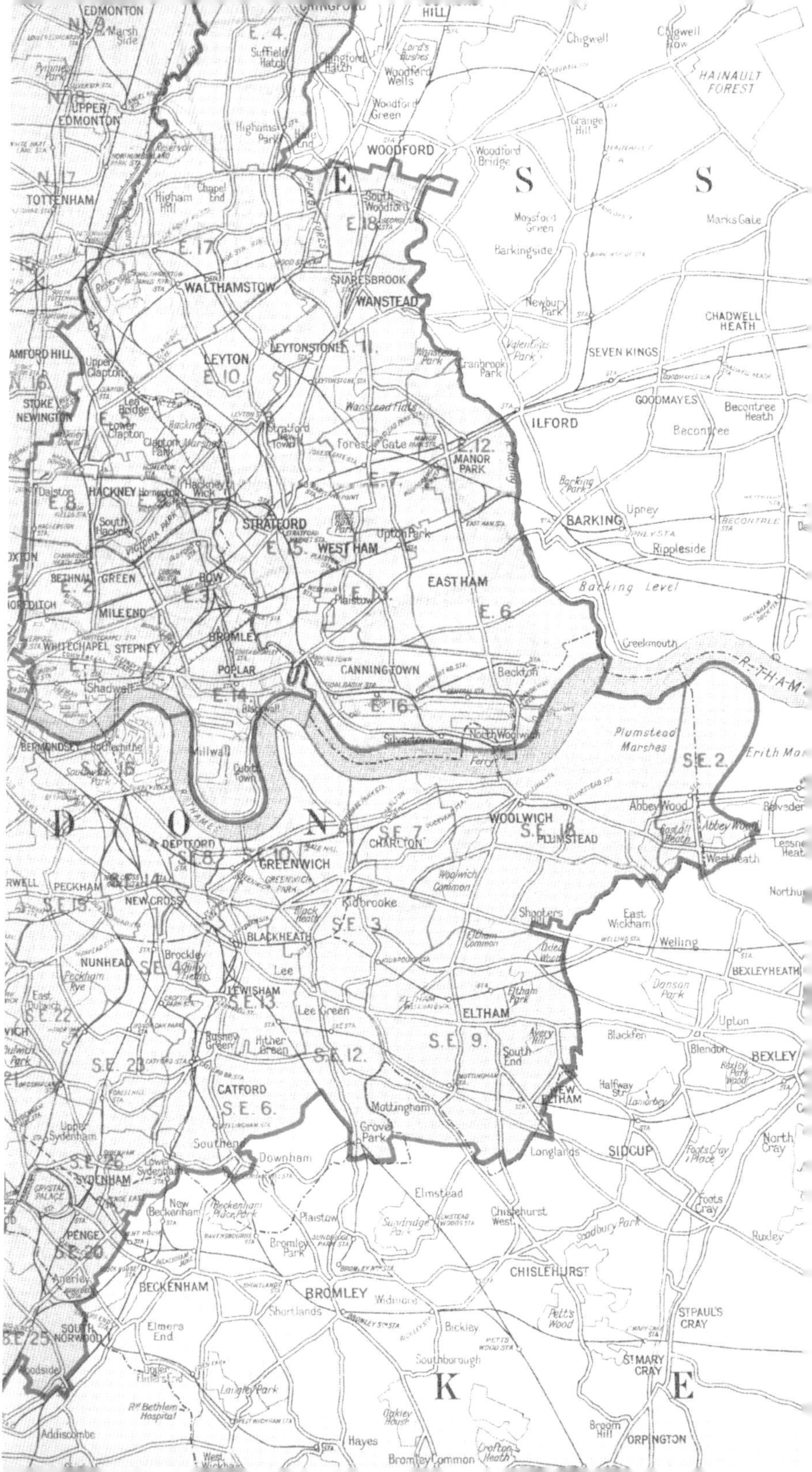
EDMONTON
Marsh Side
E. 4.
Suffield Hatch
Chingford Hatch
Lord's Bushes
Woodford Wells
Chigwell
Chigwell Row
HAINAULT FOREST
Pymmes Park
N. 18
UPPER EDMONTON
Highams Park
Woodford Green
WOODFORD
Woodford Bridge
Grange Hill
Reservoir
N. 17
TOTTENHAM
Higham Hill
Chapel End
E
South Woodford
E. 18
S
S
Mossford Green
Marks Gate
Barkingside
E. 17
WALTHAMSTOW
SNARESBROOK
WANSTEAD
Newbury Park
CHADWELL HEATH
STAMFORD HILL
Upper Clapton
LEYTON
E. 10
LEYTONSTONE
E. 11
Wanstead Park
Cranbrook Park
Valentines Park
SEVEN KINGS
N. 16
STOKE NEWINGTON
Lea Bridge
E. 5
Lower Clapton
Wanstead Flats
GOODMAYES
Becontree Heath
ILFORD
Becontree
Clapton Park
Stratford New Town
Forest Gate
E. 12.
MANOR PARK
Hackney Wick
Dalston
E. 8.
HACKNEY
Homerton
South Hackney
STRATFORD
E. 7
Barking Park
Upney
BARKING
Victoria Park
E. 15.
WEST HAM
Upton Park
West Ham Park
Rippleside
BETHNAL GREEN
E. 2
BOW
E. 3
Plaistow
E. 13
EAST HAM
E. 6
Barking Level
SHOREDITCH
MILE END
WHITECHAPEL
STEPNEY
BROMLEY
E. 1
POPLAR
CANNINGTOWN
Beckton
Creekmouth
Shadwell
E. 14
Blackwall
E. 16.
R. THAMES
Silvertown
North Woolwich
Plumstead Marshes
BERMONDSEY
Rotherhithe
S.E. 16
Southwark Park
Millwall
Cubitt Town
Ferry
S.E. 2.
Erith Marshes
D
O
N
S.E. 7
WOOLWICH
S.E. 18
PLUMSTEAD
Abbey Wood
Belvedere
DEPTFORD
S.E. 8.
S.E. 10
CHARLTON
GREENWICH
Greenwich Park
West Heath
PECKHAM
S.E. 14
NEW CROSS
Woolwich Common
Kidbrooke
S.E. 15.
Black Heath
S.E. 3.
Shooters Hill
East Wickham
BLACKHEATH
Eltham Common
Welling
NUNHEAD
Brockley
S.E. 4
Lee
BEXLEYHEATH
Peckham Rye
LEWISHAM
S.E. 13.
Eltham Park
Danson Park
East Dulwich
S.E. 22
Lee Green
ELTHAM
Upton
Blackfen
Rushey Green
Hither Green
S.E. 12.
S.E. 9.
South End
Blendon
BEXLEY
S.E. 23
CATFORD
Halfway Str.
NEW ELTHAM
S.E. 6.
Mottingham
Upper Sydenham
Grove Park
Southend
Longlands
SIDCUP
North Cray
Downham
S.E. 26
SYDENHAM
Lower Sydenham
Foots Cray Place
CRYSTAL PALACE
Elmstead
Foots Cray
New Beckenham
Beckenham Place Park
Plaistow
Chislehurst West
Sundridge Park
Scadbury Park
Ruxley
PENGE
S.E. 20
Bromley Park
CHISLEHURST
Anerley
BECKENHAM
BROMLEY
Widmore
Shortlands
Petts Wood
ST PAUL'S CRAY
S.E. 25
SOUTH NORWOOD
Elmers End
Bickley
Southborough
ST MARY CRAY
Woodside
Langley Park
K
E
Rl. Bethlem Hospital
Oakley House
Broom Hill
ORPINGTON
Addiscombe
Hayes
Crofton Heath
West Wickham
Bromley Common

temperamentally ideally suited. We'd have lived in picturesque poverty in a cramped and draughty tied cottage. Cooking would have been done on a range with variable results depending on which way the wind blew. There'd be no running water indoors. If you were lucky there might be an outside tap but more probably you'd have to get your water bucketful by bucketful from the well. The lavatory, such as it was, was an outdoor privy. And what passed for a bath was of the galvanised variety that hung up on the wall outside until it was brought in once a week for bath night. It was then laboriously filled up with water heated with some difficulty on the range. Then you had to wait and take your established turn in the increasingly dirty and chilly water, privacy of a kind being provided by a strategically placed clothes-horse draped with laundry.

If I was a member of one of the long-established village families then I could have been directly related to half the people I was at school with and with whom my parents worked. So there would have been a sense of belonging unimaginable to me when I was growing up in the suburbs of London – belonging not simply to a community but also to the land around me and the ground beneath my feet. But in the close-knit community that existed then I would have known my place: at the bottom where almost everyone else was. This was graphically demonstrated by arrangements on Sunday at the Norman parish church of St Nicholas. Morning service catered exclusively for the gentry, evensong for the multitude at the bottom of the heap and all those in between. And at the now demolished and largely unlamented village school I would have been taught just enough to fit me for a future in domestic service in the homes of the said gentry. It would have been the same for my mother and for her mother before her. A lowly-paid place would easily be found but with a bit of ambition and a few brains I might perhaps have broken out to become a shop assistant in Alresford, the small market town a mile or so down the road where I now go almost every morning.

Maybe you're wondering just who the gentry were. Well once

upon a time the gentry were defined as the social class immediately below the aristocracy and this was the class into which Jane Austen had been born in 1775. But by the twentieth century it was a term used by the labouring classes to denote any well-spoken professional person, or individual of means, who didn't have to get their hands dirty. In *Kelly's Directory* for 1935 these people are quaintly referred to as 'private residents'. By this time ownership of a telephone line seems to have become a fairly accurate indicator of social status. There were then just thirteen private residents with telephones in the parish out of a population of about 470. So, as a tribe, the gentry and their offspring perhaps made up ten per cent of the population while providing employment for the other ninety per cent. And although in the 1950s the principal landowner would no longer have been referred to as the squire and small girls no longer expected to bob a curtsey to him and his wife, the paternalistic set-up was a strong survival from Victorian times which would have been recognised by Flora Thompson who wrote about rural Oxfordshire in the 1880s. However, very soon this way of life was to be swept away by increasing mechanisation of agriculture and almost universal car ownership.

Who knows whether a sense of belonging would have prevented any desire or ambition on my part to get away? Who knows whether I would have taken the loveliness of my surroundings so much for granted that I hardly saw them? One thing is certain though: I wouldn't have had the intuitive sense of loss which I did as a child in south London – an increasing sense of grief for what had passed away.

❋

One day in the company of a girl called Pauline I came out of school to discover that the already unlovely surroundings of Coloma were being rendered even more so by the addition of parking meters. 'More junk!' I exclaimed in disgust. I didn't know Pauline particularly well but she flung her arms round me and gave me an enormous hug expressive of astonished gratitude that someone else felt the same as she did about the increasing degradation of the world around us. It's the only joyful moment of mutual self-revelation I can recall having with anyone during my schooldays. What we all talked about among ourselves I can't remember but I think it's true to say that none of us spoke about our deeper thoughts and feelings. Although you were surrounded by people almost all the time you were essentially alone. I don't remember any girlish intimacy among us about personal matters either. I coped in concealed misery with the excruciating business of adolescence, feeling as if its horrors both physical and emotional were unknown to the apparently self-confident girls around me. I wouldn't have known how to speak of these things anyway. And even if I had known how to, I don't think I would have done. I had an instinctive distaste, terror even, of giving myself away; of letting on about anything.

Without being consciously aware of it I felt that my very survival depended on keeping quiet. This way of dealing with things was mine by ancient habit. Even the most casual remark at home could have shatteringly incendiary results. For example one evening when my mother came home from work I found that she expected me to have an opinion (hers) about some new curtains that had gone up in Birdham Close where we'd been living for a couple of years. I hadn't even noticed them and said so. 'Oh don't be so ri*dic*ulous. Of course you noticed them. You couldn't possibly miss them. Even *you* can't go round with your eyes shut *all* the time.' I was then unwise enough to give her a truthful explanation which was that I hadn't noticed anything when I came up the road because I'd been thinking about something. I can't remember the exact torrent of fury that burst forth but it was an explosive version of the familiar refrain: who do you think you are? In effect who did I think I was *thinking*! So if just being caught in thought could get you into so much trouble then how much more trouble would you find yourself in if you let on about what it was you were thinking about?

I suspect my mother felt I was trying to be superior and if I had been doing that then her fury would have been both understandable and righteous. As it was, I hadn't been. Yet she'd hit on something I was finding hard to hide: that I didn't think new curtains were worthy of notice and I felt increasingly asphyxiated by having come to live in the kind of place where people thought they were. This was airlessness of the genuinely suburban kind which had been unknown to me in the flat at Sydenham although I don't think I ever felt homesick for the old place. It was as if it didn't exist any more. It wasn't somewhere I'd lived in the past so much as part of the past itself and you don't think about your past when you're trying to cope with growing up. When you're growing up you seem to shed the previous year's self at the start of the September term and it's as if all your previous selves had never existed.

Whatever it is that's going on when you're growing up seems to be going on for an awfully long time but nevertheless I can't recall any active desire on my part for it to end. I didn't find the adult world enticing and wasn't keen to enter it. It seemed a cramped and dreary place with all its work and worry and I hadn't got the faintest idea what to do with my own life except to get married and have children. This seemed the most attractive option but before that happened I just wanted to earn some money of my own, have some pretty clothes and not have to take any more examinations. It wasn't so much a matter of freeing myself from constraints – it didn't occur to me that there could be any escape from them – so much as the acquisition of a small space for myself.

I don't know what it was like for other young people then or what it's like for young people now, but I've always felt that late adolescence – the period between, say, fourteen and sixteen – is the most excruciating phase of life. I probably find it painful to recall because this was when I felt the most acute misery about bodily matters in general and anguish about my lumpy-frumpy appearance in particular. I didn't realise then that maybe things wouldn't have seemed so bad if we hadn't moved to Bickley when we did – because for me this move around the age of fourteen had involved significant change for the worse in the loss of my grandmother as part of the household. The effect of this went unremarked by me. Things were the way they were because that was the way things were and it's only now that I begin to appreciate that if we'd still been at the flat and she'd still been around then those years might not have seemed so dismal.

In spite of having a bedroom of my own at last I nevertheless felt hemmed in, not just by the small houses all around but by a new way of living. My overall impression of these years is one of acute claustrophobia induced by having to squeeze round a blue Formica table to eat food that gave no pleasure to anyone. Besides being no cook, my mother was out at work all day and so as often as not it was my father who cremated the lamb chops and served them up with boiled potatoes and frozen peas followed by tinned peach slices.

It became a strain to maintain one's privacy in such close proximity. It felt as if we were on top of each other and this was rendered worse by the fact that I could no longer make myself scarce by sliding out of the bedroom door and disappearing down to the swing at the end of the garden or jumping over the hedge into the Palace grounds. So there was no escape either from any atmospheric pressure that happened to be building up or was still hanging around – unless perhaps the weather was good enough to go off and play tennis.

I can hardly believe that I've got no recollection of missing my grandmother in my new home. I certainly didn't forget her and know that I loved her as much as I'd always done but I suppose that, quite naturally, I'd found change exciting. I wonder though how horribly thoughtless I'd been in expressing my excitement at the prospect of having a bedroom of my own at last? How casually did I say goodbye to her when she left the flat for the last time? Did I even realise it was the last time? Did I come home from school one day to find her no longer there? I just don't know. I can't remember. And yet no-one has ever meant more to me.

✻

I don't know what age I was when I first disturbed her evening seclusion by knocking on her bedroom door. I soon made the welcome discovery that she was always pleased to see me. If she hadn't wanted me around she'd have left me in no doubt about it. I'd have been told to hop it, scram, beat it, skedaddle or make myself scarce. That's the kind of thing she used to say if you got under her feet in the tiny kitchen we had. Her room may have had a very Spartan feel to it but it was nevertheless the most comfortable place in the flat as far as I was concerned. It was a place where you could be yourself. Its lino was unrelieved by any rug or carpet that I can remember. An iron bedstead was immediately behind the door with a jerry concealed beneath it. An east-facing window looking over the front garden had a white-painted chest of drawers in front of it and the wall facing south had a tiled fireplace in the middle with a small window either side through which the afternoon sun could shine. I don't recall the nature of the chair Granny sat in to the right of the fireplace but I don't think it was particularly comfortable. My own place was on a stool opposite her. In winter as we chatted away, some of the chill might have been taken off by a very small coal fire or by a tiny single-ring electric stove on which she could boil up a bit of milk if she wanted to.

    Against the centre of the fourth wall stood the only exotic item in the room – a wind-up gramophone. The cabinet in which it was enclosed stood on four legs and had accommodation for a small music collection. I don't think there were as many as half a dozen records there. Among them was the still-famous recording of *The Wings of a Dove* sung by Ernest Lough together with *The Lost Chord* and *The Isle of Capri*. Best by far though was a rather wicked-sounding tango called *La Paloma* which seemed excitingly foreign and made you want to fool about to the tune. In time, Granny's only exotic possession ended up in Heather's and my bedroom, probably because we made such pests of ourselves by endlessly wanting to use it. Heather had discovered classical music on the wireless and was beginning to acquire records of her own. So it was probably after the removal of the gramophone that I began to colonise Granny's room.

I've told you already the little that's known about my grandmother's life and about the peculiarity of her not knowing the date or year of her birth. I never managed to get anything out of her about her childhood. I remember making an attempt about a week or so after I started at Coloma and had just been introduced to some new subjects.

'What did you learn at school Granny?'
'Nothing I ever wanted to remember.'
'Did you do physics?'
'Nope.'
'Did you do chemistry?'
'Nope.'
'Did you do biology?'
'Nope?'
'You must have done geography.'
'Nope.'
'History?'
'Nope.'

She never told my mother why she, her two sisters and her brother Jack were brought up by their grandmother. But perhaps my mother, lacking all curiosity, simply didn't think to question her about it. So I'm left wondering what happened to her parents. Had there been a tragedy of some kind? Was there some hidden shame? Did Granny even remember them? Had she deliberately forgotten something that was too painful to remember – the kind of forgetting that's sometimes necessary if you're going to be able to get on with your life? Perhaps. It feels unlikely though. There was too much blitheness of spirit about her for that – some childlike quality and too great a capacity for taking pleasure in small things. She knew how to make the best of things and small jokes were a great help in this respect. I particularly remember the deep enjoyment she got from a punning cartoon on the front of a newspaper one day. An exhausted dog, apparently in recovery from a shopping expedition, says to her friend, 'Oh my paw feet!' That put a smile on her face for the rest of the day.

'Be a good girl and pop down to Mickey Mouse for me. Here's my list if you can read it.' How many times did I hear her say that to Heather or me and how many times did I go into Mickey Mouse myself? I noticed that it didn't say Mickey Mouse over the door and yet I wasn't curious about why this was so. I didn't think it at all odd. Nor did I make any connection with the cartoon character or realise that ours was the only family to know this particular grocery shop by the name of Mickey Mouse. Granny's joke was so old even she'd probably forgotten there'd ever been one. The name she'd dubbed the proprietor with many years previously had just come naturally. It was his ears. They were huge, purple and round as teacups.

Another thing I didn't think at all odd was to have a grandmother who on occasion would say 'OK Chief' to shopkeepers while raising right hand in direction of black beret by way of salute.

A few months ago, after the death of my father, I was staying with my mother, now aged ninety-four and trying to engage her in conversation. As her short-term memory is virtually extinct this is only feasible if you focus on the past. So just to start things off I brought up the subject of Granny not knowing when she was born. I was startled by the response.

'Oh that was nonsense! I didn't believe her about that. She was hiding something.'

'What would she have to hide?'

'Being under-age when she married if you ask me. That's what I think.'

If Granny had indeed been married under-age then incriminating lies must have been told to British officialdom in Dublin. And perhaps even my grandfather didn't know the truth. So if my mother's right and something like this had gone on, then it could explain Granny's tendency to resort to amnesia when it suited her.

There was though just one childhood incident I'd heard mentioned *sotto voce* over the afternoon cup of tea. This concerned her first confession which she made when she was about seven. She'd got her list of sins off her chest and was waiting for absolution but before he gave it the priest asked, 'Has anyone ever touched your privates?'

*

Although Granny lived in the same flat with us she didn't live with us. She seemed to like being on her own and to have virtually no bodily needs. She cooked almost everything we ate but seldom ate what she cooked. All her food tasted wonderful, even if it was just simple things like fish pie, apple charlotte, scrambled eggs or rissoles made from tinned corned beef. She certainly had her culinary secrets but it's my belief the flavour of her food was the result of preparation that involved the kind of care and close attention that springs from love.

And, in the absence of kitchen gadgets whose possession we take for granted now, a great deal of time was needed to make something as comparatively simple as a lemon meringue pie. In order to beat up the egg white until it was stiff enough to make meringue, she made do with a plate, a knife and a draught. Draughts weren't usually difficult to find but in their absence Granny would open doors back and front and then support herself against the hall wall for ages while whipping away with her knife until the miracle took place. Not surprisingly, special thought and patience went into the preparation of food for Christmas. Work on this started in September with the purchase of large quantities of dried fruit which had to be laboriously washed and picked over before she could begin the often strenuous work involved in mixing puddings, cake and mincemeat. But it wasn't until Christmas morning that she took out her hidden store of little silver sixpences and slipped them into the pudding for Heather and me to find.

She was never present when we found them though because

she didn't join us at the table, not even on Christmas day. I only once questioned this and was told by my father that it was the way she preferred things. Later, when I began to infiltrate her privacy I found that what she ate by the fireside in the evenings was often no more than a couple of wafer-thin slices of Hovis with a scrape of unsalted butter and a sprinkling of soft brown sugar.

I suppose she sensibly adopted this arrangement of evening and weekend disappearance when my father came home from Germany in late 1946. It was one that seemed to work very well until shortly before we moved to the new house without her. Feeling my way back to Granny in those days I find I'm in her bedroom on a sunny day. It's early afternoon in summer. The door of her room is open and she isn't in there. But she's not far away. I can feel her presence. And I can also feel the absence of anyone on the dark side of the flat. My parents are at work and won't be back for hours. There's a breeze of freedom around the place and a sense of rising joy. I'm sorry to say this wouldn't have been possible if they'd been around.

I don't know whether Granny lived in the Irish countryside as a child but she certainly had a country love for trees, birds and flowers and was generally in tune with the natural world even though she'd lived in the London area for decades. She had a particular affection for sweet-smelling plants like mignonette, lily-of-the-valley, sweet william, honeysuckle and jasmine; and it was thanks to her that every May you could inhale the tremendous scent of wallflowers as you went in and out of the front door. Every year as a child I used to make posies of wallflowers and forget-me-nots from that bed to take to school in honour of Our Lady.

One evening when I got home from school she said she'd got something to show me later. It turned out to be a copy of Palgrave's *Golden Treasury* that she'd borrowed from the library. In it she'd discovered or rediscovered Tennyson's poem *The Brook*. We took it in turns to read it out loud and then agreed to memorise it. Time and again after that we'd take delight in reciting it together, not just in her room but anywhere and any time we had the place to ourselves. As I've said, I know very little about Granny, and yet knowing how much she loved this poem perhaps tells me a great deal.

Not that Granny was always in a good mood and if you accidentally did anything to hurt her feelings she'd pay you back by being in a mighty miff with you for days. I don't know how long it was before she forgave me for forgetting to wave to her one morning on my way to the station. And if she ever did forgive me I doubt whether she ever forgot the crime. She certainly never forgot me saying how smashing Aunt Dolly's fried bread was (she did it both sides). After that it was, 'Well it's just bacon and tomato for your supper. You won't be expecting any fried bread will you since mine's not good enough for you any more? You'll have to go to Eastcote for that.' When the plate of bacon and tomato arrived complete with fried bread (as you knew it would) she'd put it down in front of you with a sniff and frustrate your fervent efforts to make peace. 'Don't go bothering to thank me. It's too late for that. The damage is done.'

✱

For years when I was young, Sunday was enlivened by the pleasing prospect of Eileen coming for tea. (We weren't allowed to call her Aunt because it made her feel old.) I'd swing on the rickety gate and wait for as long as it took before her elegant, high-heeled form descended from a number 12 at the bus stop over the road. Sensibly not accepting the grubby hand I proffered, she'd circle my wrist very lightly with thumb and forefinger as we crunched our way across the gravel towards the front door.

Eventually things began to change. Increasingly, instead of Eileen coming to us, Granny would make the journey to her dreary bed-sit in a shabby house at Notting Hill, somewhere near the Portobello Road. She couldn't have had the slightest interest in her surroundings because although she obviously spent a lot on her appearance there was no shade over the light bulb in the middle of the ceiling. No sign of comfort anywhere. Not even a cushion. The tiny room was below street level and was reached by the area steps. The front door went straight into what passed for a kitchen – a damp, mildewed hole with an inconveniently sloping ceiling. The slope was due to its having been squeezed in underneath the front steps. She must have had to share a bathroom and lavatory with the other occupants of the house but this was never mentioned. Eileen seemed to be someone who had no need of such gross appurtenances.

Her favourite form of enjoyment was reading Dickens. Next to that she liked anything she could get hold of about the life and crimes of the most notorious murderers. She was a connoisseur. If you wanted a real life story that was better than many a novel then she'd have put you onto Dr Crippen. But if you wanted to enjoy the thrill of something truly grizzly then you couldn't do better than sink your teeth into Haig and the acid bath murders. For someone so gentle, and who quite literally couldn't kill a fly, it seemed an odd field of interest.

So it was a nice irony that when I was about ten it became known that a serial killer was at work in Notting Hill. Several female bodies had been discovered at 10 Rillington Place and their killer, a man called John Christie, was at large for quite a while before the police caught up with him. During this time Eileen was too scared to go down the steps to her own door in case he lay in wait for her. She took up her landlady's offer of coming and going by the front door until he was arrested.

Perhaps it was about this time that Granny began her visits. In her bag she'd take a book or two that Eileen might like. More importantly she'd also take small parcels of food because it was pretty obvious to her that Eileen cared as little about eating as she did about home comforts. One day Granny travelled there by train and tube instead of by bus and when she arrived home she was still chortling because of something that had happened to her.

Apparently she'd been horrified to find at one of the underground stations that there was no alternative to the escalator.

# THE BROOK

I come from haunts of coot and hern,
I make a sudden sally
And sparkle out among the fern
To bicker down a valley.

By thirty hills I hurry down,
Or slip between the ridges,
By twenty thorps, a little town
And half a hundred bridges.

Till last by Philip's farm I flow
To join the brimming river,
For men may come and men may go
But I go on for ever

I chatter over stony ways,
In little sharps and trebles,
I bubble into eddying bays,
I babble on the pebbles.

With many a curve my banks I fret
By many a field and fallow,
And many a fairy foreland set
With willow-weed and mallow.

I chatter, chatter, as I flow
To join the brimming river,
For men may come and men may go,
But I go on for ever

I wind about, and in and out,
With here a blossom sailing,
And here and there a lusty trout,
And here and there a grayling,

And here and there a foamy flake
Upon me, as I travel
With many a silvery waterbreak
Above the golden gravel,

And draw them all along, and flow
To join the brimming river,
For men may come and men may go,
But I go on for ever.

I steal by lawns and grassy plots,
I slide by hazel covers;
I move the sweet forget-me-nots
That grow for happy lovers.

I slip, I slide, I gloom, I glance,
Among the skimming swallows;
I make the netted sunbeam dance
Against my sandy shallows.

I murmur under moon and stars
In brambly wildernesses;
I linger by my shingly bars;
I loiter round my cresses;

And out again I curve and flow
To join the brimming river,
For men may come and men may go
But I go on for ever.

The stairs were closed. She always avoided escalators because she was frightened about not managing to get on and off and so she was standing there in dismay not knowing what to do. Then swiftly and gently her problem was solved. A black porter with a huge smile simply picked her up and carried her laughing to safety.

In later years when Granny was being cared for by Aunt Dolly over at Eastcote it sometimes happened that she contracted pneumonia and found herself in Mount Vernon hospital. However there was no need to worry about her on these occasions. She was always perfectly happy because she loved the motherly black nurses from the West Indies who called her their darlin' and made her laugh. And so it's always been a source of comfort to me that this is where she died, quietly and with no warning just after Christmas in 1968.

❋

One day I let myself into the flat after school and was surprised to hear voices. I was particularly curious that they were coming from Granny's room. Her door was ajar and my father was in there. Their voices weren't raised but I realised almost immediately that they were having words. A row. Such a thing had never happened before. Evidently she was defending herself against some charge he was making. His shocking reply was, 'Well you're not. I'll tell you what you are. You're a very troublesome old woman.' At that point, having become aware of my presence in the hall, he left the room. Another inadvertent overhearing from around this time was my mother speaking on the telephone to her sister Dolly. 'I can't stand it any more Dol. She'll have to go. She's driving me mad.'

So there was no more cosiness over cups of tea. Instead there was silence in the sitting room. One day my mother and I were in there about six o'clock. It was late spring or early summer and the setting sun was shining from behind the house onto the horse chestnut tree in the front garden. A greenish light was reflected into the room and it shone on Granny's face when she suddenly appeared in the doorway. Her eyes filled with tears as she flung some words across the room at my mother. Before banging the door shut to go back to her own room, she hurled something horrible behind her. 'I hate you. I hate you all.' I could just about bear the thought of her hating everyone else but not the thought of her hating me.

Whatever it was all about I've never known for certain but I'm fairly sure that Granny had convinced herself that my father was carrying on with a Catholic parishioner, a Polish woman who lived nearby and whom we met sometimes on Sundays at the bus stop on our way to church.

'Who's that on the telephone?' she shot at me when I went into her room one evening.

'I don't know. Someone for Daddy.'

'Well of course it's for him. And I know who it is too. It's that woman.'

There was silence between us as she strained to catch what he was saying but the low tones of his voice and her own deafness defeated her. She may well have been right about the identity of the caller but I'd picked up from conversations between my parents that the Polish woman was in some kind of trouble and had asked my father for advice. I didn't even understand what Granny was implying because at the age I then was I had no idea about goings-on of any kind in the adult world. But I know she was wrong. Granny had an active imagination and, perhaps because she sometimes didn't have anyone else to talk to, she quite often said things to me that maybe she shouldn't have done.

'I wish your mother had had that baby' she said one evening when I was in her room. Baby? What baby? It was the first time I'd ever heard anything about a baby. I must have looked blank and she didn't say any more. Just fiddled with the poker to try and stir a bit of life into the fire. Much later on my mother told me the story which had taken place a couple of years after the war ended.

In our old flat the skirting boards were very deep with

sharply pronounced corners. Clumsy as I frequently was, I fell over and bashed my forehead on one at the end of the hallway near the kitchen. My mother was heavily pregnant at the time (something I've no recollection of noticing) and the sound of my screams and the sight of blood pouring down my face caused her to faint. A couple of days later, feeling that something wasn't quite right, she called the doctor. When Dr Allport turned up she only needed to make a brief examination to establish that the baby was dead. It had died because of the shock my mother got when she thought I might have been badly injured. Dr Allport prescribed ergot to stimulate labour and told her to go to bed. Some time later she returned to deliver a lifeless boy.

So I think this must account for several early memories I've mentioned: Heather and I having to be very quiet in our room because of what I'd done, waking up in my cot one afternoon to find I was sharing the room with my mother, having to look out for the arrival of brusque Dr Allport and finding my mother crying silently in the sitting room one afternoon. But when she told me about this decades later I had no idea then that those early memories relating to it were inside my head waiting to be recovered.

There was always a stoical element to my mother and in spite of what she'd been through she spoke of it with calm detachment. She didn't seem to pity herself as I've always pitied her. Imagine suffering the long pain of labour knowing that it's all for nothing. Imagine not being able to give the baby any sort of funeral. Imagine knowing that when the doctor takes him away he's going to be dumped in a hospital incinerator.

There was never any suggestion that by my clumsiness I was in any way to blame. What I took away from the story and the way my mother told it, and retold it occasionally over the years, was that her collapse had been an expression of how much I'd mattered to her. Yet it feels to me that her extreme irritability in all my subsequent clumsy moments originated then. Whether I'd cracked my head on yet another lamp post or demolished an elaborate display of tins on the pavement outside

Mickey Mouse it was always, 'Sally, Sally, Sally, Sally, why can't you *look* where you're *going?*

❉

So I killed my brother. It baffles me that this thought didn't enter my head until my late forties. Suddenly there it was and it shook me. So much so that I remember precisely where I was when it came to me as I was driving through Sussex on the way home from visiting my parents. It was where you have to stop to turn on to the road from Uppark which takes you down into South Harting, a pretty village at the foot of the downs. This is the half-way point of a journey that takes about an hour and which I've been doing every couple of weeks for almost forty years. On bright days it's a lovely drive and I find that while I'm bowling along enjoying the scenery I can slip into a particular, undirected, almost unconscious form of thought. It's lucky that the thought which came to me that day had never occurred when I was with my mother. If I'd let it slip out I know what her reaction would have been. 'Oh don't be so ri*dic*ulous!'

Well here's something she'd find not just ridiculous but downright preposterous. One morning when I was driving cheerfully through South Harting in the opposite direction and on my way to see her, I got a feeling of utter desolation. The trigger for this was the sight of a horse chestnut tree. The sun had gone in suddenly and a gust of wind blew all its leaves on the diagonal. As I drove on the sun came out again and the feeling passed but I found it happened again and again whenever the weather conditions were similar. I'd get a sense of total despair which I couldn't understand.

Eventually the reason revealed itself during a time of stillness in the garden here. It was as if I was no longer sitting here but was lying in my pram in the front garden at Sydenham. All I can see is the chestnut tree and the sky above it. I've been lying there for a very long time and I've had enough. There's a grey sky now instead of a blue one and there's a chilly wind that whips the chestnut leaves onto a slant. I don't like being outside now. It's cold and I want to be inside in the warm where the others are. I wish she'd come out and get me. But she doesn't come and she doesn't come and still she doesn't come. She's forgotten me.

*

When I was lying in my pram facing the chestnut tree I wouldn't have been able to see the row of bullet holes twenty or so feet above me along the front of the house. They were still there when we left the flat in 1957. Perhaps it wasn't thought worthwhile to repair the damaged brickwork because number 7, like all the other houses in Crystal Palace Park Road, was held on a lease with only a few years left to run. The bullet holes had been made by a German fighter plane which managed to evade the radar and swoop down without warning. That much I'd always known and one day, little more than a year ago I decided to bring the subject up on one of the visits to my parents.

Once they got into their nineties it was sometimes difficult to keep a conversation going with them and I found that the best way to liven things up was to go back to the past. As they were the kind of people who'd kept up with the times and weren't in the habit of reminiscing endlessly like so many elderly people do, this was a pleasant way to pass the time. It was also an opportunity for me to bring up some of my own recollections. Anyway, when I mentioned the German aeroplane I found myself listening to something I'd never heard before.

'Oh' said my father 'I remember that. I happened to be on leave at the time.' He'd been walking along the pavement outside the flat, just near the chestnut tree, when the sudden noise overhead made him automatically throw himself to the ground. The plane came screaming low over Lawrie Park Road with the gunner aiming at a barrage balloon on the corner. Once past the barrage balloon he just kept on firing as the plane whizzed past the house and then disappeared. 'You were in the garden at the time.' said my mother. 'The pram was full of brick-dust when I went out to get you.' No drama at all. No mention of fear on her part. So matter-of-fact.

When they'd finished speaking I made what I thought was a perfectly reasonable comment. 'No wonder I nearly die of fright whenever there's a loud noise all of a sudden.' 'Oh don't be so ri*dic*ulous! Babies can't *hear* anything' my mother snorted angrily. But I think she realised she'd said something pretty ridiculous herself. Of course babies can hear. She hadn't really managed to say what she meant but she didn't bother to put it in clearer form and she didn't need to because I knew what she meant. What she was repudiating so furiously was the notion that an adult could have been adversely affected by something experienced as an infant and which he or she couldn't possibly remember. It was an idea that maddened her. She was very good with babies but I suspect she thought of them rather like dolls and didn't really want them to grow up. There was certainly a sense in which she didn't think they could see or hear. (Something I shouldn't have been able to see convinced me that she was bleeding to death.) She didn't want to believe that small children were people with eyes and ears. Another thing she wouldn't have wanted to believe was that a childhood memory could lie submerged for the best part of half a century before floating up to the surface without warning. Do you remember me telling you about being in a cot in my parents' bedroom? The memory I said I'd tell you about another time? Well now's the time.

*

I wake up in pitch blackness. I can hear something. It's in the room. Something quite loud. But it's only the sound made by someone heavy turning over in bed. Him? The sheets are rustling noisily and a bedspring's going *boing*. My mother's voice says No. So the Man must be there. Yes he is. His kept-low voice sounds angry. Another No. More kept-low voice of the Man. Another No. More anger in kept-low voice. Another No.

A lot of noisy sheet business. Then silence. I think: Mummy's dead. The Man's killed her. So I mustn't make a noise when I cry or else he'll remember I'm here and kill me too.

Mummy's dead! That's my first thought on waking up next morning. But her body isn't there. There isn't anyone there and the bed's been made. What's he done with her? Everything's very quiet. I climb out of the cot and run into the hall and am shocked by what I see. She's standing at the stove in the kitchen and stirring some porridge. I stay where I am just long enough to make sure it's true, then run away and get back into the cot before she sees me.

❋

How old would I have been then? Perhaps three and a half and therefore rather too old to be in a cot in their room. It must have been shortly after my father came back from Germany and that's why he was still just 'the Man'. He hadn't turned into my father yet. In time, when I had my own bed in the room I shared with Heather he'd always come and sit on the side of it to say goodnight. After he'd read to me he'd sometimes tell me how much he loved his girls and that he didn't mind a bit not having a boy. It had never occurred to me that anyone *would* want one. Girls seemed a much better idea. I don't know what he felt about the dead baby and whether he was trying to talk himself out of its loss. Maybe, but I think it's more likely that he was preparing me for an inevitable discovery: that boys were generally considered better than girls and that women weren't thought equal to men.

This wasn't an impression I could ever have received at home. My parents were clearly in full partnership, however tetchy things might be between them in private. On Saturday mornings when my mother was working, my father would go down to Mickey Mouse and bring back two big holdalls of heavy shopping. Then, while Granny was preparing the lunch for him to finish off later, he'd get the vacuum cleaner and other stuff out to give the flat a good going-through. When he'd finished he always said, 'Now don't you girls go making any mess. I want everything to be ship-shape for your mother when she comes in.'

It wasn't until I was sixteen that the attitudes of the outside world became apparent and shocked me into furious thought on the subject.

✽

'Of course the woman is very much the minor partner in the marriage.' It was August 1959 and we were in a restaurant near the Albert Hall. The face of the young man who let this thud onto the candlelit table between us had (fittingly I've always thought) something Neanderthal about the nose. The only thing which had made him seem a suitable escort to the concert for which I'd obtained complimentary tickets was that he'd been to a public school (Haileybury) and was therefore presumably a gentleman. As it turned out he wasn't even that. He only consented to see me home when threatened by my father's wrath if he didn't, and I'm pleased to say that consequently he missed the last bus, had to walk all the way back to Beckenham and was out for a duck at cricket the next day. So that was the end of him. I'd never particularly liked him and don't know why I bothered in the first place.

Then four months later, a week before Christmas, I had the greatest stroke of luck in my life. Anthony appeared on the doorstep. I'd never had any kind of mental picture of the man I'd love and want to marry but suddenly and incredibly, there he was. He just had it all – looks, voice, manners and style. He'd still got a couple of terms to go before leaving Douai, a Catholic public school in Berkshire, and had just come back home to Bickley for the holidays. His mother, whom I had yet to meet, a frumpily-dressed and rather intimidating woman heavily involved in parish matters, had asked him to deliver something.

There seemed almost to be a tradition in our family of

meeting our lifelong partners at an early age and going on to have a lengthy engagement. My parents met at seventeen and so did Heather and Roger. I'm sure I must have been unconsciously influenced by this and as I didn't have any alternative plans I didn't hesitate to do everything I could to reach an understanding with Anthony. This only took a short while because he wanted someone of his own as much as I did and so there I was in the lower sixth, secretly engaged while plodding my dull way towards very low achievement in history, English and art at A-level. I'd only stayed on because I couldn't think of anything else to do. The grammar school experience still hadn't led to any doors that opened onto interesting prospects or provided any other means of more agreeable escape than the one I'd just chosen. Like the majority of girls in those days I didn't think in terms of a career although marriage was itself a career I suppose. By its means you got away from the parental home and gained independence of a sort by choosing a man who could support you financially. In this way you'd found the means to provide for yourself. You'd done what was expected of you.

Planning my future the way I did and particularly by hitching myself to a Catholic brought certain negative consequences. One regret I've always had is that I didn't go to art school. When my father suggested it, as few fathers would, I just replied that I wasn't good enough. It's what I mistakenly believed. Later on I was encouraged to enrol as a full-time student by a tutor at the Central School where I used to go to evening classes in life drawing. Although I'd love to have done it I was prevented by the most mundane considerations. As a matter of historical interest perhaps it's worth rehearsing them.

If Anthony and I were ever to get married and I was to get away from home then I had to go on working in order to save something every week towards an eventual deposit on a house. (Anthony meanwhile was studying law and was only being paid a couple of pounds a week.) I'd learned from my parents' experience how hard it was to do this once you had a family.

But, you might ask, couldn't I get married, not start a family and still go to art college? No, because the most cramping factor of all was Catholicism. Birth control was, and still is, contrary to the church's teaching. It was a mortal sin back then but maybe it isn't any more. Marriage meant babies. Even so, knowing this as I did, I was still taken aback as I stood in front of the altar on my wedding day in 1966 to hear Father Wright, our parish priest, pray that I be as a fruitful vine on the side of my father's house. I'd got no intention of going as far as that.

❋

After this we moved into our mortgage-laden semi on a new estate tacked on to a village a few miles from Maidstone. It was in Meadow View, a road named, as roads so often are, for what it destroyed. The nearest Catholic church was in Maidstone itself and it was here, only a few weeks after the wedding, that I abandoned Catholicism for good.

To a large extent it was the ugliness of everything I found there that made up my mind. Father Wright had paid such attention to simple beauty in his church and to the performance of ritual, music and singing that it hadn't been difficult to go on pretending to myself and others that I was still a *bona fide* member of the congregation. It also helped that sometimes Anthony served for him at mass and in cassock and surplice he made a most fetching altar boy. John Wright was a funny, provocative, fiercely intelligent, Spanish-speaking, motorbike-riding, English convert who'd been trained for the priesthood in Valladolid. It seemed a cruel fate for him to fetch up somewhere so irredeemably suburban as the parish of Petts Wood.

So the ugliness, both visual and aural, in the church at Maidstone was bad enough but it wasn't quite what finished me off. It was the sermon which did that. The relentless, dreary, monotonous, bossy drivel of an Irish priest. He and his words encapsulated everything I'd ever loathed about Catholicism and before we'd even got outside I'd made up my mind. I wasn't going to take this any more because there was no reason why I should. I'd left home and was beyond my father's jurisdiction now – so I could do as I pleased in this respect. It felt like a tremendous liberation. And so it was that, completely devoid of fear about the destination of my immortal soul, I took the first step on a convoluted journey to become myself. This took longer than the twenty-three years I'd already spent on Earth and you could say it's a process that's still going on. It can take a long time to find out who you really are and perhaps even longer to accept what you find.

✷

Sometimes I try and work out a kind of balance sheet for Catholicism; to sort out its legacy to me for better or worse, assuming that all other circumstances of home life and so on had been the same.

    I don't think there can be any doubt that educationally it was very bad. Catholic dogma is the enemy of reason and free thought which is why I've never understood how even highly intelligent people can subscribe to it. The purpose of the nuns at St Winefride's was threefold: first of all to turn us into devout Catholics, secondly to inculcate standards of deportment and manners appropriate to a lady and finally to get as many of us as possible through the Eleven plus (otherwise no-one would send their children there and they wouldn't have an income). When it came to the Eleven plus they seemed to have done very well but actually they hadn't. I'd hardly been taught anything that wasn't strictly necessary for passing the examination and so there hadn't been any need or encouragement to think or to question anything. This, and the fact that class sizes were so small, meant that I was hopelessly lost when I went on to Coloma.

    And I needn't have even gone to Coloma at all. My parents had, understandably but nevertheless lazily, made the assumption that one high school or grammar was as good as another and so the great opportunity I'd won was wasted. They didn't seem to consider sending me to a non-Catholic school and it's ironic that, in order to keep her out of a secondary modern, they'd paid for Heather to go to St Anne's, a much better convent at Sanderstead than the one I went to in Croydon. Who knows whether or not I'd have done any better at St Anne's but I still wish I'd been sent there. Its buildings made you want to be inside them and they were surrounded by lovely grounds. These things matter.

Without realising it at the time, the grounds at St Winefride's had meant a great deal to me. They contributed so much to the feeling I have now that in spite of its shortcomings as an educational establishment my time there was of great value. Existing within the bomb-damaged, hard and ugly world in which I lived, there was this enclave in which I was able to absorb its opposite – this world of order, gentleness and beauty that the nuns created around themselves in their pursuit of perfection. For better or worse I don't think I'd have been the same person if I hadn't known that place. It's all been built over now and there's no sign of it left.

❉

There was just one part of Coloma where I was always happy. This was the art room in the attic off to the right at the top of a rickety staircase called Jacob's Ladder. It smelt invitingly of splintery wood, powder paint, printing ink and warm paper. Far away from all the sweaty classrooms it smelt of freedom. It was here that I was given the only guidance I every received about what to do when I left school. It came from Thirza Simmons, the art mistress. She was so attractive, interesting to listen to and appealingly different in dress from anyone I'd ever met that everything she said made an impression on me. I suppose she was about forty at the time, a tiny woman with wavy chestnut hair over her shoulders and a slight Welsh lilt in her voice.

She did what no-one else ever did which was to try and get us to think – to open up our minds. I imagine she did this because the five of us doing A-level were a pretty dull bunch. One day she raised a question about thought itself: is it possible to have a truly original thought – one that owes nothing to the previous thoughts of someone else? Another time her subject was great men. Who did we think was, or had been, a great man? My unoriginal response was Winston Churchill. After a while she astonished me by saying, 'Do you know Sarah, I think it's quite likely that your own father is a great man.' This didn't just provoke new considerations about the concept of greatness; it made me realise that my stated opinions were not my own but my parents' – in this case my father's. I didn't know enough to have an opinion about anything and in my experience opinion wasn't something that any of us were encouraged to acquire on any subject at all.

Thirza's assessment of my father must have been made at the only time I remember him visiting Coloma. This was the excruciating occasion when, at the request of the headmistress, he came to give a careers talk about his work in the London Probation Service. I settled down to cringe at the back of the hall. As he drew to a close I began to revive. He hadn't given me cause for embarrassment after all. Then in a wholly unforeseen way he went on to do just that. With his final words he subverted the whole point of Mother Mary Cuthbert's invitation by stating that in his opinion probation work was no job for a woman.

He wasn't saying they didn't have the ability because of course they did. Indeed many of his colleagues were highly-competent women. But probation work meant coping with a very ugly side to life which he'd prefer women not to have to deal with. He'd rather they were spared from that. Men and women were different and each needed the complementary capacities of the other. He thought that in many ways women were rather nicer than men and this was one reason why it was incumbent upon men to protect them from unpleasantness if they could.

✽

In the art room one day Thirza said, 'None of you seems to have the slightest ambition. Maybe that's a good thing. Maybe not. I just don't know.' I felt she did know and that we were a disappointment to her. I couldn't find a word to say at the time. Ambition? Where would you get ambition? Ambition to do what? What I'd say to her now is that my years in the convent had done nothing to encourage the notion that I could aspire to do anything much except scrape through exams. How can you have ambition if no-one fosters a talent they see in you? How can you have ambition if no-one gives you an idea of what opportunities there are? How can you have ambition if you're schooled in obedience to a system that doesn't give you the slightest idea that you can, and may, act upon the world in some way? After all, who do you think you are?

Reflecting decades later on how important Thirza had been to me I suddenly realised that even she'd fallen short in this respect. She had so much influence over me that if only she'd said, 'You should go to art school Sarah' then I would have done so whatever the difficulties but because she didn't say this I presumed I hadn't got the necessary ability. It's a good example of how words not spoken can shout as loudly as words that are.

Anyway, noticing that I had a feel for typography and book-jacket design, she suggested publishing as a congenial destination. This appealed to me, so I followed her advice to get a secretarial qualification and eventually found myself working in the art department of Macmillan & Co. This was in their old building in St Martin's Street, just behind the National Gallery and before long I'd achieved the limited ambition of not needing to use my secretarial skills at all.

✣

Quite a long time ago now, perhaps when I was in my mid-forties, I woke up early one morning and had a ridiculous thought. I imagined I was on my deathbed (naturally at some comfortably obscure date in the future) and saying to myself, 'Well I made it then. I got through.' Underlying this thought was a vague recognition that this could only have been achieved by some kind of subterfuge on my part – at best pretence, at worst dishonesty. There was something shifty about me. Something counterfeit.

It was rather like when your mothers, Rebecca and Candida, were small. I'd found it unexpectedly draining looking after them and it fills me with sadness to remember how those perfectly sweet little girls sometimes felt like the enemy to me. At times I felt in danger of being done in by them simply because of the effort it took to survive the exhaustion involved. I thought it would never end. For what seemed like eternity but which was probably only a year or two, I'd wake up every morning after virtually no sleep and wonder how in God's name I was going to get through the day. I used to get so ratty and on days when they squabbled incessantly I'd scream at them. They never deserved this and I was a terrible disappointment to myself. I was an abject failure at the one thing I'd assumed I could make a success of.

By this time we'd moved from Kent to Hampshire and none of the women I made friends with seemed to find motherhood difficult. However in fairness to me I do think I had things a bit tougher than they did. The girls were only fifteen months apart and Anthony was never around to help. He had his job and I had mine. Still, I got through it somehow and probably managed most of the time to project a reasonable impersonation of a mother to the outside world. From which you will deduce that I felt as if I was playing a part. That's exactly what I felt. While everyone else was doing the real thing I was just pretending. I wasn't the person I appeared to be. I realise now that no-one else is either and that most people live to some extent with a sense of dishonesty and the fear of being found out.

Often, without being aware of what you're doing, you're manufacturing some kind of image of yourself to present to the outside world in order to provide a label or an alibi to satisfy or stem the actual or supposed curiosity of others. It's easy to say that you shouldn't care what other people think of you and it's true that for the most part they're far too busy thinking about themselves to give more than a passing thought to you or anyone else. However, you'd hardly be human if you didn't sometimes imagine how others perceive you. But it can get out of hand as it did with me about the time I hit forty. It was quite a while before I realised what was happening.

They'd been there for ages at the back of my head directing operations – this shadowy group of people outside the Village Hall muttering among themselves, 'But what does she *do* with herself all day?' Yet this imagined gathering wasn't entirely absurd because people *did* keep asking what I did. I felt I was being asked to justify my existence; that I was being judged. Although the truth probably was that the shadowy group wouldn't have colonised my head if I hadn't been the one who was really doing the judging.

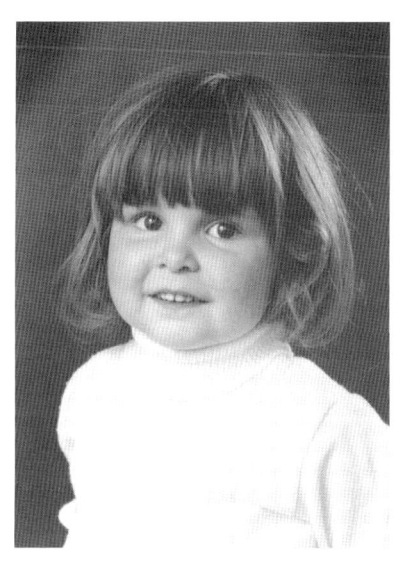

It was as if I'd dropped off the edge of the world once the girls were in their mid-teens and I'd successfully completed an Open University degree. Studying for this had provided me with a false sense of direction and accruing achievement while ultimately leading me nowhere I wanted to go. So one side of the problem was that I didn't know where to go next and the other was that I no longer had an alibi. I didn't have an answer when people said, 'Hello Sarah. What do you do?'

When people ask you what you do I think it's unlikely they're particularly interested in the answer. You could probably just make something up in the certain knowledge they'll soon be only too happy to snatch the conversational baton from you so they can talk about themselves. But as you'll understand from what I've already said, being flagrantly dishonest wasn't something that came easily to me. So this question was one which floored me every time. I just couldn't give a satisfactory account of myself. When they asked me what I did I felt they were asking me who I was. Now that's a very difficult question to deal with if you haven't got some kind of label handy by being in paid employment or involved in some form of worthy voluntary work. In fact it's one I've never been able to answer. If only people would just ask you if you've read any good books lately.

By the 1980s it was no longer sufficient to run your home, cultivate your garden, care for the family and be there for everyone when they needed you. (Things my own mother had never done.) It had been at one time and still was when I married in the mid-1960s but it wasn't any more. Times had changed and I was out of step thanks to the women's liberation movement. The person I'd thought of as myself had been blown to pieces. I felt as empty as Michael's head; just a body with a name attached.

During that chaotic and protracted phase of my inner life, I was fortunate enough to be friendly with a woman called Angela who had professional training in psychology. She was able to give me some valuable insights into my predicament. One of these was something called The Life Script. She said that by the time children are four or five they've unconsciously determined a method for survival – some way of behaving in order to ward off adult disapproval which to them constitutes the threat of annihilation. Since they aren't aware they've done anything of the kind they carry this behaviour into adulthood, by which time it may or may not continue to be useful to them.

This all sounded fairly far-fetched to me but she assured me that we could quickly discover my own Life Script. 'It works every time as long as you don't think about it. Now just close your eyes, imagine you're five years old again and complete the following sentence: Survival is …'

My response was a single word: dissimulation. And I quickly realised that it was spot on. Covering up my feelings and keeping my thoughts to myself had always seemed entirely natural – as if it were an innate aspect of myself and not a piece of acquired behaviour. I'm pretty sure I adopted it because I'd seen Heather get into trouble almost every time she opened her mouth and that it began when my father became a permanent presence in the household when I was three.

I tried this parlour trick out on one or two other people. A friend called Anne said, 'Work hard so that I'm always top of the class'. Well she's been top of the class for a long time now. She's a judge. As for Heather, well she unhesitatingly said, 'Make them laugh'. And she is indeed still making our mother laugh even though there's nothing left for her to laugh about.

Poor little Mum. I don't think she even remembers the past now but finds herself in a permanently puzzling present. We had to move her into residential care last month because we just couldn't keep her any more in her home by the sea with the beautiful garden she'd created and worked in almost every day. When she gave up paid work in her fifties and turned to domestic enjoyment for the first time in her life it was strange what a pleasing sense of rightness we all felt about it. Now Heather and I face the wretched business of breaking up the home in which our parents were so content for more than thirty-five years. I don't mind admitting I'll be glad when it's all over. Yet there's a lot to be said for the earlier stages of getting old providing you enjoy good health and don't have pressing worries. Even though you still haven't come to any satisfactory conclusions about the meaning of life, you've come to terms with it and can appreciate the blessedness of everyday things. You don't take anything for granted any more because you know how fragile life is. And even if your own life seems to have been as short on interest or incident as mine has, it can still furnish you with worthwhile material for reflection.

About the time you reach sixty a funny thing happens. You find that people younger than your own children have begun to research and write books about the decades in which you grew up. The world has changed so much since then that you've begun to become a historical resource. And so the thought comes to you: perhaps even I could make a small contribution to knowledge by leaving something about this lost world for my grandchildren. The idea there could possibly be anything in my experience worth writing about was so ridiculous that initially I dismissed it but after a while it became the impetus to get going. Since few lives could have been more unremarkable than mine the challenge seemed to lie in making something out of nothing.

✻

I've already given you some idea of the colourless and rather threadbare nature of existence in the late forties and early fifties. It was at its most colourless, not when there was snow on the ground but when one of the infamous London smogs came down for days on end. Back then I didn't realise this was a local phenomenon caused by coal being burnt in millions of fireplaces. I thought it was all over the world and for me it was yet another excitement provided by the weather. Few people knew at the time that smog killed thousands of people suffering from respiratory complaints.

Come to think of it though, smog wasn't colourless. In day time, the light such as it was, had a sulphurous tinge. The filthy stuff muffled sound and made all the traffic move painstakingly slowly and eventually stop altogether if visibility had shrunk to a few yards. This was where the excitement lay. Perhaps you wouldn't be able to go to school tomorrow. Usually you did have to go though and as you left home you'd be exhorted not to breathe in the muck but to keep your scarf over your nose all the time you were out of doors. And when you were in bed you'd keep hopping out to see how dense it was getting along the passage to the front door. It got everywhere and made everything black.

Because so little happened in those days, it meant that the smallest deviation from normal was cause for excitement. On summer days it might be an aeroplane writing *Cadburys* in the blissfully blue sky. Or it might be the prospect of the new Clarks sandals you always got at Easter from Gamages and which said that summer was on its way. Or it might be that we were expecting family to tea and my mother was making little upside-down cakes which she smothered in royal icing (half of them in white icing and half of them in chocolate). There was never enough of it left in the bowl by the time she passed it over to Heather and me to lick clean. Or it might be some toffee apples that granny had made for us as a special treat and which we were waiting for impatiently to cool down in the enamel bowl on the draining board.

Sometimes before visitors came (and it always seemed to be in early summer when they did) my father would get down on his knees to varnish the boards that surrounded the few rugs and runners we had. Because of the asphyxiating smell this job had to be done when it was warm enough to have the windows open. Indeed it was the smell that helped remind you to jump from carpet to carpet as it dried but some of the leaps proved too much and you invariably left at least one tell-tale print of crepe sole in a noticeable place. More stench was provided by the Flit gun loaded with DDT that he'd pump in and out and round about and with which he'd incidentally cover you in a fine mist of cool droplets. This felt quite pleasant but the business with the Flit gun which was intended to deal with the nuisance presented by flies didn't seem to do much good. Soon they were all back again and for some mysterious reason always congregated in irritable-looking clusters around the central lampshade in every room.

Sometimes the excitements weren't at all pleasant. One lovely summer evening when we were on our own with Granny because 'they' were out together somewhere Heather, who was never frightened of anything, let out a sudden gasp of horror. I followed her gaze and we stared aghast at a massive beetle, inches across, spread over an electric socket by the fireplace in our bedroom. I dashed to fetch Granny who acted with admirable despatch. After muttering, 'Holy Mary Mother of God' she sent for the tongs from the fireplace in the sitting room. Pausing only to make the sign of the cross she snapped the beetle up and gingerly carried it out into the garden. Heather had dug its grave and stood by with a shovelful of earth at the ready. I stood by with the brick that was to be plonked on top. 'Well that should be the end of the fella!' she said. We hoped she was right. Sadly I realise now that it was a splendid stag beetle and that we shouldn't have killed it. It hadn't meant us any harm.

Then there was the time one winter when Heather and I woke up in the middle of the night to hear what sounded like a million mice skittering about on the linoleum. Terror helped me leap with perfect precision onto Heather's bed where we clung together under the bedclothes until help arrived. As soon as my father put the light on there wasn't a mouse to be seen. I've always wondered how they managed that vanishing act. It wasn't as if there were any visible mouse-holes in the skirting boards like the ones in *Tom and Jerry*.

The cause of this sudden infestation was put down to the recent departure of a family from the top flat. It was something that was reminisced about occasionally over the afternoon cup of tea. My grandmother would say things like, 'Nancy was a card. That place of hers must have been marvellous for mice. She never did a hand's turn and didn't mind admitting it. Said she'd got better things to do. Like mooning over Marlon Brando I suppose. She was potty about that chap. And she must have spent hours in front of a mirror getting herself up. Always had her hair piled up and her face in place didn't she? Mind you I never liked those slacks. If you ask me trousers don't do anything for a woman's backside. Nancy reckoned they made her look glamorous. God knows where she got that daft idea. The fil'ms I suppose.'

Then they'd go on to marvel that Nancy used to pay a Mrs Stubbs from Penge to come in and 'do' for her twice a week. They were in agreement that Mrs Stubbs would have had to put in a lot more time than that if she was going to stand a chance of making any impression on the top flat because Nancy always left her several days' washing-up to do and the beds to make before she could get started on anything else.

Talk about Nancy invariably ended with the story of the gloves. Nancy had been appalled to notice that Mrs Stubbs was apparently so poor that she couldn't afford them. So during the bitter winter of 1947 she bought her the warmest pair she could find but still Mrs Stubbs came to work with her hands red and raw and with no gloves on. When Nancy asked her why she wasn't wearing the ones she'd given her Mrs Stubbs said, 'The likes of us don't wear no gloves Mm. Them's for the gentry.'

Anyway, the mice may have all disappeared (and never came back once traps baited with cheese had done their business) but they'd left their mark on our bedroom. The old dolls' house that our father had somehow managed to procure for us one Christmas had proved particularly attractive to them. This was because when he'd patched it up with fresh brick paper for the walls and tile paper for the roof he'd used flour and water paste. That was all any of us had for glue. It was what I always used to stick pictures of the royal family into my scrap book.

✱

It's February 1952 and I'm nine. 'The King's dead! The King's dead! The King's dead!' A girl darts round the playground at St Winefride's spreading the news. It doesn't mean anything to me. King? What king? I thought you only got kings in history and fairy tales. So I keep quiet and wait for enlightenment. This comes from the daily newspapers which are full of photographs of the royal family. I realise now that the man familiar from his appearance on news reels at the cinema was the King going round (disappointingly) without his crown on. The royal family and the impending coronation, which isn't going to take place until June of the following year, become part of the fabric of everyday life. And quite often, the first thing you hear in the morning is the national anthem. This is being played because it's some royal person's birthday. It's always played on my birthday because I've got the same one as Princess Margaret. This makes the day feel especially special.

Although I'm not particularly interested in kings and queens I'm very keen on the little princesses – Elizabeth and Margaret Rose. I cut out and stick in loads of pictures of them, notwithstanding they're grown up by now. It's a way of passing the time. There's a lot of time to pass before television comes into the household about 1956. The long winter evenings go something like this. After supper's been cleared away my father sits at the table and plays cards and board games with us. Then when I've settled down to making a mess of my scrapbook or stamp album he and my mother compete to see who can be first to complete the *Evening Standard* crossword. Sometimes this ends in laughter because of my father's outrageous cheating. If he doesn't know the answer to the last couple of clues he just makes them up, pronounces himself the winner, permits himself to be revealed as a fraudster and then in a state of mock contrition goes off to get us all a hot drink to make amends. But he would have made the drinks anyway. He always does.

When coronation day finally arrives you can't call it exciting. Street parties and that sort of thing aren't for people like us anyway. We don't belong to any kind of community – urban, suburban or rural – where they're going on. So we spend the day travelling to and from Eastcote so we can watch the event on Aunt Dolly's new black-and-white television set.

I seem to recall much more of a party feel during the Festival of Britain in 1951 but that was probably only because we went up to London after dark to see the golden Skylon suspended shining in the night sky before ending up in a crowded Lyons Corner House where we were serenaded by a violinist who played something by Ivor Novello at Heather's request. Now that's what I called exciting.

✽

This business of not belonging wasn't something I thought about or even noticed particularly when I was young. It was just the way things were. I didn't know any other kind of life. It was only later I could see things with detachment and notice the extent to which we didn't really belong anywhere except in whatever home we were living at the time. We hadn't even derived any social benefit from belonging to the Catholic Church but had only satisfied its minimal requirements. We weren't members of it in any real sense. Catholicism was something we'd been saddled with but which was never part of our identity.

It was quite different for Anthony whose dozens of un-mortal-sinning uncles and aunts provided him with a prodigious number of cousins occupying places at just about every Catholic preparatory and public school in the country. Consequently he belonged to an elite tribe, membership of which he took for granted. This was the tribe of the English Catholic. Membership of this provided them with a comfortable sense of being set apart and provided a major element in their sense of who they were. The only tribe I vaguely felt I belonged to was the Shervington family itself.

Alignment to some kind of tribe seems to be a virtual necessity in the construction of the person you think of as yourself. For the most part I think it's done instinctively. You create a version of yourself for public consumption. You do this, self-consciously or not, by living in such-and-such a house, driving such-and-such a car, sending your children to such-and-such a school and so on. By these means people send out signals about their values or aspirations. They tell you where they belong or at least where they want to belong. They provide a kind of shorthand by which like-minded people can recognise each other and tacitly help one another avoid the fundamental question of who they really are.

But I knew nothing about this until after I was married, when its potential for discomfort soon became apparent. Up until then I think I'd been able to imagine that I was simply the person I was. However, for me to say this is to forget the extent to which as a family we'd been defined by what we weren't. What you aren't counts just as much as what you are and my father had his own way of establishing who I wasn't and what I wasn't going to be by screening potential boyfriends whenever he got the chance. One evening when I was about fifteen and had just come in from playing tennis he said, 'A chap called Ian was trying to get hold of you earlier. I told him there wasn't any point in ringing again.' Ironically I'd only met this pleasant young man because of a ballroom dancing class my father had encouraged me to go to because the daughter of a friend of his went to it. I loathed these classes. I was in misery because of my awful clothes and the knowledge that I was being sniggered at. But Ian at least had seen a certain something in me. Unfortunately my father had heard a certain something in Ian's voice. So that was the end of that. It hadn't even begun.

However it can't have been much more than a year later when the Catholic Church paid its debts to me by throwing Anthony into my path. There was to be no summary dismissal for him, not least because my mother wouldn't have allowed it. He always went down very well with her. Well there's not much a father can do in these circumstances, especially when it transpires that he and the young man's father had been pupils at the same school – in this case the Cardinal Vaughan School in Holland Park. So that was my dear old Dad well and truly dished. Which isn't to say he made things particularly easy for us. Young men courting his daughters were objects of distrust and suspicion. It stood to reason they were up to no good.

❊

Now, to go back to certain social discomforts of early married life in Kent. Fortunately we didn't live in Kent for long because marriage and the move to Meadow View had introduced me to modes of being I'd no idea existed. Even Birdham Close hadn't prepared me for the world of Tupperware parties, mail order catalogues, Avon ladies calling and the daily competition to be first out with the clothes pegs in the morning. Nor had it prepared me for association with the kind of men Anthony began to meet on the train between Marden and London. I knew nothing about them and their tribe but soon discovered their numbers were legion.

Their homes bore a marked resemblance to one another and were invariably chintzy, half-timbered country cottages substantially subsidised by family money. Perhaps this is why they were furnished in styles more appropriate to an older generation. I suppose that by having hunting prints hanging all over the place and a couple of large dogs slobbering by the log fire they sought to establish their country credentials in spite of the job in the City. More credentials could generally be found in the downstairs loo where sporty pictures of one's host at prep school, public school or Oxbridge might be on display. One found these things out when they invited one to their frightfully proper dinner parties at which one was astonished to find that when it was time for coffee one was expected to troop off to the drawing room with the other ladies in order to leave the gentlemen hee-hawing over the port.

This was how I found out there were people who established your identity according to the kind of house in which you lived. So often on introduction my hostess would say, 'This is Sarah. She lives in Meadow View on the Lewis Court Estate.' Apparently this was the most significant thing about me and I presume it was designed to put me in my place; I hadn't made it the way she and the other women had. Not unnaturally, I envied these women their houses but not their husbands. When you're young and inexperienced it's difficult not to be affected by this sort of thing. It isn't pleasant to be looked down upon.

Well then we moved on to Alresford in Hampshire, which we immediately found far more congenial. Occasionally you got the same sort of comment but not nearly so often and once we moved into our present house in Bishop's Sutton I didn't expect it again. I was soon to learn I was being naive. It didn't matter what size house you had because there was always someone somewhere with something bigger or better who, by virtue of such possession, was ready to assume superiority. However, this no longer caused me much concern because I'd become rather more socially confident by this time.

We hadn't been in this house very long before we were asked for drinks one Sunday morning at the home of a brigadier and his wife along the main road. They were throwing the party because their daughter was down from London for the weekend and could help shove round the sausage rolls and things on sticks. Well the daughter was duly doing her stuff and a plate came in my direction.

'Hi! I'm Lavinia.'
'Hello Lavinia. I'm Sarah.'
'Super of you to come. Where are you from?'
'We live in the village.'
'Oh do you? Where? '
'Right in the middle.'
'Where exactly?'
'In the house nearest the telephone box'
'Oh! One of those little houses!'

In fact I don't think that in terms of accommodation our house was so much smaller than her parents' but it lacked the cachet mysteriously attaching to an old house, however ugly and inconvenient. So the sausage rolls moved off never to return and I was left to laugh at such transparency. There are times when it's a great relief to be popped into the box marked NWK. Not Worth Knowing.

❋

'And what does your husband do?' This was an even more common way of being placed. In the world in which I found myself back then a woman was defined by the social status or occupation of her husband and this question was almost invariably the first one asked at a drinks or dinner party. You were of course assumed to be of no interest or significance yourself. When a man asked you what your husband did he was trying to ascertain whether, after a decent interval of forbearance with the little woman, it was worth his while going over to introduce himself. When a woman asked you what your husband did, she was trying to find out where you stood in relation to each other and whether she might safely add you as a couple to her list of potential guests.

However, at some stage one of these husbands might ask, 'And so what do you do with yourself?' In other words what do you do with the acres of spare time your husband kindly permits you to enjoy while he slaves away to pay the costs of keeping you and your children. I'd imagined that no-one could take exception to me slowly studying for an Open University degree while the girls were at school but I soon found this wasn't so. In those days, showing signs of intelligence wasn't something likely to make a woman friends of either sex. Most people seemed to feel threatened by my harmless pursuit. (Nevertheless it came in handy as a means of diluting the stereotype of the solicitor's wife and the expectations that went with it.) I think it was men who were most bothered but one can't be sure because men had at least one virtue not shared by women. Whereas they didn't hesitate to say what they thought of you to your face, their wives would only say what they thought of you behind your back.

It's hard to believe it now but when I was young almost every man you came across, however ugly and boring, apparently felt he not only had a divine right to launch an indecent assault upon your person but also to pass judgement and lay down the law about what you ought and ought not to do. For example there was an architect I met just once who said to me, 'That university thingy you're doing. Don't you think it's *frightfully* frenetic? I'm surprised your husband lets you. I wouldn't let my wife do it.' Not long afterwards another man (unmarried, occupation unknown) with whom I had the misfortune to be dancing, had the effrontery to tell me that while I was doing all that studying I must be neglecting my children. By great good fortune, at that precise moment, we were on the outside of the raised dance floor. So it was child's play to shove him over the edge and let everyone think he was just drunk as usual.

The vast majority of men I came across in those days seemed to perceive their wives as extensions of themselves, whose principal purpose in being around was to provide them with an extra life to squander. As husbands, they felt affronted (threatened even?) by the treachery of a woman showing signs of independent existence. Their wives appeared to think this was perfectly reasonable of them and believed it was a woman's duty to do what her husband wanted her to do and be what he wanted her to be. If I expressed an unconventional opinion or said something deemed uncomfortably honest they'd say, 'Oh well of course you're one of those women's libbers aren't you?' I was bemused by this because I didn't think I was anything of the kind.

However, once the women's liberation movement got under way it wasn't long before men spotted the advantages it could bring to themselves and I reckon you could make out a good case for finding them among its chief beneficiaries. Very quickly they began to tell you that you ought to be out at work to help your poor husband pay the bills, whereas previously they would have told you that you'd got no business to go out to work at all because your place was in the home. The best thing to do was to ignore them. They didn't like that. And if you put forward, as I often did, the case that a working woman ought to be able to expect her husband to do his fair share of the housework, shopping, cooking and childcare then naturally it was guffawed out of court as a preposterous notion.

But that's enough about people like them.

✱

'People are such frightful sheep. They always follow the herd.' My mother frequently said this over the years and certainly she could never have been accused of this failing herself. She stood aloof from just about everything and seldom accompanied my father to any social events apart from family ones. Sometimes he'd say wryly but without complaint, 'Do you know Pamela, most people don't believe I've even got a wife. They wonder where I got the girls from.'

Yet apart from her beauty it had been just that aloofness or air of self-containment that had attracted him to her in the first place. So he accepted her as she was and never tried to change her but I'm sure he would have loved it if she'd been a bit more sociable because he was such a gregarious person himself. However, he was able to satisfy that side of himself at the cricket club, not only in the summer when he played there most Saturdays and Sundays but in winter too when he went up there for a drink before lunch on Sunday mornings after mass.

We never had any alcohol in the house except for a bottle of sherry at Christmas, but he'd become accustomed to whisky during the war. In later life, when I asked him about his wartime experiences he recalled that it only cost six and ninepence a bottle and was considered part of their essential supplies. 'So much so that when the bridge behind us had been blown up it came to us by ambulance, the only vehicles allowed across. Well it did help to keep out the cold and give you a bit of Dutch courage when you needed it.'

Being a strongly-built man he was able to take alcohol but I remember him doing the daftest thing under its influence. One afternoon he'd played cricket at a sports club in Bickley and in the bar afterwards one of his team mates called out, 'Bet you a tenner Pete you can't swim a length in your kit – boots and all.' Well he could and he did. Then strode home soddenly triumphant and came in the back door laughing.

There wasn't much laughter though on Christmas day 1946, the first one since he'd been demobbed. Although I was only three at the time I do remember him being in awful disgrace and not understanding what was going on. If he wasn't well, why did he have to lie in the empty bath with his overcoat on? Why was Mummy so cross with him? The answer was that it had been after three o'clock before he came back from the cricket club and on arrival he was being kept upright (after a fashion) by his friends Dick and Stuart who were told in icy tones where to dump him. Dad always maintained that someone had spiked his drinks as a joke that day and actually I believe him. Anyway, on that Christmas day we'd all waited and waited, Eileen included, to eat the dinner that Granny would have so painstakingly and lovingly prepared, but which we'd finally had to eat without him. My mother must have had to savage the turkey with a carving knife as best she could, presumably becoming more furious by the moment.

When he'd come into sight being dragged through the front gate by Dick and Stuart I thought I heard Heather whisper, 'Daddy's trunk'. Because I knew that elephants had trunks I thought she was saying that he'd turned into an elephant. Perhaps this is when I began to feel there was some sort of affinity between him and elephants. Is it something to do with the way they combine great size and strength with such sensitivity? And are so careful where they place their feet? I don't know but they always make me want to cry.

✸

I've already told you that life wasn't easy for my parents in the post-war years, particularly because they were so short of money. Once my father became a probation officer he earned less than half of what he'd been paid as an army officer in the preceding years. During the war he'd received several offers of well-paid employment when it was all over but none of them appealed to him. He didn't want to go into the world of business and make profits for the big man at the expense of the small. Nor did he want to become a professional soldier as he could have done. He'd had enough of soldiering and didn't have the stomach to go on firing guns. He'd made up his mind that if he came out of the war alive (and he never doubted that he would) then he wanted to do some form of social work. Above all he wanted to come home and lead a normal life. He wanted to leave the war behind. Of course he wasn't able to forget the war, neither what he'd seen nor what he'd had to do in its name, but he never dwelt on it. It was just something that had happened. And now it was gone. It was in the past.

So in 1984 when it came to the fortieth anniversary of the D-Day landings he seemed almost surprised to discover that what he'd been doing back then was making history. I think both he and my mother were always too preoccupied with present and future ever to bother much about the past. Consequently they had no curiosity about how and why a place had become the place it was. So it's hardly surprising that I was myself so lacking in curiosity about my surroundings as a child. If I'd been able to frame the question, 'But why is everything like this and where did it all come from?' they wouldn't have known where to begin. The teaching of history must have been every bit as useless in their schooldays as it was in mine.

Do you remember me saying a short while back that many years after the war I'd asked my father to tell me something about his experience of it? Well he let me record some conversations with him when he was about seventy and later on I transcribed them. What follows is an amalgamation of a few extracts about some things that happened after the war in Europe had ended in May 1945.

'I wasn't de-mobbed until August 1946. Quite a long part of that time since the end of the war was spent in Elmshorn and around there but later on I was sent further up in Schleswig-Holstein. We had to do various things. First of all was getting rid of all the German soldiers – getting them rounded up and demilitarised. And we had a lot of trouble with underground people up there. We were searching for various villains. We were searching for a long while for a chap called Hoess who was a very wanted man. And there was old Himmler we were looking for up there for a time. There were all sorts of things we were occupied with. And for quite a time we were responsible for sorting people out who needed repatriating.

I also sat in various military courts before the Control Commission took over from us. You were dealing with so many different offences at that time. For example there were some criminal elements among the soldiery. I sat on the court martial of a chap who'd shot a poor old night watchman. A ruthless killing of him for nothing but the fact that he was a German. We sentenced this British soldier to death. Whether it was ever carried out or not I never knew. I didn't follow it up.

Another thing which stands out in my mind is being told to hold myself ready to take some high-ranking German prisoners-of-war back to a prisoner-of-war cage in Belgium. They would be reporting voluntarily these people to Neumunster railway station at eight o'clock on such-and-such a morning. Their instructions were that they were to have hand-baggage only and that I was to be responsible for moving them down from Neumunster to Belgium, just outside Brussels.

Well when I turned up there were all these colonels, admirals, majors – you name it – all ranks. Very correct and arrogant really. They were all polished and absolutely perfectly kitted out. Some of them had got their mistresses with them – great piles of luggage, servants carrying luggage and so on. All stacked in the square at Neumunster station. The first thing I had to do was get rid of the luggage so I said, "The orders are hand-luggage only and hand-luggage it is and anyone who can't carry what they've brought – it stays there." You should have seen all these German bigwigs trying to carry all the stuff they'd brought [laughter] – well actually it had been brought for them by various family members, servants and so on. There was a great big pile left standing in the square.

Well, eventually I got them all loaded on – two hundred and eighty-nine of them – and we set off for the prisoner-of-war cage in a very broken-down train. No windows in it. Very unpleasant journey. Very slow. It took us two days or more and we kept halting and being halted because rail tracks were broken. It was a fascinating experience and I tried to get an insight into some of the officers. I invited one or two of them into my coach. I had a coach to myself. Privileged? Wasn't very comfortable I can tell you. It still hadn't got windows. I just didn't have Germans with me that's all. I had no other privileges at all. We used to have to stop the train to make tea by the side of the track and let people have sandwiches which had been put on board for the trip.

Well I had a number of them in – to speak to them. But at first they were very, very arrogant really. They didn't really accept that they'd lost the war. The fact that we were taking them down to a prisoner-of-war cage did seem to me to prove that we had won it but they said well you know it was bad luck and this, that and the other. All kinds of excuses. But a lot of this arrogance left them on the journey; it was a most salutary trip. By the time we got them down to the prisoner-of-war cage they were old men. All the polish and the uprightness had gone. Two days on the train and they were pretty tired people. They weren't bad people when you got talking to them (as much as you could do in broken English) and I thought Oh well I've known as bad in our own army. But yes, it was quite an interesting trip.

Then there were all the homeless and stateless people that there always are in a war. And during the fight up into Germany one picked up odd people who attached themselves to you and did useful things. I had a Dutchman in the Netherlands army who acted as an interpreter and I had a chap from Latvia who also acted as an interpreter. But I also had a family of Russians from one of the Baltic States. They had escaped from the Russians and joined up with us. They were with us from some time in 1945. I can't remember where we picked them up but they were with us right through into 1946. They were with us when we took our first permanent billet in Germany after the cease-fire – at Elmshorn. He was a shoe repairer and a very good one at that and there was his wife and two daughters and a grandchild. There they all were complete with a horse and how on earth we picked them up I don't know but I know we transported them all and the horse wherever we went. And he stayed with us after the fighting finished and was very useful indeed.

But at some time – and this must have been the great let-down for them – the order came that all the people from eastern Europe had to go back to eastern Europe. I remember the great tragedy of having to tell this family that much as we'd loved having them with us I was under orders to send them back. Oh the absolute breakdown! Oh terrible really having to tell them! Having to say cheerio and they knowing that they were going back into ... that their chance of survival was nil. I've never understood it. It was just an order. But it's one of the episodes one's least proud of I think.'

✻

So although things were difficult between my parents when my father came home in 1946 they nevertheless provided Heather and me with an example of equal partnership. I suppose I thought all married couples were like that. We had no way of knowing that theirs was an unusual marriage. Furthermore, far from being inferior, women even seemed to enjoy a slight edge over men. In our household it was the husband who deferred to his wife's wishes rather than the other way around. So with an upbringing like mine it's hardly surprising that once I was married I was so out of step with the kind of people I then found myself among.

In other ways though the life of my parents illustrates

exactly what it was like in the fifties. I remember particularly the sense I had of them being subject to Authority and restraint by Government. On Budget Day you were always told to shush. With pencil and paper in hand, they listened anxiously to details of the Budget being announced on the wireless. What new taxes had they dreamt up? How would these affect their plans to save enough to put down on a house of their own? Would the interest payments for hire-purchase be so high they wouldn't be able to get that much-needed item of furniture? Luxuries such as a refrigerator or television could only be dreamt of.

Then one Saturday morning in the mid-fifties, an elderly friend of my father's called Wattie (short for Watkins) dropped in unexpectedly at the flat. During the ensuing conversation over coffee, the subject of television was touched on. My mother admitted that she'd rather like one. She felt a bit out of things in the office where she worked because she couldn't join in conversations about what they'd all been watching the night before. Well that was all Wattie needed to hear and at 3 o' clock that afternoon a brand-new television arrived. The most obvious result of this was that my parents hardly ever went to the flicks again. This was a bit of a drawback because it meant they didn't go out on Saturday evenings any more. In general though it did seem to liven things up. Something else I think it did was to make us more normal.

It had been possible for me to have an almost Victorian childhood in the immediate post-war years but the advent of television meant you could no longer be insulated against the world beyond home. And by this time things had already begun to change in ways we could see for ourselves. New things were happening. Teddy boys with their knuckle-dusters, drainpipe trousers, wide-shouldered long jackets and brothel-creeper shoes had sprung onto the streets of Penge in the 1950s. And I think it was in 1956 that they tore out the seats in the King's Hall so they'd have more room in which to jive to *Rock around the Clock*. Respect for authority among young people was rapidly becoming a thing of the past. However, until the day we were married in

1966, Anthony still had to get me home by 10.30 sharp unless we were going somewhere special for the evening. And if I was foolish enough to emit so much as an audible sigh or a visible shrug in my mother's presence I'd feel the lash of her tongue and a sharp slap with a tea towel if she had one handy. Secrecy about what I thought or felt or did was still my only defence.

So not all young people had a wild time of it in the sixties as people seem to imagine. Nevertheless it was an enjoyable time to be young. Although we weren't carefree students, Anthony and I did a lot of partying to the Beatles and the Rolling Stones and it was during one of these events that I caught sight of myself in a mirror. For the first time in my life I was happy with what I saw. Without even noticing, I'd lost so much weight that I suddenly realised I didn't have to feel uncomfortable about my appearance any more. And now there was colour and style in clothes for young women. Instead of having to dress like your mother in straight grey skirt and pastel twin-set, you could shimmy into a shocking-pink dolly-rocker frock. Best of all was the introduction of tights which meant not only the death of discomfort-by-suspender-belt but also the possibility of shorter and shorter skirts.

I remember the early sixties as a time of burgeoning laughter accompanied by a feeling that for better or worse, restraint was beginning to evaporate. When I was still in the sixth form and sullenly sitting through classes in Catholic Apologetics by which the Church sought to justify its authority in all areas of one's life, younger and more worldly girls at Coloma were crazy about rock-and-roll and crying with desire for Elvis the Pelvis. One morning before classes began they managed to scrawl GREAT BALLS OF FIRE!!!!! on every blackboard in the school. And in 1960 there was the sensational trial at the Old Bailey in which Penguin Books was charged under the obscenity laws for its publication of D. H. Lawrence's rather tedious novel *Lady Chatterley's Lover*. The Crown lost its case and the result was that Penguin made a foreseeable fortune out of the immense sales that inevitably followed.

It must have been about this time that Coloma itself had a

brief moment of notoriety when photographs of its weathervane appeared in the national press. Suspended from it were a pair of navy bloomers and a chamber pot placed there as part of a rag carried out by the boys of John Ruskin School. Mother Mary Cuthbert had been sufficiently up with the times to take the revolutionary step of authorising collaboration between their sixth form drama department and our own so they could put on *Antigone* or some such worthy play. I don't remember how she handled this affront but it was probably by maintaining a dignified silence. I do remember though a moment in assembly in 1961 when she was on the stage addressing the six hundred or more girls squeezed into the hall beneath her. I suddenly felt how fragile her authority was and how frightening her situation might seem to her now. Did she wonder as I did, how much longer she'd be able to keep the lid on all the simmering sexuality and potential for revolt that we represented? I wondered what I was doing there myself and what it was that stopped us all, apart from good manners, from simply getting up and walking out of the place.

Then in 1963 the crumbling of the old order was swiftly accelerated by reverberations from the Profumo Affair. Almost overnight it seemed, deference was dead. It turned out there'd been no basis for the assumption made by people like us that all members of the ruling class were honourable men.

I won't say any more about that time because you can easily read about it for yourselves if you're interested. But what I remember about those days was the eagerness with which we dived for the morning newspapers and the amount of laughter generated in Birdham Close. By good luck two of our neighbours were Fleet Street journalists and they were a splendid source of rumour and gossip that couldn't make it to press.

While I'm on the subject of change, if you'd like a neat example of it in my family over a twenty-year period I can give you one. Just before I left school in the summer of 1961 one of these neighbours lent me a copy of Salinger's *The Catcher in the Rye*. I hadn't got beyond the first page when I passed it on to my father because he'd asked me if I'd got something he could read on the train. A day or two later he said, 'By the way, I've given that book back to Aubrey. I told him I didn't think it made particularly suitable reading for a daughter of mine.' I suspect this is exactly why Aubrey had lent it to me in the first place but I didn't bother to challenge my father's high-handedness. Perhaps I should have done but it was hardly worth it. I didn't care too much for the look of the book myself and I haven't managed to get through it to this day. But in 1981 when Becky was thirteen, I had the pleasure of hearing her snorts of laughter in the seat behind me as she read it during a flight to Santorini. By that time this supposedly subversive or at least unsavoury text was on a list of books recommended by her English teacher.

✻

POPE APPROVES NATURAL CHILDBIRTH. This headline must have appeared around 1957 because I know I was about fourteen when I came downstairs one morning and saw it on the front of the newspaper. My reaction (unspoken of course) was one of fury. What the *hell* had childbirth got to do with him? Or any other man for that matter? Ignorant as I was about sexual matters, I obviously had no idea of the extent to which the Catholic Church presumed to interfere with women's bodies and dictate the uses to which they might be put. As far as I was concerned my body was just as much part of my self as my mind. It belonged to me and to me alone and anything that happened to it was as private as my thoughts. Although I was acquainted by Catholicism with the idea that the self resided in the soul, I never found it possible to split soul from body. As much as anything else, your body defined who you were and determined what happened to you. In fact very often it felt as if my body was my self.

So this was the beginning of my rejection of Catholicism and the increasing sense of resentment I felt towards it. By the time I was sixteen I know I'd come to the conclusion that the Catholic Church was an organisation run by men for the subjection of women and so it seems strange I was so stunned by the Neanderthal pronouncement of 1959. Until then the idea that women were, or could in any way be considered, inferior to men was unknown to me. I can only suppose that I managed to split off Catholicism from the real world of which I knew so little anyway. But during the next few years my fury was fuelled as I noticed the way so many men took their superiority for granted while regarding subservience and silliness in women as the natural order of things. And then there were all those supposedly side-splitting jokes told by stand-up comedians on television about the stupidity of women, the ghastliness of the wife's mother and the hopeless ineptitude of woman drivers.

Back in those days, before the expression women's liberation was even heard of, I don't remember speaking to anyone about these feelings. I'm pretty sure that if I had then I'd have been accused of having a chip on my shoulder. I was out of step. And yet I was never 'one of those women's libbers' as I was so often assumed to be. I hadn't (and still haven't) read a single sentence from any feminist text, seminal or otherwise, and had no desire whatever to be enslaved by work. However, by the early 1970s there was no avoiding the subject, especially on Woman's Hour. Quite often when I tuned in I was bemused by the underlying assumption that all work outside the home equaled freedom for women, even for women with small children. And in a special edition about Russia we learned that women over there were so liberated they could even work as road-menders and coal-heavers. With intoxicating prospects like that I couldn't see how working mothers would be liberated into anything but exhaustion. And I could see no benefit at all for their children.

I was often to find that those women in the media who relentlessly pushed their convictions about women and work weren't speaking for me. Nor were those women acting on my behalf whom I saw liberating themselves at my first Open University summer school at Bath in 1976 where they were abusive to decent men who'd been polite enough to hold doors open for them. What I wanted was friendship between men and women and an acceptance that, in spite of their differences, they were complementary to each other and equal as human beings. I also wanted women's work as homemakers and mothers to be recognised for the critically important job that it was. But because it wasn't paid work the feminists treated it with disdain. So the way in which the feminist agenda denigrated the traditional role of women was infuriating to me. It's my opinion that instead of striving to make it to the top in a working world created by men, feminists would have been better employed pursuing economic recognition for women who bring up children and look after sick or elderly relatives. It is also my unfashionable opinion that women have never had the right to have a family as well as the right to reach the top in their chosen career. 'Having it all' as it's currently called. If they do manage to have it all then it's my belief this can only have been achieved at someone else's expense. Probably their children's. However, I doubt whether have-it-all women are representative of women as a whole today, any more than the repulsive, strident, man-hating, feminists were representative of women in the seventies and eighties.

Nevertheless no-one these days can doubt the ability of women to achieve whatever they want to achieve. There's almost nothing they can't do or aren't allowed to do now. It's all so different from how it was when I was young and when I try to recall what it felt like living in the relatively recent past it's often difficult to believe that things could have been as restrictive as they were back then.

It's just as well though that I lived when I did because I wasn't equipped by temperament, upbringing, or education to meet the demands faced by the woman of today. I've always known I wasn't made for the hurly-burly and that I need a lot of time to myself, especially outside working in the garden, to keep me in balance. In order to feel right in myself, I know I have to keep in close touch with the rhythms of the natural world. So I've been exceedingly fortunate that I've been able to slide through life without being enslaved by work. Consequently I know I can stand accused of failure in my role as grownup. Well I never did audition for the part with any great enthusiasm. My heart just wasn't in it.

*

I wonder if you feel as I did when I was young? That you're living at the end of things and just want to get your life in before it's all over? I've never been able to get rid of this sensation, which still seems to me to be a perfectly reasonable one if you look at the increasingly insane speed of life and change in the modern world. (It is of course entirely possible that everything will all be over before you're even old enough to read what I've written here for you.) Even as I appreciate all the advantages I enjoy by living in the present day, I feel life is becoming increasingly mad and unsustainable. I'm forever infuriated by the continuous process of degradation going on around me – whether it be country lanes used as rubbish dumps or the constant traffic roaring not just through the village itself but also round the bypass. Except during the night-time hours the noise level is tremendous and judging by the number of police cars that go screaming through on both roads you'd be forgiven for thinking that ours is a shockingly criminal community. And, like almost everywhere else, it's seldom possible to have five seconds free from the drone of aeroplanes. If we're really having an unlucky day then it's the turn of the military helicopters which fly so low they make the house judder.

Whether any of these things are responsible for frightening away the cuckoo from Sutton Wood I don't know but I do know why the house-martins no longer twitter to each other outside our bedroom window as they had done ever since the house was built. We always used to have three or four nests out there but the martins don't build at all now because of a house that went up in the field opposite. Before then there was always mud by the gate for them to use but there isn't any more. Every year when they came back in the spring, dipping and diving around, it felt as if all was well with the world, But that's all over now. And so is the pleasure I used to take in Sutton Wood in spring. Without the cuckoo my delight in the wood has gone. This has been replaced by a sadness that deepens day by day. So many birds have disappeared and all we seem to be left with is the droning of wood pigeons and collared doves.

But looking back on my life I can appreciate how immensely lucky my generation has been. Even though everything was overshadowed by the Cold War and fear that the world could end at any moment, our youth wasn't blighted by any actual war and the standard of living we enjoyed was phenomenal by comparison with that of our parents. And in spite of everything I've said about attitudes to women, there's probably never been a better time and place in which to be one, providing you aren't in thrall to an outfit like the Catholic Church.

I once read somewhere that it's not possible to retain two contradictory ideas at the same time but I'm not sure I agree. Don't most of us do it all the time? Split our minds in such a way that we plan for a future in which we don't altogether believe? I certainly know that I can retain two contradictory feelings at the same time (and the distinction between thought and feeling is a difficult one to draw in any case) – anxiety about the survival of my grandchildren in an increasingly hostile and degraded world, alongside an earnest desire for the imminent and painless demise of the entire human race so that Earth can rest in peace and start recovering from the depredations of mankind before it's too late.

∗

Well I think I've said everything I wanted to say but if you'd like to know the story behind the place in which Heather and I grew up then you'll find something about it a page or two further on.

Anthony and I are looking forward to seeing you all very soon when you come to stay. We'll take you down to my parents' place by the sea at Aldwick. We haven't sold it yet so you'll be able to run around in the garden which is perfect for hide and seek. And we'll go to the beach where my belovèd father used to take Becky and Candida so often when they were little girls.

Dear old Pa. Last week when I was down there I began to clear out the garage. I had to brace myself to get rid of stuff like his old gardening mac, various sets of golf waterproofs and an ancient rug that had been his mother's and which he always kept in the car. When I'd just lobbed these and other things into a hefty plastic sack I came across a white cardboard box neatly labelled by Heather PLEASE DO NOT DISTURB. On investigation it turned out to be my share of his ashes and I found myself starting guiltily in case he'd seen what I'd just done. I don't suppose I'm the only person to be so ridiculous.

✻

# Postscript

In 1996 I happened to mention to someone that my parents had been married nearly sixty years and that it was their diamond wedding in October. 'Why don't you fix up a message from the Queen? All you have to do is write to Buckingham Palace and send a copy of their marriage certificate.' So we decided to do this as a surprise for them. Consequently it was disappointing that I had partially to give the game away on my next visit when things went something like this:

'While Mum's in the kitchen Dad could I ask you something?'
'Of course.'
'You and Mummy *were* married in Sydenham weren't you?'
'Yes dear we were.'
'Well for reasons you can probably guess we've been trying to get hold of a copy of your marriage certificate but Anthony's been told there's no record of a marriage there in 1936'. Without hesitation and still looking me straight in the eye he says, 'No there wouldn't be. That's because we weren't married until 1937'.

It only takes a fraction of a second to work out the implications of this. If Heather was born in April 1938 then the astounding thing he's telling me is that at the time of their marriage my mother was up the duff.

An explosion of mirth on my part was the inevitable response. All those decades of deception! Saint Peter himself! And no wonder there weren't any photographs of those two quiet weddings. No wonder either that it hadn't been their custom to mark their anniversary in any way. Perhaps Heather and I just assumed they'd married in 1936. Well we would wouldn't we? How could we have imagined the truth?

'You old *devil*!'
'I'm afraid so dear.' [unsuccessful attempt to assume appropriately contrite expression]
'So do you mean to tell me that in 1986 when we celebrated your fiftieth anniversary it was really only your forty-ninth?'

'I'm afraid so. I did warn your mother that you were bound to find us out one of these days. [pause for thought] So there's no need to bother about a party. You can forget about that until next year. [musingly] I suppose I'll come in for quite a bit of barracking.'

'Oh I think you can count on that, especially from your grandsons. Serve you right you old fraud.'

'Yes dear'.

'If Heather and I'd known about this you'd have found it pretty difficult laying down the law the way you did when we were young.'

'Would I? Yes I suppose I might have done.' [as if this had never occurred to him]

'You know darned well you would. So you've given me quite a lot to think about.'

'Have I? Yes I suppose I might have done.' [looking at his watch] 'Well I think we've just about got time to fit in a quick drink before lunch. What do you think?'

'I think you might be trying to change the subject.'

'I think you might be right.'

 [laughter]

❋

# The Story of the Place

I don't know whether there's a particular age or stage in life when people begin to reflect on their childhood experience and wonder what part it played in turning them into the people they became. However, I suppose Heather and I were in our late thirties or early forties when we began to reminisce and discovered how deeply we'd both been impressed by the place in which we'd grown up, especially by the mysteriousness of the Palace grounds.

In this map printed in the early 1930s (pages 210/211), the area looks virtually the same as it does in today's A–Z Street Atlas of London, although not nearly as cramped. We lived at the bottom of Crystal Palace Park Road, pretty well exactly where it says Penge Entrance. The peculiar and derelict landscape that we could get to through the hedge at the bottom of the garden was of course the ruin of Crystal Palace Park, always referred to by locals as the Palace grounds.

The name Crystal Palace was so familiar to me that it didn't give rise to any pictures in my mind. I saw no palaces in the royal or fairy-tale sense as a more imaginative child might have done. For me Crystal Palace was just part of my address and was a place where bus routes ended. When you got off at Crystal Palace Parade there wasn't anything there at all except a desolate, blackened emptiness. A television transmitter reminiscent of the Eiffel Tower that came later wasn't an improvement and made the spot feel even more sinister. But for Heather, who remembers going for a walk with our father in the grounds below one snowy Christmas morning, the ivy-smothered balustrades and toppled statues were charged with romantic potential.

Nobody told us what the Crystal Palace had been and I for one didn't ask. All I ever heard was that it had burnt down in a spectacular fire in 1936 – seven years before my mother moved into the flat while she was expecting me. And if as a child I'd thought to consult Arthur Mee on the subject I'd have been disappointed because the only brief reference to it concerns a structure designed by Sir Joseph Paxton that had gone up in Hyde Park in 1851 to house the Great Exhibition. Arthur Mee had nothing to say about our own Crystal Palace. Nor (if one can trust his index) did he even have anything to say about Queen Victoria.

Anyway, Heather's fascination with what had passed away was communicated to me when she produced a coloured engraving she'd found which showed the Crystal Palace at Sydenham as it was supposed to have looked at its opening in 1854. It showed an immense glass structure that looked about a quarter of a mile long spread across the top of the hill where the now desolate Parade was and looking down over spectacular grounds resplendent with lakes and temples and sparkling fountains. We grieved over the loss of all that beauty and wondered how it had come to be there in the first place. So I began to collect what information I could.

I soon found that the success of the Great Exhibition of 1851 was due in no small measure to the delight engendered by the novelty of Paxton's iron and glass building which was hailed as the eighth wonder of the world and according to *Punch* resembled a crystal palace. Reporting on the opening ceremony, *The Times* described it in terms of awe: 'They who were so fortunate as to see it hardly knew what most to admire or in what form to clothe the sense of wonder and even of mystery which struggled within them … There were many there who were familiar with magnificent spectacles … but they had not seen anything to compare with this … above them rose a glittering arch far more lofty and spacious than the vaults of even our noblest cathedrals … It was felt to be more than what was seen, or what had been intended.' And Thackeray described it in a poem as being like 'a blazing arch of lucid glass, leaping like a fountain from the grass.'

Paxton was employed by the sixth Duke of Devonshire and by this date had become a household name as the most famous gardener in England. (And also the busiest man in England according to his friend Charles Dickens). His structure was

SYDENHAM
SYDENHAM & FOREST HILL RECREATION GD.
SYDENHAM WELLS PARK
CRYSTAL PALACE PARK
PUBLIC PARK
Alexandra Recreation Grd
KNIGHTON PARK ROAD
TREWSBURY ROAD
DACRES ROAD
SILVERDALE
BISHOPSTHORPE ROAD
QUEENSTHORPE RD.
KINGSTHORPE RD.
PRINCETHORPE RD.
DUKESTHORPE RD.
EARLSTHORPE RD.
ACACIA RD.
VENNER
HOMECROFT RD.
TREDOWN RD.
WIVERTON
BYNE
LENNARD
PARISH
CATOR
KIRKDALE
SYDENHAM HILL
PEAK HILL
COLLINGTREE RD.
JEWS WALK
HIGH STR.
CHURCH LEY RD.
HALIFAX
GROVE
LONGTON AVENUE
TAYLOR'S LANE
WESTWOOD ROAD
LAWRIE PARK GARDENS
LAWRIE PARK CRES.
LAWRIE PARK ROAD
SPRINGFIELD RD.
SYDENHAM AV.
BORDER CRESCENT
AMBERLEY RD.
Horner Grange
Orphanage
ORMANTON RD
CRYSTAL PALACE PARK
WEST
S.R. (S.E.&C.) Tunnel
UPPER SYDENHAM
The Wood
Water Wks.
FOUNTAIN
ROAD
PARADE
PALACE
Crystal Palace
Cricket Ground
Pavilion
Football Ground
Sports Arena
Intermediate Lake
Band Stand
Maze
Rockhill
Low Level Entrance
PENGE
LORINGTON
CRYSTAL PALACE (LOW LEVEL)
ANERLEY
KINGSWOOD
CRAMPTON
STATION RD.
PHOENIX RD.
LUCAS RD.
MAITLAND RD.
ALEXANDRA RD.
WESTBOURNE RD.
STUDLAND RD.
HARDINGE ST.
PRINCES RD.
Naval Asylum

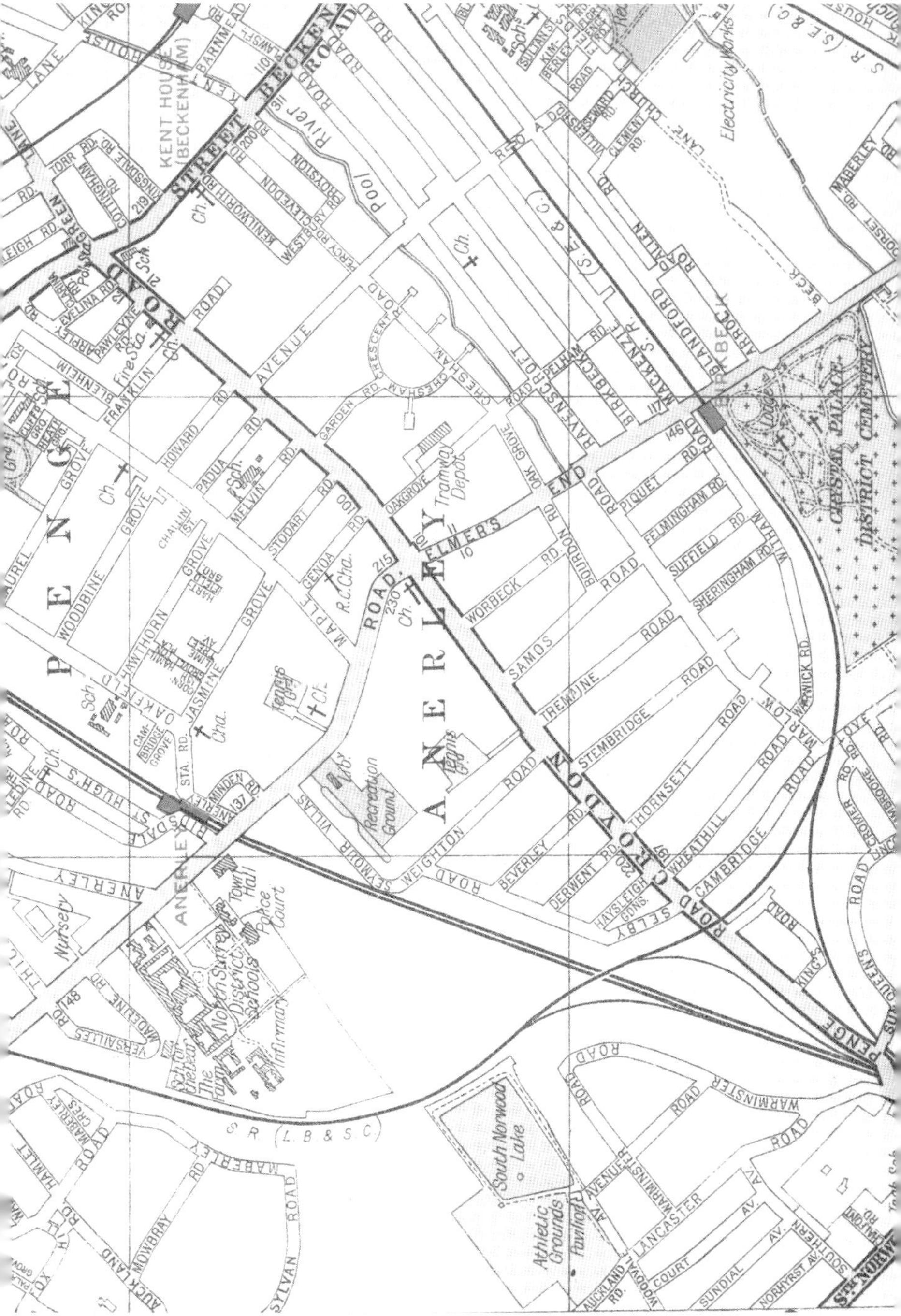

revolutionary because it could be erected with great speed on site by using prefabricated units. He based its form on that of a glass-house which he'd designed and put up at Chatsworth to house his enormous Victoria Regia lily. This design was in turn modelled on the structure of the lily itself. When the exhibition was over Paxton envisaged its retention in Hyde Park as a winter garden but the authorities wouldn't permit this and so he and various fellow entrepreneurs looked around for a suitable site on which to re-erect the people's palace as a commercial enterprise.

However, the building that went up on Sydenham Hill was a much enlarged and more complex affair than the one in Hyde Park. The intricate park overlooked by his new palace was designed with elaborate meaning and included a system of waterworks intended to rival those at Versailles and Chatsworth. There was no limit to Paxton's ambitious plans or the effort he put into realising them. The apparently unending terrace I told you about turned out to be the lowest of a series of three, through the centre of which an enormously wide staircase ran down towards the central axis of the park.

I see from the plans reproduced in a book I have that those

prehistoric monsters were referred to then as Extinct Animals. They're still there, just where it says Anerley Entrance on the map. Do you see how the railway line from Sydenham makes a loop and for a while becomes the boundary of the park? Well, because this bit of line is on an embankment visitors could get an excellent, if brief, aerial view of them just before they pulled into the splendour of Crystal Palace station.

> The visitor looking across the Extinct Animals and the Park would have been stunned by the colossal scale of Paxton's architecture and landscape. The crowning glory was the "long sparkling vault" of the Palace itself; below it was the series of horizontal lines about the spine of the Park forming the "hanging gardens, stone terraces, reservoirs, fountains and conservatories." [Piggott]

Well in my day, without any knowledge of what Park and Palace had once been, when you slithered along the damp path past the dinosaurs this railway line felt unpleasantly threatening, especially when trains rumbled along it about twenty feet above your head. And in spring there was the nasty smell of garlic in dark places. I was always glad to get away from there and reach the lake. I felt the railways blighted any surroundings through which they went but this isn't how mid-Victorians necessarily saw things. For many of them the arrival of the steam train was central to the excitement they felt about the age in which they lived and the advances that it was making. So the proximity of this line probably wouldn't have been seen as an eyesore but as part of the meaning of the place.

In fact the railway companies and the Crystal Palace Company needed each other because the Crystal Palace Company was reliant on trains to transport visitors to its turnstiles and the railway companies were reliant on the Crystal Palace Company to bring them profit through increased passenger traffic. In addition to this, directors of those railway companies, like Paxton himself, were often not only directors of the Crystal Palace Company as well but also speculators in local land for the building boom they knew would come. Another such man was Leo Schuster. He was both a director of the London and Croydon Railway (which opened in 1839 and ran over the spooky bridge I knew was going to fall down) and the owner of Penge Place, on the site of which the Palace was eventually built. He sold his house and park to the Crystal Palace Company of which he too was a director.

As if the magnificence of the station put up by the London and Croydon Railway weren't enough, its rival, the London, Chatham and Dover Railway constructed an even more monumental one at the other end of the Park. The lines became known respectively as the Crystal Palace Low Level and the Crystal Palace High Level. The new High Level brought its passengers directly to the Palace by way of a pillared and vaulted passageway beneath the Crystal Palace Parade in front of it. You can't see any sign of this on current maps because the line was torn up after the Second World War and the station demolished to make way for new houses.

So by the time the houses in Crystal Palace Park Road went up in the early 1880s, they were surrounded by unseen railway lines, bridges, viaducts and tunnels. These leasehold houses stood within the park itself and I think it's reasonable to assume they were constructed in order to provide income for the Crystal Palace Company which never made a profit and frequently teetered on the brink of bankruptcy.

The opening ceremony in 1854 was attended by Queen Victoria and accorded all the significance of a state occasion. She also attended a later ceremony to inaugurate the elaborate system of waterworks. Queen Victoria loved the Crystal Palace and visited it time and time again, frequently accompanied by foreign royalty who shared her enthusiasm. The fact that she consequently became identified with the place was probably an important factor in its becoming a focus of patriotism. However, the success of the Crystal Palace as a commercial venture depended on the steadily increasing mass of her subjects having the leisure in which to seek amusement.

Yet despite the fact that this embodiment of Britishness and Empire was a profit-seeking organisation, its avowed purpose right from the beginning was educative. It was to be an improving place – somewhere the People were able to enjoy themselves by learning as they strolled at ease through both the Palace and its Park. It was to be an instructive place. The primeval world was evoked by the Extinct Animals and the Geological Illustrations at the lower end of the park. On top of the hill rising above it shone the newest architectural and technological achievement. In between these two extremes, 'Man's position as the artificer in nature, like Adam, was to be interpreted emblematically in the garden'. [Piggott]

The Geological Illustrations account for the coal seam across which Heather had edged so fearlessly above the chasm below and also for a huge outcrop of rocks we used to jump over and hide among. And while visitors were learning about horticulture and the history of gardening they were also having their taste improved by an abundance of classical statuary. Inside the Palace, the manufactures of 1851 were replaced by a series of lofty 'Courts' leading off the nave, whose purpose was to illustrate the art and architecture of ancient civilisations. Elaborate and meticulous recreation of splendours from such places as ancient Egypt, Assyria, Rome, Pompeii, Moorish Spain, Byzantium and Renaissance Italy enabled visitors to educate themselves through a form of virtual travel. So, ironically, on the very spot I lived as a child there had been this place which would have met my educational needs, including the provision of music that hardly came my way except through the wireless. The Crystal Palace had become the centre of musical life in this country during the second half of the nineteenth century and concerts continued to be held there into the twentieth. So if I'd been born twenty years sooner things might have been very different for me.

But by no means certainly. By the 1920s Sydenham was no longer the fashionable place it had been fifty or sixty years earlier. The Palace itself was in very bad shape although by then it had been purchased for the nation and was undergoing limited refurbishment. The Crystal Palace Company had always struggled to survive and in 1911, the year of George V's coronation, it finally went bankrupt following a Festival of Empire to celebrate this event.

I find it impossible not to see the forlorn state of the Palace and its Park at this time as emblematic of the decline of Britain itself, the signs of which showed up very early on. Part of it collapsed in 1861 while Paxton was still alive and in 1866, the year after his death, fire destroyed the north transept. It was never rebuilt. In addition the grounds swiftly lost their meaning because Paxton had over-reached himself. The famous waterworks may have used six times as much water as Versailles but had rarely been operational.

The waterworks explain the presence of that horrible ruin filled with brown water near the end of our garden. It had been an engine house for pumping water to the fountains, lakes and basins. Once the waterworks proved unworkable, the great basins had no function and were filled in to provide areas for sport and recreation. It took a very short time for most of the Park to become what it was never intended to be – a place of mere amusement like a permanent funfair with fireworks.

So I wouldn't have found the Park very uplifting at that time, nor indeed at any other time in its history I think. It may look like something out of a fairytale in engravings but in photographs you can sense bombast and bleakness. Worse still, Paxton apparently went in for huge displays of gaudy bedding plants that looked like patterned carpets and which were the forerunners of those regimented salvias and floral clocks I hated so much. So I've come to the conclusion that I prefer the Palace grounds I knew as a child. Yet the whole place certainly gave pleasure and benefit to millions and I'm sorry I was too late to see the Palace itself glittering on top of the hill and changing colour according to the light.

Our house, which is still there along with most of the others on our side of Crystal Palace Park Road, passed into the hands of the London Borough of Bromley. Still there too, when I was last in the district with Heather in the summer of 2003, was the chestnut tree in the front garden. This was just as well because without it I don't think I could have identified the house with any certainty. We stood in bewilderment trying to find anything on the ground we recognised. Not only had the long back gardens been cut to less than a quarter of their original length and a conifer hedge planted at the bottom, but all fences between the houses had been taken away. There were no gates either and the gravel drives had been replaced with tarmac. Evidently this was to facilitate the progress of the council dustcart that we saw going from house to house through what had once been individual front gardens. All the old privacy had gone and so had all the verandas and balconies that previous leaseholders had added on. I thought I'd recognise our house anywhere but I couldn't – not once it had been deprived of its attachments and surrounding features.

But I'm glad it's still there. All the houses narrowly missed demolition in the sixties or seventies but are mentioned in *The Buildings of England* where they're described as Gothic mansions designed by John Norton. You've never heard of him? Neither had I but I found a lengthy article about him in the Dictionary of National Biography. Apparently his predilection for all things Gothic reached its apotheosis in Tyntesfield, described by the National Trust as a Gothic extravaganza.

I'm glad too that my intuition about the Palace grounds having some affinity with an encyclopaedia was well-grounded. According to publicity material, the aim was to create an 'illustrated encyclopaedia'. The Palace and Park would create a 'perfect Cosmos – a brilliant illustration of all that is noble and elevating in the world.'

Furthermore, I found to my amusement a neat parallel between the Crystal Palace and Arthur Mee's encyclopaedia. A month before the opening ceremony a letter appeared in *The Times* signed by the Archbishop of Canterbury, various bishops and several peers of the realm. It expressed grave concern about the nude male statuary that was to be on display 'to promiscuous crowds of men and women'. The letter ended,

> We demand but a small thing, not at all a sacrifice in point of artistic beauty – viz. the removal of the parts which in the 'the life' ought to be concealed, although we are also desirous that the usual leaf may be adopted. [Quoted by Piggott]

In our wanderings through our childhood landscape in 2003

Heather and I revisited Mayow Park and were pleased to find it hadn't changed at all apart from a block of flats overlooking it. And I got that peculiar, slightly disturbing pleasure you feel on rediscovering an object from long ago with which you were once on terms of great familiarity but had completely forgotten about. This was a massive and rather ugly drinking fountain somewhere near the spot where winding paths converged and which commemorated (if I remember correctly) whoever was responsible for saving this piece of potential building land as a public space for people's enjoyment. Mayow Wynell Adams, after whom the park was presumably named, described it as the 'prettiest Public Park in the Metropolis' and when it opened in 1878, in the presence of a crowd estimated to number 10,000, it was declared to be 'open and free for ever.'

In case you think I'm rambling on nostalgically to no purpose I can assure you I'm not. The reason I'm mentioning these things is because they illustrate perfectly the growing concern at that time about the spread of the built environment at the expense of the natural one. Land had been gobbled up, and continued to be gobbled up for building at an unprecedented rate in order to accommodate a vastly increased population and to satisfy the desire for houses in countrified surroundings within easy reach of central London. The creation of Mayow Park can be seen as a consequence of pioneering work done by the Open Spaces Society which had been founded in 1865 with the objective of saving the commons of Hampstead, Wimbledon and Wandsworth for public use.

When I came across this map which was made as part of a Survey of London by John Rocque between 1741 and 1745 my heart turned over. I gazed at it in disbelief and misery. This was what had been there before. This was the ancient landscape onto which all those roads, railway lines and ugliness had been imposed. It was onto this that the mechanical shape of Crystal Palace Park had been smashed. How, when and why did all this happen I wondered.

Well it seems that things changed hardly at all for several

decades. When change began to come in the 1800s it did so because of the proximity of Croydon about three miles or so to the south of Penge Common. In order to improve communications between Croydon and London the construction of the Croydon Canal was authorised by Act of Parliament in 1801 and its route towards the Grand Surrey Canal lay across Penge Common. A wharf was constructed at Penge which facilitated not only the movement of goods and merchandise to outlying places like Beckenham and Bromley but also the means by which to transport timber and other materials from Penge Woods.

Although the Croydon Canal was ultimately a financial failure it became extremely popular for recreational purposes. The local historian Alan Warwick gives an account of this in his book *The Phoenix Suburb*.

> The woods of Penge were a favourite place to picnic [and]… Boats could be hired, and parties were made up to row to Forest Hill through beautiful countryside, with scarcely a house to be seen on the journey. Teas were to be had in the extensive gardens of the Dartmouth Arms tavern. The walks on the banks or towing path could not be surpassed in the neighbourhood. Norwood and its grand woods were on one side, and wide, well-cultivated fields on the other. At Penge Reach the canal widened, and the journey through Penge Woods passed through country as picturesque and romantic as an American backwater. The country was varied, and the activities on the water, barges passing and repassing, boating parties, anglers on the banks, all added to the charm and attraction. The gardens of the Jolly Sailor

tavern at South Norwood, where teas were served, were visited by family parties where they would watch the various craft passing to and fro.

If you look at Rocque's map you can see large letters running across it on the left hand side saying North Wood. This referred to a great chain of oak woods bounded by ancient commons that once covered the steep ridge of clay hills that stretched from Selhurst to Deptford across what was then the Surrey-Kent border. The nearest to London of the remaining, threatened fragments of these ancient woods are on Sydenham Hill. We used to go up there as children. I remember how much I enjoyed it whenever my father took us to look down towards the Thames where we could make out the shipping on it and spot landmarks like Tower Bridge and St Paul's. So the site of the Crystal Palace had a splendid double aspect. Paxton described it as the most beautiful spot in the world for the Palace and *The Illustrated London News* wrote that: 'For beauty of scenery and

half way house
Knights hill Farm
KNIGHTS HILL
STRETHAM
Mr Wheeler
Lane
DULWICH
COMMON
THE HORNS
KNIGHTS HILL COMMON
KNIGHTS HILL POUND
STRETHAM
COMMON
Stretham Wells
KNIGHTS HILL
WOOD
N O R T H
Bewlys Farm
WHITE HOUSE WOOD
PARK OF CROYDON
COMMON
PVNERA VIRTUS
ht Honourable
d Boyle,
Viscount Dungarvon
Baron Boyle of Youghall
able Privy Council
Order of the Garter.
ly Dedicated by
obedient and
rvant

SYDENHAM
SYDENHAM WELLS
WEST WOOD COMMON
PLACE HOUSE
BECKENHAM
PENGE GREEN
COMMON
ELMS END
Kengley Bridge
Pool River Bridge
New Leave Bridge
Charlton
Peter Burrell Esq

perfect retirement, combined with an easy access from London, it is impossible to imagine a more fortunate situation.'

Easy access was provided by the railway, without which there could have been no Crystal Palace at Sydenham. And the railway had arrived because of the Croydon Canal that had been there before it. The canal had closed in 1836, been drained of its water and sold to the London and Croydon railway which began to run trains along its old bed in 1839. The prospect of profit for Joseph Paxton and Leo Schuster, who were both directors of this railway company, was undoubtedly a major factor in the choice of site for the Crystal Palace. This was particularly so for Schuster because the line ran along the valley at the bottom of his park at Penge Place. The choice of site meant that he was all set to capitalise even more than Paxton, by selling Penge Place and its park to the Crystal Palace Company for £50,000. According to the *Illustrated London News*:

> [Schuster's] … park, pleasure-ground, garden and pasture fields contain 280 acres, lying on a gentle slope … adorned with clumps of ornamental timber, and surrounded by a thick belt of plantations which completely separate it from the road and from adjoining properties … The situation, sloping down into a valley and hedged in by thick plantations affords the most perfect solitude; not a sound, not an object within view, betrays the close vicinity of a great city. The blackbirds and thrushes sing away in harmonious rivalry, and the rabbits dashing through the brushwood and wobbling along the fields complete the idea of a remote rural district only disturbed by the occasional thunder of a train dashing along the valley below unseen but marked by a following trail of vapour. The village in the valley is hidden, all but the tapering white spire of the church, by the roll of the ground and the intervening clumps of trees, but rising beyond, the Surrey hills, almost covered with wood, spread out in a vast panorama … [Quoted by Piggott]

So the spot on which our house was eventually built around

1880 had originally been on the wooded common, virtually on the path taken by a Mr William Hone (of whom more later) across it in 1827 at a time when the canal still curved, gleaming through the trees less than a hundred yards away. Within a few years this spot was inside Schuster's garden and its peace shattered by trains roaring along the route once taken by the canal. By 1854 it was inside Crystal Palace Park.

Many of the plantations and private delights enjoyed by Schuster had been made possible by the enclosure of Penge common in 1827. Usually the rationale behind enclosure of common land was that it facilitated agricultural improvements necessary to feed the rapidly-growing population. This wasn't the case with Penge Common which was simply allocated to local landowners and swiftly built upon once the railway arrived so conveniently in 1839. Essentially this was a common enclosed to provide land for building.

The significance of the growth of London is trenchantly expressed by Martin Spence in his book about the transformation of Penge:

> In the first half of the nineteenth century London's daily growth

saw not ten new inhabitants, but 100. And in the second half of the century each day brought well over 200. The population passed 3 million around 1850 and 7 million around 1900. The world had never seen anything like it ... The point cannot be over-emphasised: London is not just another city. London is unique. No other great capitalist city saw such a record of steady, unbroken growth going back over centuries to the dawn of the capitalist era itself. London is the extraordinary, teeming, filthy, brilliant, shameful exemplar of urban capitalism.

For centuries too, London had been a dirty, noisy and unhealthy place from which people of all degrees were keen to escape for recreation into the rural charm and clean air of the country south of London. Originally its pleasures were preserved to those of highest degree who built palaces there but by the seventeenth century rather less exalted people were able to enjoy its attractions at spas such as Epsom and Tunbridge Wells. Springs closer to London like those discovered at Sydenham in 1641 quickly became popular with day-trippers and were consequently considered rather less desirable. Nevertheless George III didn't disdain to visit the wells at Sydenham which was becoming an increasingly fashionable place to live and where prestigious houses were beginning to be built amongst the woods that had been there since time immemorial and which had long been frequented by charcoal burners and gypsies. The same thing was happening on the slopes above Penge Common near Norwood, a small settlement in the parish of Croydon.

Interestingly, Penge itself was not a parish nor even a village as suggested by *The Illustrated London News*. It was a detached hamlet of the parish or manor of Battersea several miles distant and had been for at least a thousand years. Its tiny population had never merited a church and the spire referred to as being visible from Penge Place belonged to one that had only gone up four years previously when the population had grown to about 1100. In the next twenty years Penge became a town with over 13,000 inhabitants. Yet a hundred years before, at the time of Rocque's survey, only about fifty people lived in Penge in a cluster of houses around the green at the foot of the wooded hills and common.

Before land at Penge became valued for its building potential in the second quarter of the nineteenth century its economic value had, for a thousand years or more, lain in its woods. As the amount of land cleared for cultivation had increased over time, so any remaining woodland (usually on the top of hills) was an increasingly valuable resource. Woods like these were not wildwood but were carefully managed by the ancient skill of woodmanship. Thus they provided renewable sources of timber for buildings and ships as well as wood for poles, tools, hurdles, fencing, firewood and so on. Before the Industrial Revolution, access to wood was vital for most communities and this would account for the acquisition and retention of Penge by the manor of Battersea. It is believed that the name given to the hamlet is of Celtic origin meaning 'Place at the end of the wood' and a charter of 957 refers to the: 'wood that is called Paenge, 7 miles and 7 furlongs and 7 feet about' on which, 'the residents of Beckenham were allowed to pasture geese, cattle and pigs, being careful to avoid the monks of Westminster who used the same common for hunting.'

As the economic value of woodland declined in the late eighteenth and early nineteenth centuries so the land it occupied was increasingly sold for building.

> The rural landscape and villages were soon overwhelmed by a new breed of "commuters" who dreamt of living in the country and working in the town. They chose to ignore the evidence that the country diminished in direct proportion to the town expanding. [Neville]

The arrival of the Crystal Palace greatly increased this trend until by 1880 Penge was completely built-up.

> Penge was no longer pretty. Where once there had been open land, woodland and rough grass, now there was a carpet of roads and houses. The only reminder of Penge Common's existence lay in street names which recalled some of its trees and plants – Oakfield Road, Maple Road, Thicket Road, Hawthorn Grove, and so on. By the 1870s one visitor went so far as to describe Penge as ' ... a waste of modern tenements, mean, monotonous and wearisome ... [Spence]

> Penge for most people is a joke, an epitome of the dreary suburban non-place. It is a reputation not quite deserved, and a journey from the Crystal Palace down the hill to the High Street and beyond yields several buildings worth a look. [Cherry and Pevsner]

The last quotation is followed by a description of the houses in Crystal Palace Park Road and serves as a useful reminder that the Crystal Palace was not built in Sydenham but in Penge. This makes me realise that in spite of our postal address we lived in Penge too and not in Sydenham. I suspect that in the 1880s when our houses were built by the Crystal Palace Company its directors realised that an address in Penge wasn't likely to prove appealing. It was still smart to live in Sydenham but it was no longer smart to live in Penge and hadn't been for a long time. (I can't help thinking too that Penge is an inherently funny/ugly name like Slough or Bognor.) Anyway, Penge New Road became Crystal Palace Park Road and this bit of Penge (SE20) became Sydenham (SE26). When I looked at the street names as a child I used to wonder how one place could turn into another place just because you turned the corner at the bottom of the road.

So the ancient countryside mapped by Rocque which had remained essentially unaltered since well before Roman times was virtually obliterated within no more than fifty years between about 1830 and 1880. Only tiny fragments remained, one of which must have been the grove of old oak trees on the edge of the meadow at St Winefride's.

It seems to me that the unobtrusive area in which I lived as a child is of considerable historical significance. The story of Penge and the speed of its transformation from hamlet to town within one generation is the story of the nineteenth century, of the optimism and ingenuity of the Victorian age, of the movement of people and tremendous social change. It is the story of the modern world itself. Perhaps there are other places that would claim the same but none with as much justification as Penge because Penge was home to the Crystal Palace – that great popular symbol of Victorian advancement and focus for patriotism and pride.

But for over seventy years now the ruined Park has been in search of meaning and purpose. All sense of its original ground plan has been destroyed by the National Sports Centre and parts of the site are probably still being eyed-up greedily by property developers, just as they have been so often in the past. However, apart from wanting what's left to remain an open, well-maintained space for local people to enjoy I can't say I care too much what happens there. I mind too much about what preceded it and how the Crystal Palace played its part in laying the area waste.

In his book *South London* Walter Besant says that in May 1827 a Mr William Hone (finding Dulwich Picture Gallery closed and deciding therefore to explore this unknown area) walked across country from Dulwich to a place called Penge. At the top of the hill, on finding a choice of three roads, he chose that which led through Penge Common. The place he entered was thickly wooded and, in his own words, "a cathedral of singing birds." But this lovely place was already doomed. The common had recently been enclosed and would soon be built upon. Besant writing in 1899 wondered whether there was anyone at all in Penge who knew there had ever been a common. And also whether there was anyone in Penge who remembered the hanging woods?

Now, more than a century later, I shall let Walter Besant speak for me by giving him the last word.

> They hung over a hillside, as beautiful as the hanging woods of Cliveden. But like the Common they are gone ... It is difficult now that the whole country south of London has been covered with villas, roads, streets, and shops, to understand how wonderful for loveliness it was until the builder seized upon it. When the ground rose out of the great Lambeth and Bermondsey Marsh – the cliff or incline is marked still by the names of Battersea Rise, Clapham Rise and Brixton Rise – it opened out into one wild heath after another – Clapham, Richmond, Putney, Wimbledon, Barnes, Tooting, Streatham, Thornton, and so far south as Banstead Downs. The country was not flat: it rose at Wimbledon to a high plateau; it rose at Norwood to a chain of hills; between the heaths stretched gardens and orchards; between the orchards were pasture lands; on the hill sides were hanging woods; villages were scattered about, each with its venerable church and its peaceful churchyard ... All this beauty is gone; we have destroyed it; all this beauty has gone for ever; it cannot be replaced. And on the south there was so much more beauty than on the north.

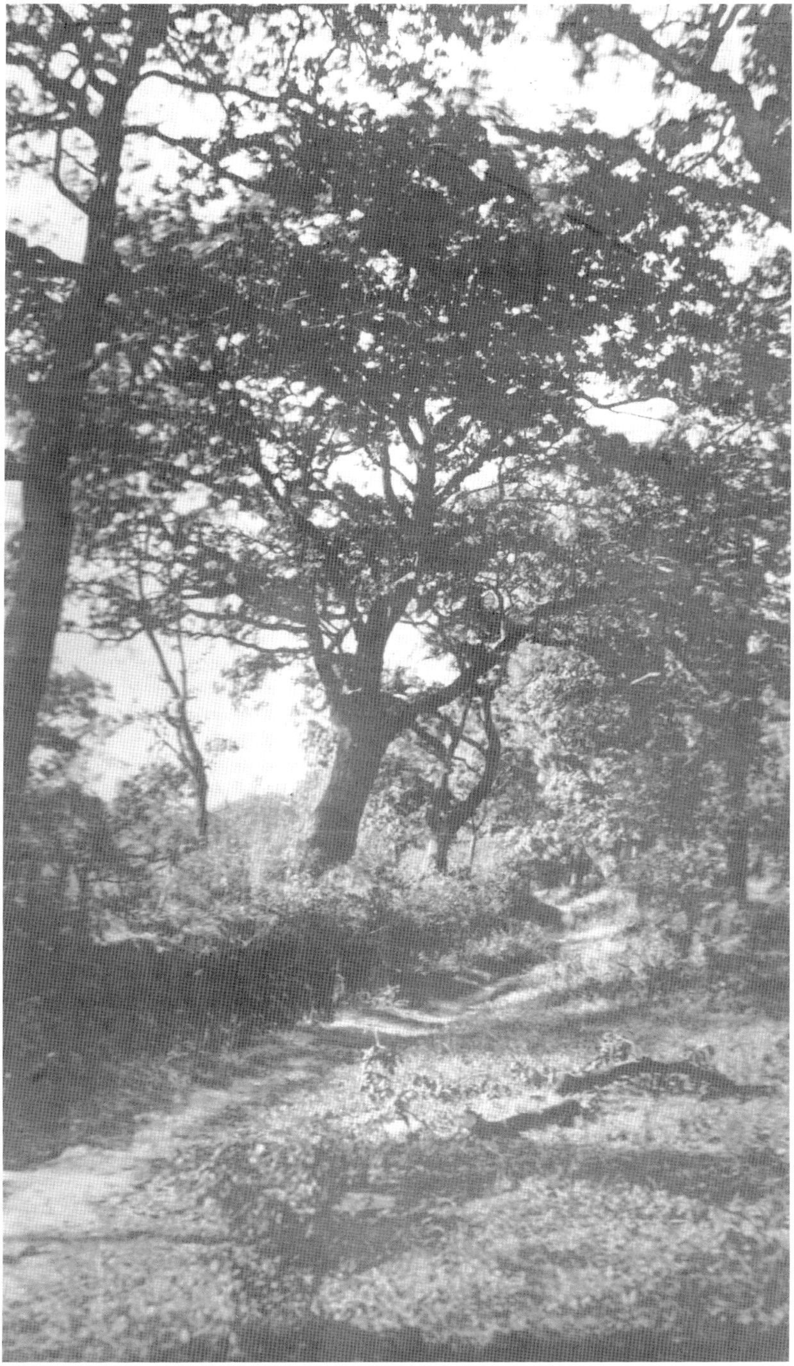

# Notes

The William Maxwell quotation comes from *The Happiness of Getting it down Right – Letters of Frank O'Connor and William Maxwell* edited by Michael Steinman, New York. Knopf 1996

**Page 103**   1925. The Shervington family at Wembley. This was taken just before George (sixth from the right) left England for Australia. My father is the sturdy boy fifth from the left.

**Page 114**   1985. Beckenham Road/High Street, Penge. Looking down towards the bend in the road where the main shopping area is. Things still look much the same here as they did forty years previously. 'Mickey Mouse' was just off to the right. Note the pavement available in front for large displays of tinned cat food just waiting to be knocked over. (Bromley Libraries)

**Page 116**   Unfortunately I was only able to find pre-war photographs but I suppose it doesn't really matter. Forest Hill station was later bombed and so its roofline was no longer like this when I used to pass by underneath the railway line on my way to St Winefride's. Nevertheless this rather sooty-looking urban scene was immediately recognisable to me and very reminiscent of the monochromatic world we seemed to inhabit in those post-war years. Cobbs Corner is perfectly recognisable too. It was named for the building on the right – the department store with the dumpy dome. (Lewisham Libraries)

**Page 117**   This building of which I could only ever seem to get the odd squint was not, of course, a Tudor palace. It was a complex of almshouses busilt about 1840 for the retirement of Thames watermen and lightermen in country surroundings. Nevertheless there was a royal connection tucked away round the corner in the form of yet another set of Tudoresque almshouses. These were put up in 1847 by Queen Adelaide in memory of her husband King William IV whose death in 1837 enabled his niece Victoria to come to the throne.

**Page 120**  September 1940. Bomb damage in Station Road, Penge. This must have been the site of the prefabs we went past so often on our way to Penge East station. (Bromley Libraries)

**Page 147**  This is part of a map reproduced from *The Authentic Map Directory of London and Suburbs 1932-1934* which shows the postal districts of London. (Bromley Libraries)

**Page 177**  May 1971. Becky on the left and Candida on the right. (Brian Champion Studios)

**Pages 210/211**  Also from *The Authentic Map Directory of London and Suburbs 1932-1934* and therefore showing the Crystal Palace and its Park just a couple of years before the destruction of the Palace by fire in 1936. North-east from there, the open space shown as the Sydenham and Forest Hill Recreation Ground is what became known as Mayow Park. If you look just north from there you will see a building called St Magnus. I don't know what that was but it looks as if it might have been the Victorian building that Heather and I knew as St Monica's. And that white space to the north of it is where the rest of St Winefride's was. (Bromley Libraries)

**Page 212**  1952. Crystal Palace Park in ruins. (Bromley Libraries)

**Page 214**  1851. The Great Exhibition in Hyde Park. A glimpse through the Coalbrookdale gates.

**Page 216**  1854. Looking south-west along Crystal Palace Parade. (Lewisham Local Studies Library)

**Page 218**  Napoleon III and his wife Eugenie at the Crystal Palace in 1855. (Bromley Libraries)

Page 220  1866. The remains of the colossi of Abu Simbel after the fire. (Bromley Libraries)

Page 221  2009. The drinking fountain in Mayow park, surrounded by some of the park's ancient oaks.

Pages 222/223  Reproduced from *Rocque's Survey of London* made between 1741 and 1745. (Motco Enterprises Limited, ref: www.motco.com)

Page 225  The Croydon Canal going through Penge Woods. (Bromley Libraries)

Page 226  Site of the Crystal Palace before construction. (Bromley Libraries)

Page 231  c. 1880 Croxted Lane. Probably pre-Roman in origin, this track was once known as Crokstrete. (Southwark Local Studies Library)

I would like to thank Iona Opie for permission to quote from *The People in the Playground* 1993 and Martin Spence for permission to quote from *The Making of a London Suburb* 2007. My thanks also to Hurst and Company for permission to quote from JR Piggott's *The Palace of the People* 2004.

In case you're interested, this is a list of publications I found useful when finding out about the Crystal Palace at Sydenham. They're in no particular order.

*The Crystal Palace* by Patrick Beaver, 1986
*The Making of a London Suburb: Capital comes to Penge* by Martin Spence, 2007
*The Phoenix Suburb: A South London Social History* by Alan Warwick, 1982

*Palace of the People: The Crystal Palace at Sydenham 1854-1936* by J R Piggott, 2004
*The Great North Wood: A Brief History of Ancient Woodlands from Selhurst to Deptford* by L S E Neville, 1987
*South London* by Walter Besant, 1899
*A Thing in Disguise: The Visionary Life of Joseph Paxton* by Kate Colquhoun, 2005
*The History of the Countryside* by Oliver Rackham, 1999
*The Buildings of England London 2* by Bridget Cherry and Nikolaus Pevsner, 1990
*Pissarro at Crystal Palace* by Nicholas Reed, 1987
*Sydenham and Forest Hill* by Joan Alcock, 2005
*The London Encyclopaedia* by Ben Weinreb and Christopher Hibbert, 1983

The old red-bound set of Arthur Mee's *Children's Encyclopaedia* that we used to have has not survived but the one I've been referring to is its exact counterpart – except that it's bound in blue.

A note of apology in case my portrait of Coloma in the 1950s has given offence to anyone. The very different school it later became appears to be one I would have been only too happy to attend and from which I would no doubt have gained much benefit.

And finally I should perhaps point out that no schoolmistress of my acquaintance went by the name of Miss Reed or Miss Hoolahan.